THE APPALACHIANS

THE APPALACHIANS

America's First and Last Frontier

Edited by Mari-Lynn Evans,
Holly George-Warren, and Robert Santelli,
with Tom Robertson

Random House

LIBRARY OF CONGRESS CATALOGING-IN-PUBLICATION DATA

The Appalachians: America's first and last frontier / edited by Mari-Lynn Evans, Holly George-Warren, and Robert Santelli with Tom Robertson.
p. cm.
ISBN 1-4000-6186-5
1. Appalachian Region–Civilization. 2. Appalachian Region–Pictorial works.
3. Appalachian Region–Biography. 4. Oral history. I. Evans, Mari-Lynn.
II. George-Warren, Holly. III. Santelli, Robert.

F106.A59 2004
974–dc22 2004041162

Major Underwriters for the PBS series *The Appalachians:*
The Sierra Club
The Sierra Club Productions
The Appalachian Regional Commission
The United States Department of Health and Human Services
Mountainmade
Vandalia Heritage Foundation

Book production: March Tenth, Inc.
Art direction: Sandra Choron
Book design: Harry Choron
Title page photograph: Chuck Conner

Random House website address: www.atrandom.com

Printed in the United States of America on acid-free paper

987654321

First Edition

To the Appalachian people, whose courage, contributions, and sacrifices have shaped our lives; and to my grandparents, William D. and LaVon Mick Currence, who inspired this book and my respect for the mountains, the land, and the culture of the great Appalachians

—*Mari-Lynn Evans*

CONTENTS

PREFACE

Currence family home, Bulltown, West Virginia
(Photographer unknown, Mari-Lynn Evans Collection)

When my colleague Tom Robertson and I first embarked on our film *The Appalachians* in 1999, the foremost thought in my mind was to document the *real* Appalachia—the land and the people I knew and loved—while its unique culture still existed. I felt it imperative to finally give us Appalachians the chance to tell our own stories of America's first and last frontier. In a world where most of us drive through towns that all look alike, with the same fast-food chains and gas stations, Appalachia is one of the few geographic

{ *Appalachian Spring*
(© Mary Almond)

regions of the country with its own distinct, centuries-old culture, still intact. The culture of southern Appalachia is not what you've seen on *The Beverly Hillbillies, Hee-Haw,* or *Green Acres*—although you can find a little bit of that if you look. It is, after all, a diverse culture.

Appalachia, in fact, represents the best of us as a society. In my own experience as a native Appalachian, there is great love of family, strong community ties, a sense that the Golden Rule is how you are supposed to live your life. And it is a quieter, more peaceful place than most areas of the country. Certainly, Appalachia contains many sophisticated urban centers, and in those communities life is not much different from that in cities across America. But there is an underlying difference that comes from our past, our heritage.

It's easy to romanticize Appalachia—perhaps as easy as it is to marginalize it, to laugh about it. But to grow up there is to know its uniqueness and what makes it precious. At least that's what my experience was. I think when you read the essays in this book you will get a sense of who we are and why I am so proud to have grown up in the hills of Appalachia.

I was raised by my grandparents in Bulltown, West Virginia. Our house, a huge white farmhouse with a wraparound porch and Ionic columns, had been built by hand by my grandfather's father and his neighbors, who immigrated there from Scotland, Ireland, and Wales in the 1800s. My grandfather had grown up on this land with his four brothers. Side by side, they'd

(Photographer unknown, Mari-Lynn Evans Collection)

worked the land along with their father; their mother traveled from house to house preaching the Bible. When their father died, the land—more than two thousand acres—was split into adjoining tracts, and the brothers labored together every day planting vegetables and raising cattle. The only time they ever left the community was to travel to stock auctions or to 4-H shows.

My grandfather's life did not really differ much from that of his ancestors. Work was every day without holiday. Primarily farmers, these landowners had lived on their land for their entire lives. Most were related to the land's original settlers, who'd arrived from Scotland and Ireland in the early nineteenth century. Every mountain, every river, every tree had a memory attached to it because my family loved that land and cultivated its every inch. I remember my grandfather taking my small hand and telling me that for as far as the eye could see, this was our land.

Our community was almost clanlike. Families had known each other for several generations, and there were virtually no outside influences. I recall, as recently as the early 1970s, men riding horses for transportation, one-room schoolhouses, and kerosene lanterns. Even then, few people had telephones or television and almost no one ever traveled to another county, let alone left the state. They believed everything they could ever need or want was right there. Everyone knew the most intimate details of everyone else's lives, and they served as a support group for one another. People would regularly travel for many miles for get-togethers to play games and visit. Every Sunday, dozens of men journeyed to our farm, some staying in a house out back so they could work the fields during the week with my grandfather, then return home on Friday evening. My grandparents hired local women to do the laundry and cook for as many as fifteen men (whipping up three meals a day). I still have that table marred by their knives. The renowned fiddler Melvin Wine, whom I interviewed for our film, told me that during the Depression my grandfather let him sharecrop, which kept his nine children from starving. It was like a message from beyond, since my grandfather had never told me that story.

My grandfather was a sweet, kind, and generous man who spent his days working the fields and his evenings telling us stories. Fourteen years his junior, my grandmother moved into his family home upon their marriage. Tall and thin with a throaty voice, my grandmother made everyone laugh with her dry wit and was admired for her great style. She loved to read, and she shared her love of words and the hills with me. She thought I was the greatest thing in the world, and I thought the same of her. My mentor, she made me believe that all things were possible.

When I was a little girl, my grandmother and I would sit and talk for hours. In the summer our friends and relatives would all gather on the front porch and chat. Neighbors came from miles around just to sit and talk, or we would get in the car and drive up hollers to visit friends, sometimes stopping to talk to people we had never met before. No one was a stranger for long. We children played softball, hide-and-seek, or caught fireflies. When it was really hot, we took our mattresses outside and slept under the stars. That was a real treat. I also helped with our cattle and horses and enjoyed working in the garden, pulling up vegetables and wiping them clean so I could sit under the sun and have my lunch. We also had an apple and peach orchard, where we collected the fruit, some of which we consumed immediately, right there under the trees. Others were canned for the long, hard winters.

Every fall we butchered a hog. Men would come from all over the county to help us in this day-long event. Afterward we would store the meat in the smokehouse. Every spring, we sheared the sheep and fed the newborn lambs with Coke bottles covered with baby-bottle nipples. Summers meant cutting and bailing the hay. I loved to go out with the workers and lift those bails into the truck. I can remember that smell so well. There was always work to do, and we children were expected to help.

My brother, sister, and I had plenty of time, though, to explore the land. We'd go down to the river, where we jumped off big rocks into the water, or we found grapevines to swing from. Sometimes we packed picnic lunches and ate by the family cemetery or by the two Indian burial grounds, imagining what it was like when natives lived on our land. After all, this land was not only where our families had settled but was the location of great Indian and Civil War battles. Many of us were raised hearing the stories of bloody massacres. Every spring, during planting, the tractors dug into the ground, unearthing an abundance of arrowheads, tomahawks, and other remnants of the Native culture. Indian burial grounds and the graves of Civil War soldiers dotted the landscape.

Just beyond a swinging bridge in our bottom-land lived two old women, Mag and Ruth. I used to visit them, and we would listen to the Grand Ole Opry. I remember them singing along to Hank Williams songs. I can also recall the smell of their coal-burning stove. They wore tiny cotton dresses with those orthopedic shoes that are all the rage now. They survived by planting a garden and canning foods for the winter. When they needed something, they would ask for my grandfather's help. He never denied anyone anything.

In the summers, there would always be tent revivals. Preachers who got so moved by the spirit that they spoke in tongues came to conduct services and to perform baptisms in the river. Sometimes my grandmother attended with me, and sometimes I walked out of the holler alone and went by myself. I loved the gospel music and all the excitement, which made it seem like God was right there in the crowd. My grandmother took us every single Sunday to the tiny white church on the top of the mountain. We had no preacher, so people took turns reading from the Bible and then we would all sing songs.

The only other big event was when the circus came in on the railroad to Burnsville, a little town where I went to school, and we would go to see it. My school was the same one my grandfather had attended, and many of my teachers had gone to school with him.

Our lives seemed very simple until the late 1960s, when the Army Corps of Engineers began to survey the land in central West Virginia for the purpose of buying it to develop lakes to attract tourism. I was about six years old at the time and I remember my grandparents telling me not to worry, that we would never have to leave our home. They were wrong. Men who believed in fairness and reason, my grandfather and his brothers couldn't comprehend that the government would actually take our land away. But in the 1970s, the government brought in people from out of the area to open an office in the county to negotiate buying the land. Many of the landowners went to court to prevent the government from acquiring their land, and my grandfather and his brothers were in court for years suing to retain what was theirs. They thought that by hiring a Washington, D.C., law firm that could speak the government's "language," they could win their fight. Then, the government successfully invoked "eminent domain," and we lost our land. After their land was bought, most of our neighbors—many of whom were in their sixties—had no means to make a living and had to move to other states. Displaced to another culture that they didn't understand, they were unable to assimilate or adjust. Their entire world had been within their community: their church, their family, and their friends. In those communities, your identity was based on two things— the value of your family name and the value of your land. The government stripped these people of what formed their very identity, and most of them died within five years. Their family members will tell you they died of broken hearts. That story is repeated so often in our region.

The day we had the auction to sell our farm equipment and the furniture we weren't taking with us, I saw my grandfather break down and cry as his friends were bidding him farewell. I remember my grandmother telling me to be strong, that this was God's will. But the saddest vision I have from that day is of my fourteen-year-old brother, who had worked the farm every day with my grandfather, holding his calf around the neck and sobbing. We moved to Akron, Ohio, to be closer to family who had gone there during the great migration of the 1950s. My grandparents bought a house with several acres of land, where my grandfather grew vegetables to give away. To feel useful again, he advertised in the newspaper that he would repair tractors and lawnmowers for free. In Akron, the kids would tell jokes about West Virginia and ask me if I'd had an outhouse. Everyone had a West Virginia joke, and no one could understand that those jokes really hurt. I missed West Virginia, my friends, my home, my family.

I both longed for and dreaded going back every weekend, which is what we did. It was so awful to sit on my uncle Paul's porch and look over to where our home once stood. The sadness was unbearable. They had moved less than five hundred feet from their homestead because their house happened to be on the boundary of the new federally acquired property. Like my family home, theirs rotted away into the ground. We would sit on their front porch and look out at "our" land. It was still right there, minus the houses. We talked and talked only of the past, and those memories seemed as if they were our present. During those quiet times, I'd often sit in our porch swing while my grandparents and aunt and uncle talked about their lives. For never having traveled far, they told marvelously rich stories. Most of the time while we reminisced, my great-uncle, in all his dignity, would silently weep. For seventy-three years those brothers worked that farm.

There was never a time when we drove off that I did not cry. Those were bittersweet times. A few years later, as my grandfather lay dying, he began talking to his dead brothers about loading up the produce truck with potatoes, telling them where the truck should be. When he left this earth shortly after that, I knew that he, too, had died of a broken heart. All the brothers were gone within five years of losing their homes.

My great-aunt Bernadine died a few years ago, and now my grandmother's cousin Cindy is the only member of that generation still alive. She is so strong, so funny, so courageous. She is an Appalachian woman full of grit and determination. She tells me there is never a day she does not think of my grandmother and miss her. And I tell her there is never a day I don't miss them all. She likes to tell me stories of their childhood, like the time they saw Grandpa Jones play at their high school, and how they used to smoke corn silk. She never lets me forget how special life is in Appalachia, and she always tells me that I have a responsibility to our heritage.

Several years ago, after returning from living in London, I went back down to the farm. It was the first time I had walked our land with my son. Except for the vanished house, it all looked the same. I walked the path that led to where my home once stood, and I lay in the grass where I used to run. I walked down the hill and sat on my "thinking rock," where I used to go when I needed contemplation time. My childhood memories were so strong that if I squinted my eyes I could see them all up there on the porch: Nanny on the swing and Pop-Pop on the glider. The din of their conversations hung in the breeze. It is

Lost Creek Bridge
(© Shelby Lee Adams)

strange that only there on that deserted farm can I see them, can I remember how they sounded. The mountains, the smells, the feel of the cool river water on my legs are all the same. When I am there, nothing, not even I, has changed at all. It is a wonderful feeling.

I tried to tell my son, Zachary, about what life was like there, what my life was like. But it's hard for him to understand a life that is like an old movie. I never ate in a restaurant until I was sixteen, and we didn't get a phone until I was ten, and then it was a party line! By the age of eight Zack had already lived in Europe. In one generation it seems as if the world has totally changed.

While working on my film and this book, I pored through my grandparents' boxes and books of photographs and journals. Included in a strongbox was a diary my grandfather had kept. This was the last entry he wrote before we left the homestead:

I looked out at my land today. For as far as the eye can see is the land my great grandfather settled. We worked this land, we built the house with our very hands. Over there is the burial grounds of Civil War soldiers, and there are some Indian burial grounds.

This land is as familiar to me as my own skin.

And now those bastards at the Corps of Engineers are burying me.

They are stealing our land. There's nothing left for me now.

I don't give a damn if I live another day. I am already dead.

—Diary of William D. Currence,
Bulltown, West Virginia,
1976

When William D. Currence died on April 18, 1980, there was standing room only in the funeral home. They said he never spoke a harsh word about anyone. Simple things like that meant something to those people. Your life was not valued by the car you drove or your bank account. The value of your life was based on the integrity of your life. When I was three months pregnant, my darling grandmother passed. It was the saddest day of my life. My grandparents are buried together in the Currence family cemetery. Every Memorial Day my cousins Kathy and Nancy take roses and peonies, grown from the clippings retrieved from the old family farm, and put them on their graves.

Today, when people ask me why I made this film, this is the answer: I made it for Nanny and Pop-Pop. I hope they are as proud of me as I am of them.

I also wanted to make this film to honor all the people of Appalachia. Virtually every other culture has been explored by the media, and I felt so strongly that it was time for our story to be told.

To aid us in this endeavor, I asked an esteemed group of scholars from major Appalachian universities and colleges to help us identify stories and people to interview. Their input was invaluable. For their assistance, we owe a great debt to Shannon Bell, Judy Byers, Chuck Connor, Howard Dorgan, Ron Eller, Laura Kohns, Ron Lewis, Gordon McKinney, Ted Olson, and Charles Wolfe. Also, we never could have completed this project without the help of Congressman Alan Mollohan, Senator Robert C. Byrd, Naomi Judd, and Bob Santelli. I especially want to thank Tom Robertson, my partner on this project. His absolute commitment is what made it a reality. Doing a project of this magnitude was overwhelming at times. When you see this film, you see Tom's heart and soul. He not only wrote the script, filmed the interviews and places, but he edited the film as well. This film is as much his legacy as it is mine.

My wish is that this film and its companion book will provide a greater understanding of the Appalachian people. An honest, complete, but not a romanticized version of our life, *The Appalachians*—the film and book—strives to tell the comprehensive history of these people through personal stories, journals, diaries, and interviews with scholars, ordinary people, and celebrated artists from the area. We cover a diverse group of people whose backgrounds are native, African, Scots-Irish, and European. Their stories help to illustrate the singularity of the culture.

This book and film, then, give a multi-faceted glimpse of the history of Appalachia: who came to the land, why they came, what they found, what they did, and why they stayed. The music, the literature, and the poetry of Appalachia also help to tell the story. We've also looked at the stereotypes to help people understand where they came from and why they have been perpetuated. Since the stereotypes are still so powerful and have had such a negative sociological and economic impact on the region, we felt it was valuable to address them. We also wanted to include some topics, like that of the Hatfields and the McCoys, which are not of major historical importance but which have become entrenched in our history.

One of the most sensitive issues we look at is poverty. So much of what we see in the media about the region focuses on impoverishment, and we were concerned about perpetuating that characterization. Yet poverty does exist in Appalachia, and it would be dishonest not to show it. We have explored the causes of it and the forces that have contributed to it, as well as the reasons people continue to live in an area where such economic downturns exist.

During the filming of *The Appalachians*, I remembered in a visceral way what it is that makes Appalachia so special. After about two hours of driving into the region, I slowly became a different person. No present and no future existed for me on that drive back home—only an overwhelming feeling of clarity. I knew who I was and where I came from. All the trappings and worries of this life dissipated.

Several incidents that occurred while making this film will always stay with me. Filming in Copen, West Virginia, for example, we took with us a production crew with high-definition cameras. On that hot summer night as we were driving up hills, down rutted one-lane roads, all we could see was the moon hanging in a pitch-black sky. Nearing the little community center where we were filming a dozen old fiddlers, the strains of their music drifted through the air. It was magical. After we interviewed several and filmed them playing for a couple of hours, one of the cameramen told me how lucky I was to have grown up there. He said he wished he could have been raised in West Virginia.

I thought about how much I hoped that everyone who sees the film and reads this book would feel that way. It is this feeling—and all the other richness that is Appalachia—that I hope *The Appalachians* conveys to you. Please join me in traveling those country roads through Appalachia, to West Virginia, the place where I belong.

—*Mari-Lynn Currence Evans*
Akron, Ohio
September 2003

INTRODUCTION

(Van Slider)

The early morning mountain mist is spread over the valley like a large, gray blanket. Underneath it, the tiny hamlet, snug and settled, rests easy. It is early autumn and the rich greenery of summer is beginning to give way to brown, red, orange, and gold hues that will become more pronounced as the sun comes up over the mountains in the eastern sky.

A dog barks, and then another. In the air there is a faint smell of burning wood. But there are no visible signs of smoke that might taint the picturesque landscape. The view is indeed gorgeous. You'd be hard-pressed to find a visitor who would disagree. Yes, he'd say, this is quite beautiful, postcard pretty. Then tell him this place is Appalachia and watch a look of surprise sweep across his face.

The *idea* of Appalachia as a particularly unique American place is deeply embedded in American popular culture. It began a century ago, perpetuated mostly by Northern journalists who found that sensationalizing life in Appalachia was a good way to sell newspapers. Since then, the media have continuously put forth the notion that life is homespun, simple, and a bit "different" in Appalachia, giving rise to cultural stereotyping on the grandest scale. We've laughed, for example, at the antics of "hillbillies" in newspaper comics. Snuffy Smith quickly comes to mind, as does the always likable Lil' Abner. (Even though Abner's story was, technically, set in Arkansas, his character is certainly attributable to Appalachia.) Those of us who grew up in the 1960s might remember the Hanna-Barbera cartoon *The Hillbilly Bears.* Speaking of television, Andy Griffith, Barney Fife, Aunt Bea, Opie, and the bootlegging Darling family warmed our hearts and made us smile with each episode of *The Andy Griffith Show.* Like Lil' Abner, *The Beverly Hillbillies* was also set in Arkansas, but, again, the connotation was equal

Scotty with banjo and Tom, 1992
(© Shelby Lee Adams)

parts Appalachian. Each week, we tuned in to the trials and tribulations of the Clampetts, those lovable country innocents who settle in the upscale suburb of Los Angeles and wreak havoc on California culture and everything having to do with modern convenience, while outsmarting Mr. Drysdale every time.

Then there was *The Waltons,* one of the most beloved and embraceable Appalachian families ever to surface in American popular arts. We've chuckled at some of the family's antics, to be sure, and sometimes we've cried with them, too. But mostly we learned about values and integrity from characters like Grandpa Walton and Tom—about them and their family, and about ourselves and our families.

Appalachia also made its mark in the movies. *Deliverance,* that particularly unsettling tale of survival starring Jon Voight and Burt Reynolds and featuring the hit theme song "Dueling Banjos," certainly affected our thinking about Appalachia—both good and bad. Beyond film, we've heard about the Hatfields and McCoys and their family feud, one of the longest in American history. We've laughed at the many hillbilly jokes—too numerous to repeat here.

When it comes to popular culture and the media, then, Appalachia, more times than not, seems to exist merely to entertain the rest of us, to remind us how good *we* have it compared with those unfortunate souls who live in the region's hills and hollers. The region might also be likened to a strange, cross-eyed, and unruly child not in the least like any other offspring. The analogy would be made even better if such a child were illegitimate, dirty-faced, and dangerous in some degenerate way.

This is a book about the real Appalachia, however, not the one described above. *The Appalachians* is the story of the people of this wonderfully unique region—their history and culture, their land, their hardships and triumphs. It is about Appalachia yesterday, and Appalachia today.

The spine of Appalachia is the Appalachian mountain range, which begins in the Saint Lawrence Valley, in Canada, and runs right down the eastern part of the United States. Appalachia begins north in upper New England, where the Green Mountains of Vermont and the White Mountains of New Hampshire dominate the landscape. The Appalachian Trail, one of America's great hiking challenges, actually runs from Maine to northern Georgia. Included in the Appalachian system are the Allegheny Mountains, the Blue Ridge Mountains, and the Great Smoky Mountains, along with the Great Valley, which takes in the Shenandoah, the James, the New, and the Tennessee valleys.

About twenty-three million people live in this two-hundred-thousand-square-mile region. All of West Virginia and parts of twelve other states—Alabama, Georgia, Kentucky, Maryland, Mississippi, New York, North Carolina, Ohio, Pennsylvania, South Carolina, Tennessee, and Virginia—can claim Appalachia as both a geographical and cultural identity.

Historically, Appalachia was America's first frontier. The region's original inhabitants were Indians. The Iroquois, Chickasaw, Choctaw, and especially Cherokee tribes created thriving indigenous cultures there before the arrival in the early 1700s of English, Scottish, and Irish settlers, who, along with Germans, were attracted to the verdant valleys, the rich, green hills, and the mountains. Protestant was the dominant religion; Presbyterians, Methodists, Lutherans, Baptists, and Pentecostals were among the Christian denominations that established rural churches in Appalachia.

Appalachian culture largely has its origins in the British Isles. Not just religious practices but social customs, traditions, and music came across the Atlantic to Appalachia largely intact. Thanks to the geographical isolation that the mountains provided, such things were virtually free of outside meddling in Appalachia.

Isolation—it is a word that figures large in the Appalachian legacy. In the eighteenth and early nineteenth centuries, Appalachia's mountainous terrain caused deeply rural settlements to sit isolated from other small communities and, certainly, the rest of America. Prior to the War for Independence, the vastness of the Appalachian mountain range hindered any large-scale westward expansion, although tales of Daniel Boone's exploits and his exploration of the Cumberland Gap are a vital part of early Appalachian history and folklore. Like first- and second-generation Appalachian settlers, Boone was fiercely independent and rugged. He led the crossing over the mountains and provided the inspiration to move the frontier farther west. (Eventually, thousands upon thousands of eager settlers, many of them fresh from Europe, followed Boone's trail, and just about all of them traveled over and through the mountains and kept on going.) After the War for Independence, many soldiers given land grants settled onto homesteads in Appalachia. There, they tended the land and lived their lives, generation after generation.

The Civil War was a difficult period for Appalachians. Poor white mountain people were torn between staying loyal to the Union and fighting on the side of their Southern brothers. In sections of Virginia, Tennessee, and North Carolina, there seemed to be no dividing line at all. Some Appalachian families chose one side, while their neighbors chose the other. In some cases, it was truly brother fighting against brother.

Part of the problem was the unique situation of blacks in Appalachia. Although there were slaves in virtually every county in Appalachia, there were fewer of them than elsewhere in the South, because there were no huge plantations and because fewer families could afford slaves. Most slave-owning households owned fewer than five, although there were some plantations in Alabama, Georgia, and Tennessee on which slaves numbered ten and twenty times that amount. In all, it is estimated that perhaps 10 percent of Appalachia's population at the outset of the Civil War was black.

It could be said that the Civil War started in Appalachia, with John Brown's raid in 1859 on the United States Armory and Arsenal at Harpers Ferry, back then located in Virginia, today, in West Virginia, which was created in 1863 as a separate state. Brown, a fanatical abolitionist, hoped to rouse slaves and to inspire an insurrection that would lead to emancipation. What Brown did was make a dangerous situation even worse, pushing the nation past the point of no return. Two years later, Americans were fighting Americans, and the key issue was slavery.

Appalachia wasn't without its war heroes or famous battlefields. Confederate general Thomas "Stonewall" Jackson, second only to General Robert E. Lee in terms of military genius on the Southern side, was Appalachian born and bred, and defeated Union forces at Winchester and Front Royal in the Shenandoah Valley, among other Appalachian-based battles. Confederate forces also won a key victory at Chickamauga in northern Georgia. In all, dozens of battles and countless skirmishes were fought in Appalachia during the Civil War. Both the Union and Confederate forces drew more than one hundred thousand Appalachian soldiers to the conflict, with the South holding a considerable edge in recruits. After President Lincoln was assassinated in 1865, it was Andrew Johnson from the east Tennessee section of Appalachia who led the country into its Reconstruction era.

Following the Civil War, isolation became less

of an issue in Appalachia. Yet, even though the region grew increasingly involved in economic, political, and cultural matters that affected the rest of the nation, most Americans outside Appalachia continued to subscribe to the belief that mountain people there were cut off from the world.

The fact is there was more to Appalachia than barely surviving farms and turnip patches. During the Reconstruction years, coal mining attracted Appalachians and outsiders alike, forcing dramatic changes not just in the landscape but also in the makeup of Appalachian society. European immigrants and African Americans streamed into Appalachia in the late nineteenth and early twentieth centuries. For many men, it was better to risk going into the earth and digging out the coal that heated America's homes than to struggle with the uncertainties of farming. Newly arrived southern European immigrants found the mountains of Appalachia and prospects of earning a living mining coal more attractive than settling in the ghettos of New York, Boston, and other eastern cities and working in factories there.

America was quickly becoming an international industrial power that rivaled the greatest countries in Europe, and demand for energy grew at a furious pace. To get the coal from the mines of West Virginia and the rest of central Appalachia to urban markets necessitated the arrival of the railroad and the creation of coal company towns, further changing the way of life in Appalachia. Families lived in coal company towns, which supplied the essential needs of Appalachian families. Children went to coal company schools, and instead of money the men were paid with scrip that had to be spent buying goods in coal company stores. Almost overnight, Appalachians who had prided themselves on being independent in the traditional sense of mountain people were now caught in a culture where they had little control over their lives.

Coal wasn't the only industry in booming Appalachia in the late nineteenth century. Even earlier, timber, cut from Appalachian forests, became a big business to supply America with building materials. Furniture making matured in North Carolina, providing some skilled craftsmen the opportunity to avoid the fields, forests, and mines. A growing textile industry employed Appalachian women, upsetting their traditional roles as keepers of the family and bearers of children. Appalachian towns supported small Appalachian business enterprises, but the big money being made in Appalachia was going into the pockets of outsiders intent on exploiting both the region's natural resources and its people. Absentee ownership of the forests and mines was the norm; management of the lumber mills, factories, and mines came from the outside as well.

Given their resilient personal pride and rugged determination to remain self-sufficient, it's not surprising that Appalachians resisted exploitation, especially economic exploitation. Beginning in the 1890s, coal or mine wars flared in Alabama and Tennessee. In the early 1900s, right on through the 1930s, conflicts between miners and management exploded often in West Virginia and Kentucky and stained the region with bitterness and blood. Labor-strife roots were embedded in the struggle by miners to gain better wages and working conditions and to unionize, and in management's denial of such improvements. Thousands of miners spent hard years below the ground; when disease struck, a man's ethnic background or skin color made no difference. Down in the mines, almost everyone had black faces—and black lungs.

During the Depression, poor people in Appalachia got even poorer and workers' rights were even harder to come by. There were a few victories, however. The protracted coal war in Harlan County, Kentucky, eventually led to some improved conditions for miners, and with the passage of the federal government's Wagner Act in 1935, unionization finally came to Appalachia. President Franklin Roosevelt's New Deal forever changed Appalachia with the advent of new economic and social programs and laws designed to make less painful the economic blight brought on by the Depression. In Appalachia, Roosevelt's Civilian Conservation Corps initiated the idea of conservation there. The establishment of the Tennessee Valley Authority meant electricity for thousands of Appalachian families still using kerosene lamps for light.

The changes in Appalachia brought about by the Depression continued through World War II. Thousands of young Appalachian men served in the armed forces during the war. They saw how things were outside their region. They broadened their view of the world and brought back home new ideas and visions. Others, however, never returned to the coal mine or family farm. After World War II, an Appalachian exodus occurred, spurred by better economic opportunities in cities such as Detroit, Akron, Dayton, Cincinnati, and Pittsburgh. Back home, coal mining had become more and more mechanized, meaning many old jobs in the mines weren't there anymore, anyway. And America was seeking cheaper, cleaner sources of energy, further cutting into the Appalachian coal mining industry. For more than half a million Appalachians, the future lay not in the country but in the city.

Although Appalachia made significant strides in the middle of the twentieth century to modernize and make daily life there easier, some outsiders still viewed the region as stuck in time. In 1960, Senator Jack Kennedy, while campaigning for the presidency, visited West Virginia and singled out both the state and the region as unjustly impoverished. The media, never wanting to miss an Appalachian story, capitalized on Kennedy's attention to the area with follow-up reports on the dismal economic climate there. A few years later, President Lyndon Johnson had Appalachia in mind when he launched his War on Poverty programs. During the sixties the federal government created the Appalachian Regional Commission to focus on the ills of the region. Social missionaries in the form of VISTA (Volunteers in Service to America) workers, plus teachers and doctors, swarmed to Appalachia to "save the region from itself."

Many Appalachian families, though happy for the help, saw things differently. To them, the world was on a reckless course; it moved too fast, paid little or no mind to tradition, and sacrificed neighbor, family, community, the church, and the common good for a chance at personal enrichment. Many Appalachians were poor when it came to material objects and money. They suffered when it came to education, medicine, and modern convenience. Some were downright destitute and became poster children for social activists who demanded that the difference between the haves and have-nots in America be dramatically reduced. But underneath their poverty, Appalachians often maintained an intense personal pride in their rural identity and affinity for the land, and a determination to overcome hardship, which is what most people there always did and continued to do.

In 1966, in northeastern Georgia, a teacher and his students gave birth to a little magazine that was published quarterly. They called it *Foxfire.* The prevailing ideas that spawned *Foxfire* were the need to preserve on paper the old ways of Appalachia, the desire to teach rural self-sufficiency, and to show Appalachian youth the value of their own heritage. Techniques for plowing a rocky field, pickling and canning vegetables, and salting a freshly butchered pig were described in *Foxfire;* local recipes and remedies for common ailments were also provided. A curious thing happened to *Foxfire.* It became an

Bill Monroe (with guitar) *and the Bluegrass Boys at the Grand Ole Opry, circa 1940*
(Photographer unknown, Charles Wolfe Collection)

unintended, how-to guide for the burgeoning, youth-driven counterculture, intent on returning to the land, or at least celebrating the idea of such a noble ambition. Eventually published as a book in several volumes, *Foxfire* became incredibly popular, making the bestseller lists by selling hundreds of thousands of copies and bearing proof that Appalachia's cultural heritage and folklore were desired both inside and out of the region.

Foxfire's commercial success inspired the publication of other books with similar visions. Suddenly, in the midst of a deluge of machines, massive transportation systems, fast food, and culture in a can, many Americans became interested in investigating how to do things the old-fashioned, Appalachian way.

Interest in Appalachia came in other forms,

too, especially music. The early sixties folk revival not only celebrated the nation's rich treasury of folk music, but also instigated a widespread attempt to seek out talented but obscure traditional musicians and present them outside their regions on folk festival stages like the one at Newport, Rhode Island, each summer. Middle-class college kids gorged themselves on authentic American folk music, marveling at the salt-of-the-earth sounds of fiddle and banjo players, guitar pickers, and singers, whose "high lonesome" wails sounded as haunting as centuries-old troubadours' laments.

Appalachia had always been a musical hotbed. Anglo-Scots-Irish ballads brought over from the British Isles by the earliest settlers of Appalachia formed the region's musical foundations. Songs passed from one generation to the next, as did instruments and the idea that music was a means of not only celebrating Appalachian culture but preserving it, too. With the advent of radio in the 1920s and the popularity of WSM's Grand Ole Opry show out of Nashville, mountain music, along with other forms of early country music, was spread throughout the South each Saturday evening.

The most important musical event in Appalachia occurred in 1927. It was in that year that the Carter Family of southern Virginia, quite possibly the most famous musical family in American history, and a former railroad worker from Meridian, Mississippi, named Jimmie Rodgers made their debut recordings in Bristol, Tennessee. These legendary sessions set in motion the birth of country music, the establishment of modern folk music, and the eventual arrival of bluegrass music. The husband-and-wife team of A.P. and Sara Carter and Sara's cousin Maybelle were a living repository of mountain ballads, Appalachian church hymns, and songs from the hearth and front porch of materially poor but musically rich Appalachia.

Appalachia contributed mightily to the American music canon throughout the twentieth century. In addition to the Carter Family, the father of bluegrass, Bill Monroe, hailed from Appalachia, creating a new American music form dug out of the region's hills and mountains. Bluegrass greats Lester Flatt and Earl Scruggs followed in the path blazed by Monroe. Add to the list Ralph Stanley, Doc Watson, Loretta Lynn, Dolly Parton, Jean Ritchie, the Delmore Brothers, the Judds, Ricky Skaggs, Dwight Yoakam, Patty Loveless, and so many other folk, blues, bluegrass, gospel, country, rockabilly, and old-timey musicians. Together, they have made certain that Appalachia's exceedingly rich musical legacy is a big part of the American music tradition.

Appalachia's contribution to American literature is nearly as impressive as its musical gifts. Storytelling has always been an essential part of Appalachian culture; colorful characters and rich motifs and themes fill out Appalachian tales passed on orally from generation to generation. The occasional publication of journals and diaries provided a personal and intimate glimpse into Appalachian life. Then, beginning in the 1930s, recognized works of literature with Appalachian settings and characters by Appalachian writers began to appear on the nation's bookshelves. James Agee, Thomas Wolfe, and Harriette Arnow, among others, chronicled the transformation of Appalachia into the modern world, and did not suffer sentimentality in the process. Agee's *Let Us Now Praise Famous Men*, Wolfe's *Look Homeward, Angel,* and Arnow's *The Dollmaker* are powerful works that provided valuable insight into Appalachia and the rest of the South, triggering further literary interest in the region. Later, the poetry and short stories of Fred Chappell, and the novels of Lee Smith, Janis Grubb, and Mary Lee Settle continued the Appalachian literary movement. The work of Annie Dillard, James Dickey, Wilma Dykeman, James Still, Louise McNeill, and Tony Earley has also played an important role in articulating the diversity of Appalachia.

Not all the attention and aid that was heaped on Appalachia in the post–World War II period was positive. The government allowed the unsightly practice of strip mining, which largely replaced digging for coal in mines, to continue in Appalachia without many restrictions. The Army Corps of Engineers reshaped wide swaths of land with the creation of man-made lakes. Where development was encouraged, it often ran rampant with little thought given to zoning, planning, or traditional Appalachian culture. Today, many sections of Appalachia are a hodgepodge of old and new, where people struggle to retain their sense of identity.

Which is why Appalachia, America's first frontier, is probably its final one, too. In the years prior to World War II, America was a nation rich in regional contrast. Traveling from one section of the country to another was a journey of exploration. Different accents and vocal expressions made talking with locals an adventure. Customs that ran deep in one region of the country were nonexistent in other parts. America was defined by the diversity of its regions—distinct areas of the national landscape, each giving to the whole unique strengths and attributes, art and culture, beliefs and ideas.

In some ways America in the twenty-first century is more multicultural and diverse than ever. But thanks to the dominance of technology and instantaneous communication in the form of the Internet and cell phones, plus the proliferation of national restaurant, hotel, and retail chains, cheap travel, and the drive to homogenize our national culture, America's regional differences are disappearing at an alarming rate.

Appalachia is the last holdout. The region is engaged in a furious cultural conflict: How does it achieve a higher standard of living for its people and attract jobs and industry? In other words, how does it fall more in line with the rest of America, without sacrificing a distinct way of life? How does it keep its young people from emigrating north or west? How does Appalachia gain the respect of the rest of America, without selling its soul and becoming a place it was never meant to be?

The Delmore Brothers
(Photographer unknown, Charles Wolfe Collection)

Two recent events elaborate Appalachia's cultural and economic dilemma. In 2003 Congress passed a resolution proclaiming it to be the "Year of Appalachia." That summer, at the Smithsonian Institution's annual Festival of American Folklife, Appalachia was celebrated over the two-week event, in late June and early July, in the form of concerts, crafts demonstrations, historical displays, and homespun activities such as recipe and song swaps. Thousands of people congregated on the Mall in Washington, D.C., to sample slices of Appalachian culture and to celebrate the region as a wonderfully original part of America.

At the same time, the CBS television network, eager in its desire to capitalize on the craze for reality TV, turned its attention to Appalachia. The network's idea was to create a sort of "real Beverly Hillbillies," not a fictional family like the one that first aired on American television in 1962 and became one of the most successful sitcoms in television history. This one, hoped CBS executives, would enable the nation to gape at a true-to-life, genuinely poor Appalachian family as it scratched its collective head at such widespread staples of contemporary life as computers, microwave ovens, and perhaps, if they got the right family, indoor plumbing. CBS was offering the "lucky" family television stardom, a half-million dollars, plus plenty of perks in return for cameras running day and night in their shotgun shack. An unexpected uproar, not just from native Appalachians but also from many other people around the country who believed reality TV about poor people wasn't even close to being entertaining or funny, forced CBS to backtrack. The idea for the show was shelved.

The four-part PBS series *The Appalachians* serves the nation's new interest in Appalachia. Mari-Lynn Evans, who conceived and produced the film and is one of this book's editors, was born and raised in West Virginia. Having spent nearly four years researching and filming *The Appalachians,* Evans sees the film project—and this book—as the culmination of a lifelong ambition: to tell the story of her people in such a way that brings honor and dignity to them.

"The place in West Virginia where I grew up rarely changed," says Evans. "Our neighbors had known each other for generations. There is a special definition of 'home' in Appalachia that I wanted to run through the film. Appalachia isn't a godforsaken place like many outsiders would have you believe. It is home—and has been home for generations—for many families who love it, despite the hard times surviving there. In order to understand Appalachians, you have to understand that first. We love the mountains. They are a part of our soul."

Evans' documentary film seeks to reveal her Appalachia by examining its past, observing its present, and hinting at its future. She and her team, which includes numerous Appalachian authorities, some of whom contributed essays to this book, present the story of Appalachia as a distinct American place, yet one that has contributed significantly to the story of America. The time is right for a fresh view of the region. Thanks to the gargantuan success of the film *O Brother, Where Art Thou?* and its soundtrack, both of which, at least in part, pay mind to Appalachia, plus renewed interest in Appalachian art, folklore, and music, Appalachia is finally being welcomed into mainstream American culture.

"Appalachia doesn't seem so detached anymore," adds Evans. "The film and the book are solid evidence that interest in Appalachia, not just the myth of Appalachia but the truth, has

grown deeper than it's ever been. The stereotypes still linger, it's true. But people outside Appalachia have come to appreciate its culture rather than mock it."

In the essays that follow, you'll hear firsthand from Appalachian scholars, journalists, historians, musicians, novelists, poets, songwriters, and common folk with stories to tell. There are essays on religion, coal mining, the Civil War, music, the Pentecostal practice of serpent handling, moonshining, and much more. In no way is *The Appalachians* meant to be definitive. Rather, the book complements the film and seeks to broaden, even inspire, the possibilities of a further exploration of Appalachia.

Pay special note to the photographs and artwork that fill out *The Appalachians*. Rather than merely embellish the essays, they provide insight all their own. As you'll see, Appalachia is a most photogenic region; the many memorable photographs that grace this book document the undeniable dignity of the people and the poignancy of the Appalachian landscape, as well as the hard times they and the land have endured.

In the end, Appalachia is the story of struggle and triumph. If this book captures just a small part of the natural beauty of the place and its people, it will have been worth the effort.

—*Robert Santelli*
Seattle, Washington
July 2003

EDITOR'S NOTE

Martha Jean Holland, 1936
(Photographer unknown,
Holly George-Warren
Collection)

Being the daughter of an Appalachian native from the hills of western North Carolina, I had many flashbacks while working with Mari-Lynn Evans, Bob Santelli, and Tom Robertson editing the book *The Appalachians.* As I saw the images in Mari-Lynn and Tom's marvelous documentary series, perused countless articles and writings on Appalachia, gazed upon hundreds of photographs of the land and its people, and listened to the haunting mountain ballads, it all took me back to Rutherford County, where I spent weeks every summer and Christmas visiting my grandparents' farm and aunt and uncle's home. (The photo on the preceding page is of my mother, red-haired, green-eyed Martha Jean Holland, the daughter of Beulah Mooney and Herbert Roland Holland, when she was the five-year-old mascot of the senior class of Tri High School, Caroleen, North Carolina.) Learning of Mari-Lynn's experiences coming of age in West Virginia, I was struck by both the similarities—and differences—between our lives in two very distinct mountain regions.

Our goal for *The Appalachians,* then, was to capture the diversity of Appalachian culture, history, and experiences. As we assigned and selected text and images for this book, we also hoped to create a volume that would complement the material in the film. We found natives of North Carolina, Virginia, Kentucky, West Virginia, Tennessee, Georgia, South Carolina, and Pennsylvania to contribute words and images. The writers' opinions vary, and on some topics they flat-out disagree with one another. It's no wonder, because, just as our contributors hail from a variety of geographical locations in Appalachia, they also come from diverse backgrounds and occupations. We are lucky to have essays from scholars who served as consultants to the documentary, as well as poets, novelists, photographers, journalists, environmentalists,

naturalists, songwriters, musicians, politicians, historians, and artists. To give even more texture to our tome, we've included the lyrics of ancient Appalachian folk songs and early twentieth-century topical pieces. Poems, artworks, and excerpts from nineteenth-century writing on Appalachia are also here. Rounding out the mix are quotes from subjects interviewed for the film, ranging from retired coal miners, to the grandson of a slave, to members of the infamous Hatfield clan, to well-known musicians such as Patty Loveless, Loretta Lynn, Ricky Skaggs, and Little Jimmy Dickens. This book is also graced by the work of some masterful photographers, including Shelby Lee Adams, Jim Marshall, Stephanie Chernikowski, Van Slider, Chuck Conner, Karl Badgley, Mary Almond, Ted Olson, Jonathan Jessup, and Andy Sabol.

For those of you who are new to the culture and history of Appalachia, we hope this book will serve as an informative introduction that starts you on a path to learning more. And to our fellow Appalachians (past and present): May this volume take you back up into the hills for some downhome fun—as well as some "book larnin'" about an area or topic you may not know well. Enjoy the trip.

—*Holly George-Warren*
Phoenicia, New York
September 2003

Part One

THE FIRST FRONTIER

Blackwater Falls State Park, West Virginia, 1982
(Van Slider)

I t is no surprise that a region as rich in natural splendor and resources as Appalachia would, from early on, attract settlers, in particular those who sought not just bounty from the land but also a more meaningful relationship with it. Later on, historians and social observers would call this establishing a "sense of place."

Such a thing certainly occurred in Appalachia, like it did elsewhere across America, and as customs and rituals grew into culture and took root in the land, the identities of the people and

Spencer, West Virginia, 1978
(Chuck Conner)

their link with the land they inhabited grew stronger and clearer. Over time, it would become impossible, for instance, to separate New Englanders from New England, Californians from California, or Midwesterners from the Midwest. Unique things and ideas flourished in these regions. It could be something as significant as a music form or a dance, or as simple as a recipe made from indigenous vegetables or herbs.

In Appalachia, the same cultural process took place; namely, the people absorbed the place where they lived into their collective soul. It began with the earliest settlers—the Indians—and it continued as Europeans came to the region, intent on building new lives and creating opportunities. Eventually, what these settlers brought with them blended with what nature had provided, and what was created was a seamless bond between land and people that grew stronger and stronger as the years passed. By the middle of the nineteenth century, there was no way to pry either loose without causing damage to both, or worse, killing the connection. This happened in other parts of America as well. But in Appalachia, such a connection between people and place became so dramatic and deep as to become the perfect living example of a sense of place.

The Southern author Eudora Welty once wrote that "place absorbs our earliest notice and attention; it bestows on us our original awareness; and our critical powers spring from the study of it and the growth of experience inside it." In the essays that follow, a foundation is laid from which to better understand Welty's astute observation. Ted Olson, in overviews on the geography and the unique people of Appalachia, provides the historical facts concerning the development of Appalachia. Ireland's John Trew uses journeys he's taken through Appalachia to trace the region's Scottish and Irish roots. Gordon McKinney details Appalachia's role in the Civil War, while Dr. Judy Prozzillo Byers presents the history and significance of storytelling in Appalachia. Bill Richardson provided a picture of the geography of the Appalachian mountains, which still appear much as they were described by nineteenth-century travel writer T. Addison Richards.

Throughout The First Frontier (as well as throughout the rest of this book) are embellishments—poems, personal recollections, song lyrics—that bring additional meaning to the essays and further demonstrate the origins of the sense of place in Appalachia. Taken together, the essays and sidebars provide the necessary bricks and mortar from which to build an understanding—and appreciation—of Appalachia.

THE LAND

BILL RICHARDSON

Blue Ridge Mountains,
North Carolina
(Ted Olson)

**From Stars to Whiteness
to Words**

One summer midnight when I was
   young
(sleeping-bag cocooned in the
   woods
behind our house), I stared up—
through the silhouetted leaves
of a giant pin-oak—
into the clear, incomparable
   vastness
of speckled night.

Soon I was falling, falling *up*
into an enormous carapace of
   darkness,
pulled bodily away from the earth,
yet crushed as well,
strained through dimensions of
   thought
for which I was ill-equipped and
   fearful.

The Appalachian Mountains are some of the oldest mountains on earth and stretch from Canada to Alabama. They are made up of a series of ranges that can be divided into three major regions: the northern, central, and southern Appalachians. The mountains were formed by alternating periods when the land was uplifted and then worn away by erosion. Much of the present character of the northern Appalachians was influenced by glacial movement; the central mountains show more evidence of water erosion; and in the south you can still see many areas where the layers of rock have been pushed up and folded by the upheaval of the earth's crust.

In central Appalachia the mountains are very steep, and sometimes the valleys are only a hundred yards wide. It is a very formidable, almost impassable area. If you think about the way people traveled 150 years ago, it was nearly impossible to cross this region, and the only way to move within it was to follow the rivers and creeks or walk along the ridge tops.

In southern West Virginia, we joke that you can stand in a valley and almost touch the mountains on either side. There is just enough room between them for a creek, a road, a railroad track, and a narrow strip of houses. As a result, when you drive there, it seems as though people live in every nook and cranny, but in reality more than 85 percent of the land is uninhabited. If you get up on a high ridge and look out into the distance, you can see wave upon wave of mountains with no evidence of people in sight. In other parts of

Appalachia, however, the mountains are much gentler and there are even huge, open valleys such as the Shenandoah Valley of Virginia.

The geography of Appalachia has impacted nearly every aspect of life there. The early isolation caused by the mountains led to the development of distinctive cultures and types of speech. The terrain influenced settlement patterns and heredity. The land provided the means for survival–farmland, game, and later the trees and minerals that would become the basis for the area's economy. So throughout history, the mountains of Appalachia have shaped the lives of the people who live there–and such is still the case today.

The magnetism of each pinhole of
   a star
sucked me through the sieve
of countless light-years.

Now as a grown man,
no longer afraid of the dark,
and resigned to implications of the
   infinite,
I feel the same fear I felt that
   summer
long ago. The scope of the
   unwritten,
or the to-be-written, is unmitigated;
too many words and too many
   choices,
too many stars, and paths replete,
with ignominious doom, too much
   darkness
like too much whiteness. And
   worst of all,
where to begin, where to end?

An abyss of whiteness, relative and
   demeaning,
awaits causation's jab of context.
A page of white light
blinds with its ghost-glow
of long-ago imploded word-stars.

In beginning: if all mass has energy
and all energy has mass,
then the smallest speck of the first
   letter
of the first word
is incumbent upon what energy,
what mass? *Idea*, perhaps—
matriarch of all else, swimming
through an ocean of irreducible
mystery.

And in ending: all this considered,
how do these words ever get to
   this page?
Is its whiteness—like the stars—
the light that glows
from the words that aren't even
   there?   —John Sokol

Shenandoah National Park, near
Old Rag Mountain, Virginia
(Ted Olson)

THE LANDSCAPE OF THE SOUTHERN APPALACHIANS

T. ADDISON RICHARDS

The distinguishing mark of the mountain scenery of the Southern states as contrasted with that of the North is its greater picturesqueness and variety of form and quantity. The grand ranges of the Catskills and the Adirondacs *[sic]* and the peaks of the Green and the White Mountains are but outer links of the mighty Alleghenian chain, which, centering in Virginia, rears its most famed summits in Georgia and the Carolinas.

Blue Ridge Mountains, Virginia
(Ted Olson)

The Alleghenies in the northern states move on in a stately and unbroken line, like saddened exiles whose stern mood is ever the same and whose cold features are never varied with a smile; while in their home in the South, every step is free and joyous. Here they are grouped in the happiest and most capricious humor, now sweeping along in graceful outline, daintily crossing each other's path—or meeting in cordial embrace; here gathered in generous rivalry, and there breaking away sullenly in abrupt and frowning precipice.

All is Alpine variety, intricacy, and surprise. Seen from the general level, the mountains are ever sufficiently irregular in form and course to offer grateful contrasts; here and there in their unstudied meetings, leaving vistas of the world of hill and dale beyond; while the panoramic views command vast assemblages of ridge and precipice, varied in every characteristic—the large in opposition to the small, the barren in contrast with the wooded, the formal and the eccentric, the horizontal and the perpendicular; while a fairy valley in which the Abyssinian Prince might have rambled, a winding river, a glimpse of roadside or a distant hamlet, lend repose without monotony to the landscape.

–Excerpted from "The Landscape of the South,"
Harper's New Monthly Magazine,
1853

"Beau Catcher, a small mountain, which overlooks the little city of Asheville [North Carolina] and commands quite a fine view . . . is the resort of the 'Beau Catchers' and the 'Beauty Lovers' every evening, who drive there, ride there, and walk there and do their courting there. Old folks are tolerated too, so I went up the other evening and witnessed from it a most glorious sunset. But old as I am, I admired the round limbs and tapering waists and merry faces of the girls more than the grandeur of the mountains in the distance. Such is the frailty of poor mankind—a slave to woman, no matter how silly, if she has a pretty face and ankle."
—Western North Carolina judge David Schenck, 1877

WILD THING: THE JOYCE KILMER MEMORIAL FOREST

TED OLSON

*Little Santeetlah Creek,
flowing through the
Joyce Kilmer Memorial
Forest, North Carolina*
(Ted Olson)

Most people who travel the Skyline Drive in Virginia's Shenandoah National Park or the Blue Ridge Parkway for the first time are amazed to see so much forest growing close to the eastern megalopolis. Indeed, the parkway provides excellent access to many wild places, including, in Virginia, St. Mary's Wilderness Area, Peaks of Otter Recreation Area, and Rock Castle Gorge, and, in North Carolina, Linville Gorge Wilderness Area, Shining Rock Wilderness Area, and Middle Prong Wilderness Area, as well as the Great Smoky Mountains National Park. Among the other nearby wild places is the Joyce Kilmer Memorial Forest, located in an isolated area of the Nantahala Mountains in Graham County, North Carolina, a little more than an hour away by car from the southern terminus of the Blue Ridge Parkway. Arguably, it is the most impressive of all the wilderness areas in the eastern United States and virtually the only one that is, in actuality, a wilderness. The Joyce Kilmer Memorial Forest boasts a fascinating history that illustrates the extent of environmental change in the Appalachian region since the arrival of white people. When Europeans first settled the Appalachian frontier in the eighteenth century, the coves in which they built their cabins looked much like the Joyce Kilmer Memorial Forest does in the present day. In fact, the Kilmer Forest is virtually the only never-logged cove remaining in all of Appalachia.

In 1913, a simple twelve-line poem appeared in *Poetry* magazine.

The poem's first couplet is as famous as any other lines written in English: "I think that I shall never see / A poem lovely as a tree." Although many people today can name the title of the poem—it is, of course, "Trees"—few people can remember the name of the poet who wrote it; after all, none of his other works are popular today. Nowadays, Joyce Kilmer's name is brought up mainly in game shows (people seem amused that such a sentimental poem was written by a man named Joyce). Nonetheless, "Trees" is among the most widely known American poems. Fans of serious literature may scoff at such an assertion, but few other twentieth-century American poems have been as frequently anthologized, as widely memorized, as often translated. "Trees" has been read by millions; countless others have come to know the poem as the lyrics of a popular song. Although critics have generally considered it to be a sapling in a forest of literary sequoias, "Trees" has achieved for its author an honor no other American poet can claim: an ecologically important forest named after him.

The Joyce Kilmer Memorial Forest is the largest and most spectacular stand of virgin deciduous trees in the United States. Located just south of the Great Smoky Mountains National Park in Nantahala National Forest, near Robbinsville, North Carolina, the 3,840-acre Kilmer Forest occupies both sides of a fast-flowing stream called Little Santeetlah Creek, which drains a watershed (formerly known by locals as Poplar Cove) bounded on three sides by three different mountain ranges: the Unicoi Range to the west, the Snowbird Range to the south, and the Cheoah Range to the north. Little Santeetlah Creek flows eastward into Big Santeetlah Creek and then, after the latter stream empties into the Cheoah River, northward into the Little Tennessee River (where its waters run westward, eventually becoming part of the Tennessee River,

"It was a pleasing tho' dreadful sight, to see mountains and hills as if piled one upon the other."
—*Frontiersman Robert Fallam, 1671*

(Andy Sabol)

A giant yellow poplar in the Joyce Kilmer Memorial Forest
(Ted Olson)

then the Ohio River, and, ultimately, the Mississippi River). On its way out of Poplar Cove, Little Santeetlah Creek supports a magnificent, never-harvested forest featuring an amazing diversity of tree species—as many as in all of Europe. More than one hundred species of trees grow in Kilmer Forest, including yellow poplar, eastern hemlock, red maple, Fraser magnolia, American beech, yellow birch, northern red oak, and Carolina silver bell. Individual representatives of most of these species reach near-record size in Poplar Cove's fertile, well-watered bottomland soil; for example, several yellow poplars are so massive that it takes five or six people to reach their arms all the way around the trunks.

Many other Appalachian coves, before being logged around 1900, contained trees as stately as those now legally protected in the Joyce Kilmer Memorial Forest. Because it was never logged, the Little Santeetlah Creek watershed is today a living museum, offering visitors the opportunity to study and appreciate an aboriginal Appalachian cove forest and its undisturbed ecosystem.

Before logging companies came to Appalachia, sheltered mountain coves like Poplar Cove permitted numerous tree species to set their roots deep and flourish. In many of these coves, for example, centuries-old yellow poplars towered more than 125 feet high, the girth of their trunks measuring 20 feet or more in circumference. Such enormous trees dwarfed the Cherokee, who hunted game and gathered nuts beneath them long before the arrival of whites. European settlers, though, cleared the cove forests more than they hunted in them, for trees stood in the way of their longed-for farmsteads. The destruction of the Appalachian forests, quietly begun by eighteenth-century settlers, was dramatically increased in the late nineteenth and early twentieth centuries by logging companies. In just a few decades, using far more sophisticated equipment than the early mountaineers had, these companies harvested the vast majority of the Appalachian cove forests.

Only by a fluke of circumstance did the Joyce Kilmer Memorial Forest escape the fate of these other forests. Unlike most mountain coves, the Little Santeetlah Creek watershed went relatively untouched by European settlers because of its remoteness; in fact, only one small homestead was ever established there. The rugged southwestern corner of North Carolina, originally the domain of the Cherokee, was settled by Europeans later and less heavily than most other sections of the southern Appalachians. White people did not reside in the vicinity of present-day Robbinsville until 1840 (after the forced removal of the Cherokee by the U.S. government during the late 1830s). This was nearly a century after Europeans, journeying down the Great Valley of the Appalachians from Pennsylvania, settled other parts of the North Carolina mountains; it was more than sixty years after Daniel Boone built the Wilderness Road from the Blue Ridge Mountains to Kentucky to encourage settlement west of the Appalachians.

By the first decade of the twentieth century, logging companies had purchased large tracts of forest in and immediately south of the Great Smoky Mountains (because of its geographical isolation, this was virtually the last area in western North Carolina to be logged). Continuing the process begun elsewhere in Appalachia, the first companies to log near Robbinsville constructed railroads, rendering remote cove forests more accessible. The Little Santeetlah Creek watershed was one of the targeted areas. Around the turn of the century, the Belton Lumber Company bought and made plans to log all of Poplar Cove, but as soon as its splash dams were set in place, the company went bankrupt. In 1915 the Babcock Lumber Company began to log immediately to the north of Poplar Cove, on the banks of Slickrock Creek and its immediate tributaries; by 1922 Babcock had removed about two thirds of the trees in its Slickrock Creek tract when the construction of the Calderwood Dam on the Little Tennessee River destroyed the company's railroad access from the north. Further delaying the logging of the Little Santeetlah Creek watershed, which Babcock never reached, was the damming of the Cheoah River into Santeetlah Lake, which restricted railroad access from the east. Then, in the 1930s, with the Gennett Lumber Company about to log the enormous trees in Poplar Cove, the U.S. Forest Service intervened.

By the 1930s, Joyce Kilmer had become an American hero—not only to those who loved his poem "Trees" but also to those who remembered his patriotism during World War I. In 1917, after the tragic sinking of the *Lusitania* by the Germans, an enraged Kilmer quit his job at *The New York Times* and signed up for the National Guard. Noted as a journalist as well as a poet, the New Jersey native was offered a position as a statistician for the U.S. Army, which would have kept him a safe distance from the battlefront, but Kilmer turned it down, opting instead to work as an intelligence officer. In that position, he was stationed, on July 30, 1918, near the front lines in France, his mission to locate enemy machine-gun nests. There he died, victim of a sniper's bullet. His comrades buried him in France, among war-mangled trees quite unlike the ones he had in mind when he wrote his famous poem.

Answering the pleas of the Veterans of Foreign Wars, who wanted a memorial site in which to commemorate Kilmer, the U.S. Forest Service purchased the Little Santeetlah Creek tract from the Gennett Lumber Company in 1935. At the 1936 dedication ceremony for the establishment of the Joyce Kilmer Memorial Forest, a letter written by President Roosevelt was read, acknowledging Kilmer's

"The very first industry in West Virginia and much of Appalachia in the mid- and late 1800s was timber. The central part of Appalachia has the second largest hardwood forest in the world. Thus in the late 1800s, armies of men came to cut the trees. Since there were no regulations, the forests were clear cut. There are old photographs of men standing on tree stumps that were five and ten feet wide.
The forests were completely virgin at that time; after logging, there was an ocean of empty stumps as far as the eye could see, mountain ridge after mountain ridge. Today, it's hard to find a tree in Appalachia that is more than 100 or 150 years old."

—*Geologist Bill Richardson, West Virginia University, 2002* dual role as beloved poet and war hero: "It is particularly fitting that a poet who will always be remembered for the tribute he embodied in 'Trees' should find this living monument. Thus his beloved memory is forever honored, and one of nature's masterpieces is set aside to be preserved for the enjoyment of generations yet unborn."

A boulder was the site chosen to place a plaque commemorating Joyce Kilmer.
(Ted Olson)

Today visitors to this living monument may not know much about its namesake, but they will certainly be impressed by the grandeur of its trees. Oleta Nelms, official hostess of the Kilmer Forest, states that "people feel awestruck when they enter this forest. I have never seen conduct here that wouldn't be permissible in church." A retired schoolteacher who lives in Robbinsville, Nelms was hired by the U.S. Forest Service to greet some of Kilmer Forest's fifty thousand annual visitors and to explain to them the significance of the place they are entering. She particularly loves to talk about the only non-Cherokee who have ever lived in the Little Santeetlah Creek watershed: her grandparents, John and Albertine Denton, who lived in a small cabin just off the Stratton Bald Trail. Nelms explains that the Dentons were self-sufficient farmers who also raised their own horses, livestock, and poultry. Although she never knew them, Nelms has heard that John Denton was a master craftsman, and that the cabin he built was so solid—being held together with two-inch black-locust pins—it was able to withstand all the punishment the Dentons' nine children could give it. The cabin is gone now, having rotted away; only the chimney remains, with a yellow poplar sapling growing through it.

When visitors first enter the Joyce Kilmer Memorial Forest on

A rotting hollow tree trunk covered in moss now provides a home for insects and animals. (Ted Olson)

the wood-chip-blanketed foot trail, they encounter a wooden sign warning them to watch out for the trees: "This trail provides hikers a unique opportunity to observe an aging virgin forest; however, it does pass near dead or dying trees that may fall or drop limbs. Natural processes, such as trees dying, are allowed to operate freely within Wilderness."

As visitors soon discover, Kilmer Forest is no secondhand stand of trees, like most of the woodlands east of the Rockies. Although many forests in the eastern United States are now federally designated as wilderness areas, very few can be considered authentic wilderness, which would mean that they possess substantial stands of virgin timber. The logging companies' exploitation of the great eastern deciduous forests was so extensive that today virtually nothing remains of the aboriginal American wilderness.

Yet Kilmer Forest *is* wilderness, unadorned and unadulterated by humans. A stroll down the Joyce Kilmer Memorial Trail (a two-mile figure-eight loop through the heart of Kilmer Forest) will suggest to the visitor what the American wilderness was really like. From the small parking lot at the end of U.S. Forest Service Road #416, the shortest distance to the legendary big trees is the Joyce Kilmer Memorial Trail, walked in a counterclockwise direction. The first trees that visitors see along this walk are quite unimpressive—a stunted grove of yellow birch, eastern hemlock, and American beech. Growing in soil disturbed by the construction of rest rooms and a parking lot, the roots of these young trees have been exposed to the impact of heavy hiking boots, tree diseases, and insect pests. Fortunately, only a hundred yards farther into Kilmer Forest, the visitor encounters far fewer traces of human interference: Except for the trail itself (built by the Civilian Conservation Corps in the 1930s) and a few benches, bridges, stairs, and handrails

(all constructed out of wood to blend in with the environment), the Little Santeetlah Creek watershed, having never known the environmental degradation of logging, has hardly changed since the time of Columbus. The cascading creek still gouges out the streambed rocks as it did millennia ago. Now, as then, huge trees, rising up through lush rhododendron thickets, continue to attain impressive girths and heights, the creek's prolific moisture encouraging them to grow to gigantic size.

And when some agent of death—old age, insects, disease, fire, or lightning—hastens their decline, these trees will still play a vital role in the forest ecosystem, providing food and shelter for numerous species of animals, especially for woodpeckers, whose holes are everywhere in Kilmer Forest. Even after these trees cease to stand,

It

drifts into your world
like the invisible dust of stars,
the rust of time,
ether from ancient jars.
It surrounds you—
after lightning, before thunder;
in the darkness, before dawn.
Midge of unmanageable
    rumination,
it settles behind the marbles
of your eyes, nests in the
canyons
of your ears, makes itself a
    kingdom
in the interstices
of your gray matter.
It arrives in the vague hours
and becomes palpable
as it sharpens itself
on the intensely specific minutes;
as it counts—out loud—
while you try to sleep;
as it becomes
your unbearable guest.
                    —*John Sokol*

A majestic tree canopy in the
Joyce Kilmer Memorial Forest
(Ted Olson)

their rotting trunks, returning to the soil that originally spawned them, will support whole colonies of smaller plants: mushrooms, moss, lichens, ferns, even small seedlings of future giants. Because they allow a new generation of forest inhabitants to gain a foothold, such trunks are aptly called nursery logs by foresters. Examples of this regeneration are common in Kilmer Forest: Perhaps the most dramatic nursery log visible along the Joyce Kilmer Memorial Trail is the decaying yellow poplar stump (at ground level, more than seven feet in diameter) out of which is growing a healthy eastern hemlock sapling. Unless it is stopped by some natural occurrence, such as lightning, or by some human-caused problem, such as the accidentally introduced insect pest known as the hemlock wolly adelgid, this sapling will someday tower over Little Santeetlah Creek like its host tree. But it will become one of the huge trees only if people continue to safeguard the Joyce Kilmer Memorial Forest. For this to happen, people must continue to appreciate—in the spirit of Kilmer Forest's namesake—the beauty of *all* trees, saplings as well as giants.

THE MOUNTAIN MELTING POT:
APPALACHIA'S DIVERSE ETHNIC
AND RACIAL GROUPS

TED OLSON

Indigenous people lived in Appalachia as early as 8000 B.C., and several distinctive Native American cultures emerged in the region during subsequent centuries. In A.D. 1539, the first Europeans to enter Appalachia—explorer Hernando de Soto and his army of Spaniards—encountered the Cherokee, the region's predominant tribe during the period of European exploration and settlement in Appalachia.

The Cherokee's traditional culture was not only complex but also radically different from European ways of living and thinking. For instance, the Cherokee people's political system was less centralized than any European model, with each member of the tribe belonging to one of several autonomous tribal organizations (often referred to as "towns"). Each of these organizations possessed its own council and its own ceremonial center, and decisions affecting a given organization had to be unanimous among all the people within that town. While male elders dominated the councils, all town members could speak at council meetings. Hence, during the early years of European exploration and settlement in Appalachia, the Cherokee did not have a central political figure to negotiate between the tribe's various towns. Before the Revolutionary War, tensions between the Cherokee and settlers led to violence, as Cherokee warriors attempted to defend the tribe's historic territory against the influx of Europeans—particularly English and Scots-Irish settlers.

Settlement into the Appalachian frontier, though, increased dramatically after the Revolutionary War. The political and military leaders of the new nation became increasingly interested in obtaining the natural resources—especially the gold—found on Cherokee lands. These white leaders, projecting European perspectives onto the Cherokee, attempted to identify tribal leaders in order to negotiate treaties with those individuals, ignoring the traditional Cherokee practice that no one person could speak for the whole tribe.

By the end of the eighteenth century, as the expanding American nation increasingly threatened to displace the Cherokee, tribal elders, hoping to strengthen the Cherokee's ability to contend with dramatic change, formed new politically centralized organizations led by respected individuals within the tribe. Despite such efforts, in 1845 a small splinter group of Cherokee in 1835 signed the Treaty of New Echota, which authorized the selling of all Cherokee lands to the U.S. government for a fee of $5 million. Efforts by the Cherokee to disclaim that treaty went unheard, and from 1838 to 1839, an estimated 16,000 members of the tribe were forced by the U.S. Army to march on the "Trail of Tears" to Indian Territory (present-day Oklahoma). Escaping this plight were approximately 1,400 Cherokee, who hid in the Great Smoky Mountains of western North Carolina and who were ultimately allowed to remain there by the federal government. The descendants of the latter group of Cherokee, still residing in the Smokies today, are known as the Eastern Band (to distinguish them from the Oklahoma Cherokee). Tourists regularly visit a section of the tribe's historic territory now known as the Qualla Boundary, incor-

Cherokee posing with visiting musicians, North Carolina
(Photographer unknown, Charles Wolfe Collection)

"They settled here in the late 1700s, and, of course, it was strictly a wilderness. One of the first things they had to do was build a temporary house, which was soon followed within a year or two with a permanent dwelling. Most of them were one room, and the traditional size was about eighteen-by-twenty-four. They learned to be totally self-sufficient. I don't think you can name a single necessity that they couldn't make or acquire or gather from the land. One of the first things they did was to build a gristmill— a water-powered mill to grind the corn or wheat. They perfected the art of gardening. They saved every scrap of ashes for the garden for fertilizer. You could take a small plot on a hillside and raise enough turnips and potatoes to do you pretty much all year."
—*Museum of Appalachia historian John Rice Irwin*

Farm in Ulster, Northern Ireland
(John Trew)

porating the area immediately surrounding the town of Cherokee, North Carolina, in part to learn of the Cherokee's distinctive cultural heritage.

Most of the people who explored and surveyed Appalachia before the Revolutionary War were English-born or the New World–born descendants of English-born colonists, and approximately one third of the region's eighteenth-century settlers were of this ethnicity. Several factors would strengthen the ability of these settlers—most of whom were dispossessed agricultural workers or artisans from the borderlands of northern England—to assimilate in Appalachia, including their familiarity with the new frontier society's dominant European language (English) and the prevailing legal, political, and economic systems.

English "borderers" migrated into Appalachia from the coastal ports of the colonies at the same time, in much the same way, and for many of the same reasons as another group of settlers, the Scots-Irish from Ulster, Ireland, whose numbers in Appalachia exceeded even those who immigrated to the region from England. Having landed in Philadelphia or Charleston only to find little available property or satisfactory work in already settled, socially stratified eastern Pennsylvania or South Carolina, the Scots-Irish headed into the mountainous backcountry of the southern colonies to claim homesteads. The Scots-Irish were products of a political experiment from the late sixteenth century, when England's Queen Elizabeth I encouraged Protestants from the British Isles—mostly Presbyterians from the borderlands of southern Scotland—to settle in the northern part of Ireland (Ulster) to serve as a buffer between English territories and the Irish, most of whom spoke Gaelic and were Catholic. Fighting the Irish and living the difficult life of tenant farming, Scots-Irish people in Ulster soon sensed that they would have little opportunity to improve their social or economic standing while remaining in the Old World.

Scots-Irish settlers strongly influenced the evolution of Appalachian identity, given that people of other ethnicities saw that group as particularly valuing independence, resourcefulness, faith, family, and tradition. These qualities are exactly the same ones that by the twentieth century would form the core of the positive and negative stereotypes held against the Appalachian people by "outsiders" and the mainstream American media.

Germans were among the earliest European settlers in several sections of Appalachia, including central Pennsylvania, where they were establishing farmsteads by the early eighteenth century. By the mid-1700s, those settlers' next generation, along with subsequently arriving German and Swiss immigrants, had moved southwestward from Pennsylvania down the Great Valley of the Appalachians into western Virginia and the Carolina mountains, where they settled on the finest farmland available. Many German immigrant Protestant sects—including Amish and Mennonites—settled in Appalachia (particularly in parts of Pennsylvania and Ohio) as whole communities, with the intention of securing religious freedom while maintaining a self-sufficient way of life; some of these communities are extant today. Recent census records suggest that approximately 13 percent of Appalachian residents claim German ancestry.

The Melungeon people reside today primarily in a few rural counties in northeast Tennessee and southwestern Virginia. The ethnic background of the group remains unclear, since neither

Melungeon ancestors nor past governmental officials kept satisfactory records of the group's bloodlines. Melungeons, according to a popular notion, descended from the intermingling of people from several ethnicities (likely Native American, African American, Anglo-American, and possibly Portuguese and Turkish) in colonial Virginia. Sometime after the Revolutionary War, yet before the Civil War, the Melungeons migrated into relatively unpopulated sections of the Appalachians to find more suitable locations in which to maintain their tight-knit communities and their self-sufficient, agriculture-based way of life. Stereotyped historically within popular literature and other media for their apparent differences from the national norm, Melungeons today are culturally indistinct from many other Appalachian people. In recent years Melungeons have attempted to ascertain their genetic ethnicity through DNA sampling, the results of which have thus far been inconclusive.

Having been present in Appalachia for nearly as long as white people, African Americans have markedly influenced Appalachian culture. Before emancipation, the institution of slavery was practiced in many parts of the region, though plantations in Appalachia were less common and much smaller (from one to five slaves per family) than those in the Deep South. Although most people in Appalachia did not own a plantation, many owned at least one slave to assist in manual labor on small farms. Other blacks worked temporarily in the region, brought there by coastal and piedmont planters as servants at summer estates or as laborers-for-hire in various trades, including herding. After emancipation and through the turn of the century, younger generations of blacks migrated into Appalachia to find work in emerging industries, including railroading, mining, and logging. Racially discriminatory penal systems forced many black convicts into Appalachia to build railroads and tunnels. Cultural sharing between blacks and whites–evident before the Civil War, when whites adopted the African banjo–continued after emancipation, with widespread exchange of musical styles and song repertoires (including the well-known African-American blues ballad "John Henry," which commemorates the heroism of a black laborer during the 1872 construction of a railroad in West Virginia).

Slaves work the fields of a small Appalachian farm.
(Photographer unknown, Mari-Lynn Evans Collection)

Several other ethnic groups have had a significant presence in at least one section of Appalachia, historically or in recent years. In the mid-eighteenth century, French soldiers resided temporarily in present-day western Pennsylvania, though in the late 1700s, the efforts of French Huguenots to construct permanent communities in southeastern Ohio failed. In the last half of the nineteenth century, thousands of Welsh immigrants with considerable mining experience in Wales found work in the Pennsylvania coalfields. Also lured to Appalachia toward the end of that century by the promise of industrial employment were Italians (who initially worked in central Appalachia on railroads and, later, as coal miners and stonemasons), as well as Hungarians and Greeks (who worked in the same mines as Italians).

A more recent wave of immigration started circa 1970, as people from countries such as India, Iran, Japan, and Jamaica found work in Appalachia. Since 1990, the largest influx of immigrants into the region has involved Hispanics from numerous Western Hemisphere countries–primarily Mexico, but also Central and South American nations as well as from the Spanish-speaking West Indies. While many Hispanics have worked temporarily as seasonal agricultural laborers, others have settled in the region as carpet manufacturers or poultry processors.

A pair of anonymous amateur musicians, southwest Virginia, circa 1925
(Photographer unknown, Charles Wolfe Collection)

Unknown musicians in a train station in Appalachia, circa 1920
(Photographer unknown, Charles Wolfe Collection)

Regardless of their reasons for venturing into Appalachia, new-comers, both historically and in recent years, have encountered discrimination and stereotypes, and many people felt compelled to leave the region during difficult economic times to seek employment in more prosperous parts of the United States.

Yet immigrants who stay in Appalachia tend to develop a deep identification with their adopted region. And most are proud to call themselves Appalachians.

APPALACHIA'S SCOTS-IRISH ANCESTRY

JOHN TREW

During the 1970s, when my job as editor of the *Belfast News Letter* became particularly stressful—it was the height of the Ulster troubles—I would slip away from the cacophony of telephones and typewriters to seek the serenity of the strong-room archives for an hour or two.

There, within the leather-bound volumes of the world's oldest surviving daily newspaper (founded in 1737), I could read contemporary reports of momentous historic events, such as the French Revolution, Britain's exploration and settlement of Australia, and the coronations of English kings.

Scots-Irish farm at the American Frontier Museum, Staunton, Virginia
(John Trew)

For pure escapism, however, I preferred the delightful descriptions of lavish entertainments provided by local music halls, revelations about fashions in ladies' linen undergarments, and prize-fighting results ("Driscoll expired after less than an hour, much to the dissatisfaction of the assembled multitude"). Most of all, I loved to read about the settlement of North America and the huge and heroic parts of its destiny being played by my kinfolk, the people known in their homeland as Ulster-Scots, and across the Atlantic as the Scots-Irish. These were mostly Presbyterians whose forefathers had migrated from Scotland to Ulster, the northern-most province of Ireland, in the 1600s, to find religious freedom and fertile farmland. Through their energetic work ethic and dogged determination, the Scots transformed the commercial, industrial, educational, and cultural face of Ulster. In the early 1700s, though, a series of crop failures, compounded by conflicts with both their Irish-Catholic neighbors and their English rulers, led to the start of a lengthy exodus to the New World. Disembarking at often-unwelcoming British-Colonial ports, they eventually moved into the Appalachian frontier, creating tiny communities beginning in 1718. By the 1740s, almost every issue of the *Belfast News Letter* featured advertisements from the owners of many different emigrant sailing ships, with most notices accompanied by the same woodcut illustration of a sturdy-looking vessel.

From the Ulster ports of Belfast, Carrickfergus, Larne, Portrush, and Londonderry, migrants faced at least a six-week voyage to Boston, Philadelphia, or Charleston. Conditions for passengers traveling on vessels built to carry bulk cargo were generally poor—often horrendous—and there was a high mortality rate when North Atlantic storms caused havoc.

"Some years ago . . . in the mountains of North Carolina, I passed by a large number of 'coves' . . . which had been cleared and planted. The impression on my mind was one of unmitigated squalor. The settler had cut down the more manageable trees and left their charred stumps standing. The larger trees he had girdled and killed. He had then built a log cabin, plastering its chinks with clay, and had set up a tall zigzag rail fence around the scene of his havoc, to keep the pigs and cattle out. . . . He had planted the intervals between the stumps with Indian corn . . . and there he dwelt with his wife and babe—an ax, a gun, a few utensils, and some pigs and chickens . . . the sum total of his possessions.

"The forest had been destroyed; and what had 'improved' it out of existence was hideous . . . without a single element of nature's beauty. Ugly indeed seemed the life of the squatter . . . beginning back where our first ancestors started and . . . hardly better off for . . . the achievements of . . . intervening generations.

Scots-Irish immigrants to Appalachia brought the music of their homeland with them. (Photographer unknown, Charles Wolfe Collection)

"THE SEAFLOWER: Bound for Philadelphia. Comfortable Voyage Assured" was a typical promise published on the *Belfast News Letter*'s front page. Alas, in 1741, food and fresh water ran out during the *Seaflower*'s tempestuous winter passage to Pennsylvania, a popular destination for the Northern Irish, and six of the dead passengers were cannibalized by the crew.

In spite of such deterrents, however, a quarter-million Ulster farmers, clerks, tradesmen, and their families had crossed the Atlantic by 1800. Many survived piracy, mutiny, seasickness, disease, pestilence, and unimaginable delays (one 1773 voyage took seventeen weeks!). Northern Irish shopkeepers William Carson and John T. Pirie survived a shipwreck off the coast of Maine and later crossed the Appalachian Mountains into Illinois, establishing the

"Then I said to the mountaineer who was driving me, 'What sort of people . . . make these new clearings?' 'All of us,' he replied. 'Why, we ain't happy here unless we are getting one of these coves under cultivation.' I instantly felt that I had been losing the whole inward significance of the situation. Because to me the clearing spoke of naught by denudation, I thought that to those whose sturdy arms and obedient axes had made them they could tell no other story. But when they looked on the hideous stumps, what they thought of was personal victory. The chips, the girdled trees, and the vile split rails spoke of honest sweat, persistent toil, and final reward."
—*Philosopher William James, circa 1880*

Author John Trew posing outside Davy Crockett's cabin, near Limestone, East Tennessee (Courtesy of John Trew)

world's first chain store, Carson Pirie Scott (which still exists in the Chicago area).

Because of these character-building experiences and the Presbyterian passion to be masters of their own destiny, it's no wonder that the Ulster-Scots and their descendents became the kings of the wild Appalachian frontier. They also later pioneered the trails westward to Ohio, Indiana, Illinois, and Missouri. David Crockett, the best known of Appalachia's frontiersmen, descended from Tyrone-born grandparents who took the Great Wagon Road from Pennsylvania, settling Rogersville, Tennessee, where they were killed by Cherokee in 1777. After a colorful career as an adventurer and politician, "Davy" gave his life alongside many comrades of Ulster origin at the Alamo in San Antonio in 1836. Appropriately, the Alamo massacre was avenged by Sam Houston, born in Virginia's backcountry, the grandson of a County Antrim farmer. Sam became, in turn, governor of Tennessee *and* Texas. He was by no means the first son of Ulster from Appalachia to wield political power in America. Indeed, so many Ulster settlers were involved in the American War for Independence that an English general said, "This is not a revolutionary war, it's a Scotch-Irish Presbyterian rebellion."

Andrew Jackson, born in the Waxhaw settlement of the Carolinas just two years after his parents emigrated from Carrickfergus, was the first U.S. president of Ulster-Appalachian descent. At least fifteen—one third of all presidents—have had a large measure of Scots-Irish ancestry, including George W. Bush, whose maternal ancestors settled in the foothills of the Great Smokies in the 1770s. Other chief executives from Appalachian states who shared what James Buchanan called "my precious Ulster heritage" include James Knox Polk, Andrew Johnson, and that great son of the Shenandoah Valley, Woodrow Wilson. Hailing from Staunton, Virginia, President Wilson combined scholarship with statesmanship, displaying many Ulster characteristics in his espousal of "faith and freedom."

Familiar Ulster-Scot surnames can be seen on mailboxes throughout Appalachia: Armstrong, Bell, Bailey, Dickson, Wallace, Patterson, Stewart, Rogers, and dozens of familiar Macs—McNally, McCain, McEntire, and McCoy. Today's McCoys don't like to be

"They were a grim, stern people . . . strong and simple . . . powerful for good or evil . . . swayed by gusts of stormy passion, the love of freedom rooted in their hearts' core. They were of all men best fitted to conquer the wilderness and hold it against all comers."
—*Teddy Roosevelt, on the Scots-Irish*

associated with the Kentucky mountain men famous for feudin' with the Hatfields, but most appreciate the fact that only the best moonshine whiskey was called the Real McCoy!

Whiskey-making skills helped Ulster settlers tolerate severe winter weather while awaiting the Appalachian spring. Elijah Craig—a Baptist minister—was the first to distill whiskey in Bourbon County, Kentucky, a decade before hundreds of Scots-Irish moonshiners arrived from Pennsylvania, following the Whiskey Rebellion of 1794. "Why should we pay tax for drinking our own grain instead of eating it?" was their seemingly reasonable argument, but it didn't wash with the new U.S. government, desperate to raise revenue, so bootleggers headed for the hills.

"The first thing the Irish Presbyterians do when they progress west of the Cumberland Gap in their Conestoga wagons," wrote a puritan land agent, "is to build their cabins and a church, then set up their stills and raise a barn in which to play their devilish music."

It's not surprising, therefore, that 250 years later, the most enduring aspects of the Ulster-Scots legacy are often characterized as bourbon, the Bible, and bluegrass. Also, "hillbilly" is said to come from the popularity of the names Bill, Will, Billy, and Willy, among Ulster mountain men descended from Williamite soldiers of the Irish war of 1690.

Today, about twenty-five million Americans can claim descent from those early pioneers. Like Ulster-born Charles Thomson, who copied the drafts of the Declaration of Independence, and John Dunlap, the Tyrone man who printed it, Ulster-Scots continue to leave an indelible imprint on every aspect of American life.

THE CIVIL WAR IN APPALACHIA

GORDON B. MCKINNEY

The years between 1859 and 1865 were a time of terror and destruction in the southern Appalachian Mountains. In many areas, neighbors and family members supported opposite sides of the Civil War, which officially began on April 12, 1861. Communities were destroyed by confrontations as large armies marched across the mountains throughout the war, leaving behind desolated farms and towns and thousands of dead and wounded soldiers and civilians.

John Brown
(Photographer unknown, Boyd B. Stutler Collection, courtesy of the West Virginia State Archives)

The Civil War actually started in Appalachia earlier than in any other part of the South. In 1859, John Brown and his companions seized the United States Armory and Arsenal at Harpers Ferry, Virginia (which now is in West Virginia). This group of abolitionists sought to spark a slave uprising and planned to use the arsenal weapons to arm the freedmen. Instead of being greeted by joyous slaves, Brown and his men were surrounded by the Federal army, led by Colonel Robert E. Lee. After a short skirmish, Brown was captured, and some of his men, including two of his sons, were killed. Convicted of treason, Brown was executed after he issued a warning that the country would soon be drenched in blood.

In the 1860 presidential election, many mountain voters supported the Constitutional Union Party, which sought to preserve the Union. During the secession crisis following Abraham Lincoln's election, the majority of mountaineers opposed quick action to form a Southern nation. In east Tennessee, northwestern Virginia, western Maryland, and southeastern Kentucky, most of the people supported the national government. In the Shenandoah Valley of Virginia, western North Carolina, northern Georgia, and northern Alabama, most were reluctant to leave the Union, but they accepted the reality of the Confederacy in their states and supported the Southern war effort.

The earliest military campaign in the region had immediate and permanent results. A Federal army under the leadership of General George B. McClellan routed Confederate forces at the battles of Philippi and Rich Mountain, leaving Unionists in control of northwestern Virginia. A convention met in Wheeling to begin the process of creating a new state. After the state convention approved an amendment requiring a gradual end to slavery, the Lincoln administration recognized the new state of West Virginia on June 20, 1863.

For Unionists in east Tennessee, resistance to the Confederacy brought terror instead of liberation. After initiating a sabotage campaign directed at the railroads in their region in November 1861, many of the Unionist perpetrators were seized and hanged after failing to receive assistance from Federal forces.

Large armies first came to the mountain regions in the spring of 1862. The most successful of these campaigns was directed by Confederate General Thomas J. "Stonewall" Jackson, a native of Appalachia. Jackson, using a smaller and highly mobile force, humiliated Union armies at the battles of Winchester and Front Royal, in Virginia's Shenandoah Valley. After Jackson easily captured Harpers Ferry in September 1862, Robert E. Lee led his Confederate army into western Maryland. Suffering a minor defeat at South Mountain, Lee fought a tactical draw with a larger Union army at Sharpsburg, Maryland. When Lee withdrew from Maryland, Abraham Lincoln issued the Emancipation Proclamation, thereby declaring that this war was a crusade against slavery.

On the Appalachian home front, the war placed enormous pressure on fragile communities. Many men from mountain hamlets volunteered for military service—about 150,000 for the Confederate army and 100,000 for the Union forces. Adding to the strain was the conscription imposed by the Confederacy in 1862 and the Federal government in 1863. This policy upset the delicate economic balance within mountain societies. The drafting of skilled craftsmen meant that these mountain families found it increasingly difficult to secure shoes, furniture, milled grains, and other necessities provided by subsistence-economy mainstays.

The removal of men from the mountain areas resulted in other negative consequences as well. Without sufficient labor to maintain the bridges and highways in many parts of Appalachia, trade in necessary commodities virtually ceased. The most important of these goods was salt, used to preserve meat. Conflict over salt led to a horrifying incident of internal violence in western North Carolina. In January 1863, a shipment of the valued white substance arrived in Marshall, the seat of Madison County. The county leadership decided not to share the salt with the pro-Union population of Shelton Laurel, whose residents then raided Marshall and seized the salt, causing the death of two small children. When Confederate soldiers from Marshall returned to the county, they marched into the Laurel area and tortured women, arrested old men and boys, and shot thirteen unarmed civilians. Many other such violent incidents took place throughout the southern highlands, and thousands of civilians suffered violent deaths before the war's end.

For the women who remained at home, life was difficult throughout the conflict. Some accepted the challenge and, with the help of family and neighbors, provided enough food to keep

The stars of heaven are looking
  kindly down,
The stars of heaven are looking
  kindly down,
The stars of heaven are looking
  kindly down,
On the grave of old John Brown!

(Chorus)

He's gone to be a soldier in the
  army of the Lord,
He's gone to be a soldier in the
  army of the Lord,
He's gone to be a soldier in the
  army of the Lord,
His soul is marching on!

(Chorus)

John Brown's knapsack is strapped
  upon his back,
John Brown's knapsack is strapped
  upon his back,
John Brown's knapsack is strapped
  upon his back,
His soul is marching on!

(Chorus)

"After the Civil War, my father stayed in Appalachia. Oddly enough, he went back to his former master and asked for a job. That was unusual. But he got this job and he started working. Then he began to buy land from his former master, who was surprised that a totally illiterate slave wanted to buy property, so he sold him land for five dollars an acre. There was plenty of land up in those Pine Hills."
  —*African-American Appalachia resident Dewey Fox*

Former slaves clear a field of the remains of fallen soldiers.
(Photographer unknown, Mari-Lynn Evans Collection)

their families intact. Others found conditions so unbearable that they sought escape to lowland regions or to Union territory nearby. Family groups from northern Georgia and western North Carolina were intercepted during two of these attempts and were massacred by local defense forces. Another incident illustrating this desperate struggle and great privation occurred in April 1864 when fifty women in Yancey County, North Carolina, broke into a Confederate warehouse to steal grain. For many thousands of mountain women, the greatest distress came from the death of a husband, father, son, or brother in the service.

For enslaved African Americans, the war brought relatively little change. In areas through which large armies marched—the Shenandoah Valley, eastern Tennessee, and northern Georgia—some slaves achieved freedom by escaping into Union army lines. Others in Union-held areas joined the Union army. But most of the enslaved people remained under traditional restraints and endured greater hardship because of the economic privations created by the war. Thousands of slaves from lowland areas were taken by their owners into the mountains—particularly into western North Carolina—for safekeeping. Thus, in some parts of the mountain South, slavery actually increased during the war.

As the Confederacy weakened, another major invasion of the mountain South took place. The Union army outmaneuvered Confederate troops and seized control of Chattanooga and Knoxville, Tennessee, in September 1863. A successful counterattack by the Confederate forces at the Battle of Chickamauga in northern Georgia forced the Federal army back into Chattanooga. In late November 1863, a heroic charge up

Missionary Ridge by Union troops forced the Confederates to retreat to northern Georgia. In May, the strengthened Union army, under the command of William T. Sherman, moved against Confederate lines, slowly pushing them back to the defenses around Atlanta.

By 1865, Appalachia's economy and society were on the verge of collapse. Significant portions of the mountain region had little political structure. Raids by organized armies and guerrillas only made things worse. Peace did not return to the region, even after the surrender of Confederate armies under Robert E. Lee and Joseph Johnston. Some of the most notorious terrorist organizations refused to disband and had to be exterminated by local forces. Tragically, the conflict had been a civil war at the local level as well as for the nation at large. So searing was this experience that loyalties forged during the conflict still influence Appalachian politics today.

"All day long the battle raged. Occasionally there would be a lull for a short time; but the cannons were never entirely hushed. They would break out in increased thunder, and the roar of musketry would roll up and down the lines, vibrating almost regularly from one extreme to the other. All day long the ambulances continued to discharge their loads of wounded. At last night set in, and the musketry ceased, but the Federal gunboats continued shelling awhile after dark. Nearly midnight when we got through with the wounded, a heavy rain set in. I was tired, sick, and all covered with blood. But I was in a far better fix than many that were there. I sat on a medicine chest in the surgeon's tent and 'nodded' the long night through."
—*Bardstown, Kentucky, native John S. Jackman, from* Diary of a Confederate Soldier at the Front, *on witnessing the battle at Shiloh*

Confederate soldiers
(Photographer unknown, Mari-Lynn Evans Collection)

STORYTELLING IN APPALACHIA

DR. JUDY PROZZILLO BYERS

The institutionalization of storytelling can be found throughout America. Originally the primary means of communicating and recording the beliefs of a people, storytelling informed, taught, and entertained. In the Appalachian region, storytelling maintains a presence far beyond that in other parts of the country because of the area's rich folkloric heritage from which it was born. Chiseled out of an ancient mountain range, at one time more towering and massive than the Rockies, the Appalachians contain a variety of lush green vegetation and timber that blanket a striking blend of rock and fertile earth, which in turn house deposits of coal, oil, and gas. Into these rolling hills and deep valleys came migrations of people who brought distinctive oral traditions and mores perpetuated through the storytelling process. The mountainous range served both as a protective band to embrace what was there and as a barrier to block outside influences. In this isolated rural environment, language patterns, storytelling variants, and their motifs were easily preserved and perpetuated. In Appalachia, therefore, storytelling comes close to replicating its original art form.

It has flourished for a number of reasons. During the late 1600s

Extended families such as the one in this 1905 photograph gathered under a canopy of trees to tell stories and play centuries-old ballads, often with new words that reflected life in the Appalachian mountains.
(Photographer unknown, Mari-Lynn Evans Collection)

and early 1700s, Anglo-Celtic (English, Irish, and Scots) and Germanic settlers migrated into these western hills. The pioneering people became farmers; wilderness explorers; raisers of hogs, cattle, and horses; and austere, often ruthless, hunters, trappers, Indian traders, and fighters. As early explorers of the Appalachian "western frontier," they were strong and brave individuals who prized courage and independence, as well as family loyalty and a fierce love of God. With a stoic self-reliance as untamed as the hills surrounding them, these men and women, with children by their sides, cleared the dense vegetation, built their cabins and communities, planted their hill crops, raised their farm animals, hunted, fished, trapped, and survived.

These "mountaineers," as they were termed early on, also possessed a romantic insight characterized by an imaginative nature, wit, humor, verbosity, and vivid humanism. Often educated with and having an inborn love for the written and oral word, many brought with them into the hills such books as the Bible, works of

"Knobby Hill (Cheat River)"
(Archie L. Musick, courtesy of Judy P. Byers, from the Archives of the West Virginia Folklife Center, Fairmont State)

Stories were set to music by numerous amateur pickers such as this anonymous Tennessee string band, Eagleville, Tennessee, circa 1890. (Photographer unknown, Charles Wolfe Collection)

Legends and traditions from Native Americans living in the mountains were passed along to Appalachian immigrants and contributed to their stories. (Photographer unknown, Mari-Lynn Evans Collection)

ancient history, and selections of world literature, along with an abundance of oral tales, or folktales. As these people were naturally great talkers, storytelling was an expedient and nostalgic way to transmit memories of their Celtic roots across the sea. After the evening meal, the family members typically gathered around the open hearth on winter evenings, or outside under the stars in the summertime, to hear the old-world tales. Even during the day, as they were going about their domestic chores, stories were spun to make the hard work bearable. Storytelling was thus a clever skill to learn, for in the rough, calamity-ridden lives of these first mountaineers, much pleasure was derived as kin and kith informed and entertained one another.

Even though most of the folktales of these early mountaineers were European in origin, collectively they began to take on a rugged, experiential flavor to fit the local setting, and the old-world variants that survived were slowly transformed to fit the needs of the mountaineers. Unlike written stories, whose printed words become permanent as soon as the ink is dry, the oral tales have always been as changeable as the individual personality of each storyteller. Slowly, then, many of the flamboyant stories of kings and treasures were replaced by tales dealing with human conditions and emotions with which the mountaineers could identify. The trials and tribulations of daily frontier living, ranging from birth to death, were orally recorded in sagas reflecting their new lives.

The new settlers also became influenced by the nature stories from the Native Americans in the hills, for they explained much of the cultural geography of the region. Such tribes as the Iroquois, Cherokee, Tuscarora, Shawnee, Delaware, Seneca, and Mingo, who hunted, fished, and buried their dead among the Appalachians, not only marked many trails, rivers, and valleys with place names but also left legends to glorify the names and mythology.

Early Appalachian storytellers, forever true to their romantic Celtic nature, also spun yarns about adventure and the unknown, especially during the long winter evenings. Examples of the strange, suspenseful, or unexplainable whetted their imaginations. Tales of the supernatural and preternatural, homegrown from these hills, suited their frontier imaginations. The humid, misty climate with its patchy valley fog rising from the riverbeds into the silenced dawns were often inspirations for the tales of spirits and will-o'-the-wisps encountered at daybreak or dusk. The rolling topography, ever changing against the four seasons, held mystery in the deep valleys that always reflected the sun's shadow but never the sun. Could that shadow really be the face of an old man or the strange witch lady up the hollow? Dense wooded areas contained hidden secrets, bewilderment, and sometimes fear, just ripe for storytelling.

By the mid-1800s, outside influences brought about by the Civil War and the Industrial Revolution began to affect all modes of mountain life, including the storytelling traditions. The hills that had isolated Anglo-Celtic and Germanic frontier farmers for generations were opened to other areas by the laying of railroad tracks. Soon, churning steam engines wound their way among the hills, carrying timber and coal. Equally rich veins of natural gas and oil were discovered amid the coal beds. Since much more manpower

"The Crying Baby of Holly" was a yarn spun by residents of West Virginia's hollows. (Archie L. Musick, courtesy of Judy P. Byers, from the Archives of the West Virginia Folklife Center, Fairmont State)

Immigrants from specific areas of the British Isles or Europe often formed societies or organizations for the purposes of telling their stories and keeping alive traditions from the Old World. This group was photographed in Caroleen, Rutherford County, North Carolina, February 7, 1909.
(Photographer unknown, Holly George-Warren Collection)

was needed to mine these new natural resources than the mountaineer grangers could provide, western and southern European immigrants, who had recently flocked to America to escape the crop famines that had plagued their lands, were wooed to the region. They were native to such countries as Hungary, Czechoslovakia, Poland, Yugoslavia, southern Ireland, Austria, Russia, and many others. In the central Appalachia of West Virginia, 30 percent of immigrants were from Italy. For security and expediency, they usually lived in ethnic communities, close to the natural resource deposits, all of which were managed by wealthy industrial barons. In the valleys, along the riverbeds, and nestled beside ridges, these camps later became towns.

These new settlers immediately displayed many of the same stoic qualities as their mountaineer neighbors before them. From various walks of life, they, too, were the most courageous and independent of their old-world families to have demonstrated enough faith and individualism to cross the ocean, seeking a new life in a strange and relatively untamed land. Each new cultural group also brought a rich folklore of beliefs and oral traditions, often in stories about family loyalty, dominance, and pride, mixed with deep love and fear of God. Unlike the dominant Celtic mountaineers, however, who all shared a common language, each new ethnic group was naturally segregated from the others because of language barriers. Plus, since living in separate nationality communities within the same coal camps gave the people little opportunity to enculturate, the old-world tales told in the vernacular by the oldest family members existed longer. The typical first-generation ethnic miner lived in a duality of answering to an Anglicized version of his name and attempting to converse in a new language during shift work but returning to the security of his native tongue and folkways when away from the mines. Stories from the old country, then, usually told in the warmth of the family setting away from the coldness of the mines, brought comfort to these foreigners and perpetuated their cultural memories.

The African Americans who settled in the Appalachians also contributed oral traditions to the already overflowing stew of cultures. Their oral literature was rich with songs, chants, and tales used to ease the drudgeries of fieldwork and house chores. Their

This unidentified young West Virginia woman possibly learned folk reels on the fiddle from her grandmother. (Photographer unknown, Mari-Lynn Evans Collection)

"The music that left here from Scotland and Ireland went over to the mountains of North Carolina and Kentucky and all around the Appalachian mountains. The tunes have changed slightly, as has the style of playing, but note for note many of the tunes are exactly the same."

—*Irish musician Ronnie Crutchley*

These two anonymous musicians wearing Spanish-American War uniforms are among African-American pickers who helped to popularize the guitar in southern Appalachia.
(Herb Peck, Charles Wolfe Collection)

themes generally showed a longing for a better life, even if this dream could only come true in the afterlife of heaven. Fear of the night, the unknown, and the devil who always tried to block heaven triggered in the black storyteller's imagination powerful images of the supernatural and the preternatural. Unlike the rich tidewater and piedmont areas east of the mountains, where slavery predominated, the poor soil and harsher climate of Appalachia did not yield enough capital to warrant slavery as an important business. After the Civil War, however, an abundance of black labor from the Deep South came into the hills as part of the industrial workforce called upon to build railroads and mine coal. They were often treated poorly, receiving commissary food plus low wages and lodging in shacks in segregated sections of the coal camps. Out of these harsh conditions even more stories evolved, often immortalizing the strength and courage of such local heroes as John Henry at the Big Bend Tunnel in Talcott, West Virginia, who stood up against steel-driving machinery and died "with a hammer in his hand, Lord, Lord."

Down through the years, many of the Appalachian tales have been perpetuated by the traditional tellers in family, school, and community settings, passing then to folklorists, who have been responsible for extending and preserving the tales for posterity by collecting and presenting them in retellings and interpretations. In particular, the works of three folktale scholars give us a panoramic sampling of the storytelling tradition in Appalachia: Richard Chase, Leonard Roberts, and Ruth Ann Musick. All three folklorists, being contemporaries, knew and respected the work of one another and were passionate about keeping the oral traditions of Appalachia alive.

The major contribution of Richard Chase (1904–1988) to

Appalachian storytelling was the preservation of the mountain variants of the Anglo-Celtic "marchen" in the actual dialectal patterns of the tellers. These wonder tales of magic and courage show how an ordinary fellow, Jack, along with his brothers, Will and Tom, outwit all types of adversaries greater than themselves and become mountain heroes. Chase, born in Huntsville, Alabama, and trained in botany at Harvard and Antioch, was powerfully drawn to the oral traditions of the Southern highlands. He explored the Blue Ridge Parkway along the ridges of Virginia into the mountains of northwestern North Carolina, past Grandfather Mountain, toward Cherokee country, finally settling in the Beech Creek and Mountain area. There, he promoted the work of the Southern Highland Handicraft Guild and the Council of the Southern Mountains, an organization devoted to all phases of life in the Appalachian Southland, from which, much later, he started the

The Fiddlin' Power Family, of Dungannon, Virginia, typified the kind of musicians who played the songs that were handed down from generation to generation and finally collected by folklorist Cecil Sharp.
(Photographer unknown, Charles Wolfe Collection)

This photograph of an anonymous musician in Bristol, Tennessee, in 1891 is almost a story in the making: Why is he holding a pistol, and who made his fretless, primitive banjo? (Photographer unknown, Charles Wolfe Collection)

Folk Toys Home Industry, as a community wage-earning project. At first he traveled the area for the council, encouraging the preservation of the English folksongs from the work of Cecil J. Sharp, the great English folklorist who had made an important collection of Scots-English ballads in the southern Appalachians from 1914 to 1918. In the spring of 1935, after Chase had spoken before a group of teachers about the importance of saving the oral traditions of the southern mountains, Marshall Ward, a young fellow from western North Carolina who was in the audience, told Chase that his family knew a lot of old stories that had been handed down from generation to generation, just like the old songs. The stories were mainly about a boy named Jack who had many more adventures than just the "Jack and the Beanstalk" everyone knew from the English tradition.

So, from one basic informant family, Chase made a unique contribution to American folklore by collecting this oral literature from people in a remote area who still practiced it as a living art. He made many visits to R. M. "Uncle Mon-Roe" Ward, of Beech Creek, North Carolina, and other descendants of great-grandfather Council "Old Counce" Harmon (1803–1898), to whom many of the tales could be traced. As he continued to collect these stories from the Ward family members and other Beech Mountain families, such as the Harmons and the Hickses, Chase began to retell these tales, imitating the picturesque language patterns that became known as the dialect of Appalachia. Found in isolated communities that remained relatively stable, this speech contained an unusually large mixture of ancient forms, usually English but often Scottish, not only in its vocabulary but also in the syntax and pronunciation.

Believing that the telling of stories would keep them alive more than the mere reading of the printed word, Richard Chase spent much of his career traveling throughout the United States lecturing and retelling these old tales at schools, colleges, universities, libraries, and clubs, using the same idioms, phrases, intonations, and rhythms that Uncle Mon-Roe Ward had evoked. Among his publications of folksongs, games, and tales were the two collections told by the Ward family, linguistically transcribed from many recorded versions: *The Jack Tales* (1943) and *Grandfather Tales* (1948). I saw Richard Chase perform at Fairmont State College in the mid-1970s. He immediately charmed the audience as he stood before us wearing an old handmade sweater and toting a knapsack of puppets, wooden toys, and such folk instruments as a banjo, fiddle, shepherd's pipe, and English flute. He sang the old folksongs and demonstrated party games. Then, in the soft drawl of the laconic mountaineer, slower than the lowland speech, often high-pitched and nasal, Chase told us about Jack, an easygoing country boy with dreams, desires, and experiences, who in meeting and conquering his foes was just living the mountain way of life, thoroughly human and unassumingly representative of a very large segment of the American people.

"Blackie" the bear was the type of enemy faced by mountaineers whose exploits became favorite family tales passed along at get-togethers and later recorded by folklorists.
(Archie L. Musick, courtesy of Judy P. Byers, from the Archives of the West Virginia Folklife Center, Fairmont State)

Folklorist and educator Dr. Leonard Roberts (1912–1983) collected the oral traditions and folkways of his native eastern Kentucky, where he lived and taught, except for several short teaching stints in North Carolina, Georgia, and West Virginia. Like Richard Chase, he was concerned with preserving the folklore of these fringe Appalachians before it was totally homogenized by modernization and technology. After receiving an A.B. from Berea

College and a Ph.D. from the University of Kentucky, he turned his attention for three decades to recording the folklore of the most isolated settlements in Kentucky's Leslie and Perry counties in the Pine Mountain range's north slope. He considered these areas the last stronghold for white, English-language folktales in North America. Many of his tales came from student informants in his folklore and English classes who led him to traditional storytelling families in an area of a few hundred square miles along the head-waters of the Kentucky River—areas such as Cutshin, Greasy, and along the Middle Fork itself, from Bledsoe to the mouth of Hell-for-Sartin Creek in Leslie, and Big Leatherwood Creek, draining into the North Fork. His first important collection of Kentucky mountain tales, *South from Hell-fer-Sartin* (1955), contains all types of old-world variants and experiential accounts, jokes and anecdotes, legends, ghostly and ghastly encounters, myths, morals, and even fables, along with examples of the Jack tales.

Black and white musicians traded folk tunes, helping to create new sounds, such as bluegrass, later in the twentieth century. This is the only known photo of Arnold Schulz (left), who reportedly influenced Bill Monroe's music, depicted with fiddler Clarence Wilson, Kentucky, circa 1930. (Photographer unknown, Charles Wolfe Collection)

Two of Roberts' collections emphasize the oral traditions and folkways of one informant family, the Couches, who lived on the headwaters of the Kentucky River in the picturesque valleys of Cutshin and Greasy. Here, for almost a decade, Roberts had explored the culture, discovering many strange and lingering folkways, primitive farming and folk handicrafts, lumbering and hunting, funeralizing and moonshining. The most valuable collecting, though, was a large repertoire of old-world storytelling and ancient ballad singing introduced to him by Mandy Couch Hendrix. She directed him back across the Pine Ridge to Putney,

This Cumberland Mountain family, circa 1933, probably played songs they learned from their parents and grandparents, who were taught by their parents and grandparents. (Photographer unknown, Charles Wolfe Collection)

on the Cumberland, a string-town lumber camp some eight miles above Harlan, to her brothers, Jim and Dave Couch, who shared the family store of folklore. Roberts preserved this folklore in two collections: *Up Cutshin and Down Greasy* (1959) and *Folk Stories and Songs of the Couch Family* (1959).

Even though Leonard Roberts was a storyteller, unlike Richard Chase, who remodeled the storytelling techniques of his informants, Roberts directed his passion toward preserving the old narrative traditions through folklore research and leadership in such organizations as American Folklore Society; National Folk Festival

"Seven Bones" is among the many scratchboard illustrations created by Archie L. Musick to illustrate his sister Ruth Ann Musick's folktales.
(Archie L. Musick, courtesy of Judy P. Byers, from the Archives of the West Virginia Folklife Center, Fairmont State)

Association; and the Kentucky, Tennessee, and West Virginia Folklore Societies; as well as becoming director of the Appalachian Studies Center of Pikesville College, Kentucky.

Dr. Ruth Ann Musick (1897–1974), like Richard Chase, was an adopted Appalachian who came from Missouri to central Appalachia, where she taught at Fairmont State College for nearly thirty years, archived the West Virginia Folklore Society's holdings, and edited its *West Virginia Folklore Journal*. Her Scots-Irish heritage inspired her to collect her family folksongs as part of her dissertation work at the State University of Iowa, and later, the eminent Midwestern folklorist Vance Randolph encouraged her to continue researching Celtic lore as it was rooted in the Appalachians. Like other parts of this region, West Virginia contained many of the same rich oral traditions, and Musick utilized her students as some of her best informants. Her weekly folklore columns in several state newspapers comprised her first collection, *Ballads, Folksongs, and Folk Tales from West Virginia* (1960).

Even though Ruth Ann Musick was fascinated by all aspects of Appalachian folklife, she noticed in it the predominance of supernatural legends, which she recorded in two collections, *The Telltale Lilac Bush and Other West Virginia Ghost Tales* (1965) and *Coffin Hollow and Other Ghost Tales* (1977). As the region's mystical atmosphere of fog and shadows added to a rugged, isolated topography, which had always sparked the imaginations of the early mountain storytellers, so had the violent deaths, murders, and unusual circumstances of

"Coffin Hollow" illustrates the title story of the Ruth Ann Musick Collection Coffin Hollow and Other Ghost Tales *(University Press of Kentucky, 1977).*
(Archie L. Musick, courtesy of Judy P. Byers, from the Archives of the West Virginia Folklife Center, Fairmont State)

the Industrial Revolution shaping the history of central Appalachia greatly influenced local storytellers to weave tales of helpful ghosts, vanishing hitchhikers, and restless poltergeists haunting the hills and valleys. Emerging out of the struggles of the Civil War, which often pitted brother against brother, West Virginians faced industrial disasters, such as railroad accidents, coal explosions, mine wars, and timber feuds. Along with this local material, Musick found many local storytellers, especially among the Italian coal miners and other ethnic settlers, who were anxious to weave compensatory tales of guardian angels returning to help loved ones in despair, vengeful spirits seeking justice, and wandering spirits finding peace. They also nostalgically remembered the old country with fantastic tales of magic, valor, and love, as presented in Musick's collection *Green Hills of Magic: West Virginia Folktales from Europe* (published in 1970 and reprinted in 1989). Musick recorded many of these tales on tape, in the original language of the tellers from ethnic families, who recounted them with childlike enthusiasm. This was the case in my own family. When I was just a child, Musick began to collect the oral tales of my maternal grandmother, aunt, and mother. In more than a decade, she recorded hundreds of examples of my family's ghostlore.

Unlike Richard Chase and Leonard Roberts, though, Ruth Ann Musick retold each tale she collected in a literary style instead of the folk idiom, usually combining the different variants of each tale. Thus, her collections were rendered highly readable, fun to tell, and universally popular. She traveled extensively around the region relating these tales and encouraging youthful listeners to retell them. I became one of those inspired to continue the storytelling traditions of my family and of my Appalachia. Since I became the executrix of her folklore estate and then the director of the West Virginia Folklife Center and its academic folklore studies program at Fairmont State College, I have carried on her folkloric programming, research, and archival efforts. We have enough ghostlore from her original unpublished estate for at least a dozen more collections, and the center continues to record this regional living art: the storytelling tradition of Appalachia.

One night in the early 1940s in Wetzel County, West Virginia, five or six teen girls decided to have a "dumb supper." Without uttering a sound to each other, they prepared for the supper by doing everything backwards. They walked backwards, dressed backwards, and set the table backwards. At midnight, they were all to sit down silently at the table. The first one to see a casket would be the first one to die.

At midnight, they all sat down. A sixteen-year-old girl, Thelma Sapp, saw a casket floating through the room. No one else saw it. In a few months, Miss Sapp died of pneumonia.

Three other variants of "The Dumb Supper" have been found in the oral traditions of Wetzel County:

It's an old superstition in the hills of Wetzel County that if you go into the sage garden on the first day of May, take some sage into the kitchen, make sage tea, and fix yourself a midnight supper, you will know what is to be. If you are to be married within a year, your husband will come bearing your coffin. There was a young woman who wanted to try this. While she was fixing her midnight supper, she looked out the window and saw four men coming up the road, bearing a long box in their arms. Within a week, the young woman was dead.

My grandmother told me of a very interesting incident in her life known as the dumb supper. All the young girls who wished to see the image of their future husbands would hold this supper. The girls had to be silent while they set the table and could include but two items, bread and water.

My grandmother attended one of these suppers, and at the stroke of midnight a black cat came into the room and crossed over near one of her friends. This was considered a bad omen because it was supposed to mean that the girl's husband would kill himself. It proved right because a few years later the young lady's husband shot himself in the head with a shotgun.

⚬

My great-grandmother used to tell me this story of her two girl-friends. It was said that their grandmother had told them an old superstition, and just for fun they decided to try it. They were supposed to stay up late one night together and, at twelve o'clock on the dot, set the kitchen table for four people and put some food on the table. This was called a dumb supper. At twelve o'clock, or shortly after, they were supposed to sit down at the table and wait. Then, as the story goes, they were supposed to see their future husbands.

So, on the night the two girls had picked out, they set the table and prepared for an evening of mystery and fun. At midnight, to their utter surprise, the wind began to blow very hard. This was very strange because it had been such a mild day. Then the curtains began to move about, and even the tablecloth waved backward and forward. About that time the fun and laughter had died down between the girls and cold shivers began running up their spines. One of the girls was even said to have burst into tears, but for some reason they couldn't move out of their chairs.

At exactly fifteen minutes after twelve, the girls heard a strange noise, and when they looked around, there were two men sitting beside them. Although these men were a bit transparent, the girls could plainly make out their features. When they were gone, the girls decided they had just imagined it all, for the food was still on the plates.

"Besides," said one girl, "I'd never marry a man with a moustache."

They decided to forget the whole episode.

However, my grandmother said that six years later, one of the girls met and married a man who had blond hair and blue eyes. The next year, the other girl, who had said she would never marry a man who had a moustache, met and married one who did.

THE HUNKITCHY MAN

Many years ago, there lived at the edge of a virgin forest a little girl and her mother. The little girl's name was Marigold, because her hair was a golden yellow and her disposition was sunny. Marigold's mother warned her of the dark forest that contained a strange man of the jungle, known as the Hunkitchy Man, and Marigold promised to pick only the flowers close to the house.

But one day, she kept finding lovelier flowers close to the edge of the forest. Then a butterfly seemed to beckon her to come deeper into the forest where the flowers nodded a welcome. She hadn't gone far until she saw something move in the underbrush. A long, hairy arm seemed to envelop her, and she found herself looking at a man who seemed to be half-animal. She didn't scream because he carried her tenderly, but he made this *hunkitchy* noise as he strode through the forest.

He came to a cave in the mountains that seemed to be his home. He cooked supper of herbs and wild meat. Marigold ate a little, but she was thinking of how to escape. Soon the jungle man stretched out to rest. Marigold observed his long fingernails that had never been

Examples of Dialect Traditional to West Virginia

- *Back a letter:* address an envelope
- *Backset:* relapse
- *Bad off:* ill
- *Bees are goin' to swarm:* a baby is expected
- *Boughten:* purchased at a store
- *Bollix:* to ruin, to mess
- *Doins:* a party or gathering of people
- *Feather into:* fistfight
- *Fire and tow:* a spirited person
- *Fox fire:* phosphorescent light found on rotting wood
- *Fur piece:* long distance
- *Hell roarin' trots:* diarrhea
- *Lopper jawed:* lopsided
- *Painter cat:* panther
- *Peart:* lively, in good health
- *Poke:* sack or paper bag

"Settlers coming to the New World brought various aspects of their culture with them—folkways, clothing, building techniques, and architectural styles. Music was especially important because it gave them comfort—something they could do themselves. They could sing and play their fiddles on the front porch."
—*Country Music Hall of Fame and Museum curator John Rumble*

cut, his long, white beard that was matted with sticks and burrs, and his teeth that looked like the fangs of a wolf.

She started singing the evening lullaby her mother had taught her. *"Kum-qua, kum-qua, kum-qua-a."* The jungle man started snoring. So Marigold tiptoed lightly past the hunkitchy man and down the side of the rocks. But just as she started through the forest, a stick cracked. The jungle man gave a snort, and with five big steps, picked up his captive. When he scolded her for running away, Marigold said she was looking for flowers.

Then Marigold started to sing her lullaby again. The jungle man's head started to nod, but Marigold kept singing until she was quite sure he was sound asleep. This time she was able to get halfway home, when she heard the horrible *hunkitchy, hunkitchy* noise again. She felt his hot breath down her back, and this time the jungle man was quite angry.

Marigold waited a third time for the jungle man to drop off to sleep, while she sang more sweetly than ever the same lullaby. This time she kept singing it as she walked softly through the woods. When she got to the edge of the forest, she could see her home and her mother. She could hear the jungle man coming, but she knew this time she would get to her mother's arms. Needless to say, Marigold never left her own backyard again.

The Evolution of a Folk Song

John Hardy was a real person, a folk hero of sorts from the West Virginia minefields. Not some upstanding kind of hero, but a rumble-tumble gambler, fighter, and hard-drinking man who had a reputation for being handy with his fists and his gun. Near Eckman, West Virginia, he got into a tussle after a game of chance with a fellow miner from the Shawnee Coal Company. Hardy shot and killed him, then was captured, tried, found guilty, and sentenced to hang. On January 19, 1894, his sentence was carried out. In the folksong tradition, his story became the lyrics of a well-known ballad passed down to the next generation. Some confused John Hardy with John Henry, the steel-driving African-American train worker. According to some reports, Hardy, too, worked on the railroad—the Big Bend Tunnel of the C&O (Chesapeake and Ohio) Railroad, in fact. The Carter Family popularized the song further by recording it in the late 1920s. Woody Guthrie later took the tune for his own story song, "Tom Joad," and a whole new group of music lovers discovered "John Hardy" when it was selected by Harry Smith for his *Anthology of American Folk Music* in 1952.

Here are the lyrics, presumably close to the original version, and most like those as recorded by the Carter Family.

JOHN HARDY

John Hardy was a desperate little man.
He carried two guns every day.
He shot a man on the West Virginia Line.
And you ought a seen John Hardy getting away.

John Hardy he got to the East Stone Bridge,
He thought that he would be free,
And it's up steps a man and took him by his arm,
Say, "Johnny, walk along with me."
He sent for his poppy and his mommy, too,
To come and go his bail,
But money won't go a-murderin' case,
And they locked John Hardy back in jail.

John Hardy had a pretty little girl,
The dress that she wore was blue,
As she came skipping through the old jail hall,
Sayin', "Poppy, I've been true to you."

John Hardy had another little girl,
The dress that she wore was red,

An unidentified banjo player hailing from the Cumberland Mountains (Jean Thomas, the Traipsin' Woman Collection, courtesy of Charles Wolfe)

She followed John Hardy to his hangin' ground,
Sayin, "Poppy, I would rather be dead."

I have been to the East and I been to the West,
I been this wide world around.
I been to the river and I been baptized,
And now I'm on my hangin' ground.

John Hardy was felled on his scaffold high
With his loving little wife by his side,
And the last words she heard her John-o say,
"I'll meet you in the sweet by and by."

"The Hunters of Kentucky," written by Samuel Woodworth in 1826, became Andrew Jackson's presidential campaign song during the hotly contested election of 1828.

THE HUNTERS OF KENTUCKY

Chorus:
Ye gentlemen and ladies fair who grace this famous city,
Just listen if you've time to spare while I rehearse a ditty,
And for the opportunity conceive yourself quite lucky,
For 'tis not often that you see a hunter from Kentucky.
Oh, Kentucky, the hunters of Kentucky.

We are a hardy, freeborn race,
Each man to fear a stranger;
Whate'er the game we join in chase,
Despoiling time and danger;
And if a daring foe annoys,
Whate'er his strength and forces,
We'll show him that Kentucky boys
Are alligator horses.

(Chorus)

I s'pose you've read it in the prints,
How Packenham attempted
To make old Hickory Jackson wince,

But soon his scheme repented;
For we, with rifles ready cocked,
Thought such occasion lucky,
And soon around the gen'ral flocked
The hunters of Kentucky.

(Chorus)

You've heard, I s'pose, how New Orleans
Is famed for wealth and beauty,
There's girls of ev'ry hue it seems,
From snowy white to sooty;
So Packenham he made his brags
If he in fight was lucky,
He'd have their girls and cotton bags,
In spite of old Kentucky.

(Chorus)

But Jackson, he was wide awake,
And was not scared of trifles;
For well he knew what aim we take
With our Kentucky rifles;
He led us down to Cypress Swamp,
The ground was low and mucky;
There stood John Bull in pomp,
And here was old Kentucky.

(Chorus)

A bank was raised to hide our breasts,
Not that we thought of dying,
But that we always like to rest,
Unless the game is flying;
Behind it stood out a little force,
None wished it to be greater,
For every man was half a horse
And half an alligator.

(Chorus)

They did not let our patience tire,
Before they showed their faces;
We did not choose to waste our fire,

*An anonymous early Tennessee
string band, circa 1900.*
(Photographer unknown,
Charles Wolfe Collection)

So snugly kept our places;
And when so near we saw them wink,
We thought it time to stop 'em,
And 'twould have done you good, I think,
To see Kentuckians drop 'em.

(Chorus)

They found, at last, 'twas vain to fight,
Where lead was all the booty,
And so they wisely took to flight,
And left us all our beauty;
And now, if danger e'er annoys,
Remember what our trade is,
Just send for us Kentucky boys,
And we'll protect ye, ladies.

(Chorus)

Appalachian Ballads

Story songs, or ballads, in Appalachia often are based on true events or people, as in the case of "John Henry," or are sung as a way of commiserating with neighbors and kinfolk about common hardships, as in "Paddy Works the Railroad," which was inspired by the experience of many Scots-Irish immigrants who helped build the extensive railroad system through the mountains of Appalachia.

JOHN HENRY

John Henry was a railroad man,
He worked from six 'til five,
"Raise 'em up bullies and let 'em drop down,
I'll beat you to the bottom or die."

John Henry said to his captain:
"You are nothing but a common man,
Before that steam drill shall beat me down,
I'll die with my hammer in my hand."

John Henry said to the Shakers:

"You must listen to my call,
Before that steam drill shall beat me down,
I'll jar these mountains till they fall."

John Henry's captain said to him:
"I believe these mountains are caving in."
John Henry said to his captain: "Oh, Lord!
That's my hammer you hear in the wind."

John Henry, he said to his captain:
"Your money is getting mighty slim,
When I hammer through this old mountain,
Oh, Captain, will you walk in?"

John Henry's captain came to him
With fifty dollars in his hand,
He laid his hand on his shoulder and said:
"This belongs to a steel-driving man."

John Henry was hammering on the right side,
The big steam drill on the left,
Before that steam drill could beat him down,
He hammered his fool self to death.

They carried John Henry to the mountains,
From his shoulder his hammer would ring,
She caught on fire by a little blue blaze,
I believe these old mountains are caving in.

John Henry was lying on his death bed,
He turned over on his side,
And these were the last words John Henry said:
"Bring me a cool drink of water before I die."

John Henry had a little woman,
Her name was Pollie Ann,
He hugged and kissed her just before he died,
Saying, "Pollie, do the very best you can."

John Henry's woman heard he was dead,
She could not rest on her bed,
She got up at midnight, caught that Number Four train,
"I am going where John Henry fell dead."

They carried John Henry to that new burying ground,
His wife all dressed in blue,

She laid her hand on John Henry's cold face,
"John Henry I've been true to you."

PADDY WORKS THE RAILROAD

In eighteen hundred and forty one,
I put my corduroy breeches on,
I put my corduroy breeches on,
To work upon the railway.

Chorus:

Fil-i-me-oo-re-i-re-ay
Fil-i-me-oo-re-i-re-ay
Fil-i-me-oo-re-i-re-ay
To work upon the railway.

In eighteen hundred and forty-two,
I left the old world for the new,
Bad cess to the luck that brought me through,
To work upon the railroad.

(Chorus)

When we left Ireland to come here,
And spend our latter days in cheer,
And bosses they did drink strong beer,
And Pat worked on the railway.

(Chorus)

Our contractor's name it was Tom King,
He kept a store to rob the men,
A Yankee clerk with ink and pen,
To cheat Pat on the railway.

(Chorus)

It's "Pat do this" and "Pat do that,"
Without a stocking or cravat,
And nothing but an old straw hat,
While Pat works on the railway.

(Chorus)

One Monday morning to our surprise,
Just half an hour before sunrise,
The dirty devil went to the skies,
And Pat worked on the railroad.

(Chorus)

And when Pat lays him down to sleep,
The wiry bugs around him creep,
And devil a bit can poor Pat sleep,
While he works on the railroad.

(Chorus)

In eighteen hundred and forty-three,
'Twas then I met sweet Biddy Magee,
And an illygant wife she's been to me,
While workin' on the railway.

(Chorus)

In eighteen hundred and forty-six,
The gang pelted me with stones and brick.
Oh, I was in a hell of a fix,
While working on the railroad.

(Chorus)

In eighteen hundred and forty-seven,
Sweet Biddy Magee, she went to heaven,
If she left one child, she left eleven,
To work upon the railway.

(Chorus)

In eighteen hundred and forty-eight,
I learned to take my whiskey straight,
'Tis an *illygant* drink and can't be bate,
For working on the railway.

Roy Banks and friends, 2003
(© Shelby Lee Adams)

Part Two

FEUDS, COAL, WHITE LIGHTNING, AND GOOD OL' MOUNTAIN MUSIC

Canaan Valley, West Virginia
(Van Slider)

olk culture is, plainly speaking, the culture of folks, a rich, earthy composite of traditions, stories, myths, music, dance, and other elements that define a people's existence. In early America, including Appalachia, folk culture also marked the eventual transition of Old World ways into New World ways. Such a shift took many years and almost always gave more than a respectful nod to the mother country. Appalachian folk culture grew from a European fountainhead, particularly that of the British Isles. But it also included various

Ohio River at Sisterville, West Virginia
(Van Slider)

contributions from Native Americans, African Americans, and, most recently, Latino immigrants.

Over the years, outsiders have characterized Appalachians as being overly isolated and removed from the goings-on of the rest of America. But no one could ever say that the region and its people weren't culturally responsive, or that they didn't contribute substantially to America's overall folk culture. In this section—Feuds, Coal, White Lightning, and Good Ol' Mountain Music—are essays that reveal some of the core elements of Appalachian folk culture.

The part begins with an overview of what writer/director Tom Robertson calls "The Great Mountain Feud." Interest in the family feud that existed, seemingly forever, between two Appalachian families, the Hatfields from West Virginia and the McCoys from Kentucky, not only ran through Appalachia like a cool mountain stream but overflowed into mainstream America and its popular culture. In Appalachia, feuds are lively, occasionally deadly affairs; the one that kept the Hatfields and the McCoys baiting and battling each other turned out to be the most famous family feud in American history.

Robertson also contributes another essay to this section, one dealing with mountain-style Appalachian whiskey making. "Moonshine on the Mountain" is a brief account of the history of this tradition and includes a north Georgia recipe for cooking up your own batch of moonshine. Ronald L. Lewis' essay, "Appalachian Myths and the Legacy of Coal," traces the region's all-important story of coal. The extraction from the earth of coal, the fossil fuel that helped turn America into an industrial power in the late nineteenth and early twentieth centuries, not only created an economic seesaw for Appalachian miners and their families but also fostered a number of myths and stereotypes that remain embedded in the way the rest of America views Appalachia.

One of Appalachia's richest cultural treasures is its music. Taken together, the lonely notes of a fiddle, the plaintive sound of a mountain ballad, the simple strum of a guitar, and the frolic of a five-string banjo form one of America's strongest musical traditions, one that has traveled well beyond the mountains and valleys of Appalachia. In the essay entitled "The Bristol Sessions," noted country-music scholar Charles Wolfe describes one of the most important series of recording sessions in Appalachian—and American—music history. In short, what resulted from the 1927 Bristol Sessions, as they've become known, was the birth of country music. Jimmie Rodgers, the "father of country music," and the Carter Family—without question, the first family of country music—cut their earliest records in Bristol, Tennessee, setting the stage for the transition of this folk-derived collection of songs that so beautifully captured rural culture into a commercial enterprise with pop music overtones. And, as if Wolfe's words weren't enough, there are personal testimonies here to the importance of the Carter Family in Appalachian music, including one by the late Johnny Cash, whose words come from the interview he did for the film *The Appalachians* just two months before his death. Sara and A. P. Carter's granddaughter, Rita Forrester, has also provided recollections of her legendary family.

From moonshine to music and feuds to folktales, Appalachia has been a wellspring of folk culture.

THE GREAT MOUNTAIN FEUD

TOM ROBERTSON

In the era following the Civil War, the backwoods of Appalachia captured the lurid imagination of big-city newspaper editors, who brandished salacious and wildly distorted images of a lawless land filled with hillbilly barbarians whose "ignorance . . . isolation, and inbreeding" spawned unbridled lust and violence. These tabloid editors, trying to sell papers, created a distorted mythology based on the lesser reality of a few notorious family feuds scattered up and down the Appalachian ridge.

From left to right: *Ock Damron, "Devil" Anse Hatfield, Jim Vance, W. B. Borden* (Photographer unknown, courtesy of the West Virginia State Archives)

The Tug Fork River was such a place, snaking a crooked line between West Virginia and Kentucky, through a brash and sometimes lawless land. In the late 1800s, the isolated valley hosted America's most infamous family feud, between the kin of Kentucky's Randolph "Old Ranel" McCoy and that of West Virginia's Anderson "Devil" Anse Hatfield. The Hatfields and McCoys would not only captivate the newspapers of the day but inspire more than a century of movies, books, cartoons, and songs, all of which perpetuated this exaggerated legend.

Devil Anse Hatfield was a man of mythical proportion, who could tame a bear far sweeter, ride a horse far harder, and shoot a gun far straighter than any man in the Tug Fork valley. He was also a prominent landowner with five thousand acres and a lumber mill. But when he gathered up his sons and handed out guns for newspaper pictures, he became the personification of the violent hillbilly. "He was a clever old man," said Anse's grandson Jack Hatfield with a wry smile. "He never killed anybody, but he was the leader, so he got the reputation."

Historians have described the feud, which occurred in a remote area where vengeance was hardly restrained by law, as a struggle for power and land during the Industrial Revolution's uncertain times. Some scholars trace the cause of the feud to hard feelings over the Civil War and the unsolved murder of Asa Harmon McCoy (Ranel McCoy's brother), who had fought for the North. Yet both Ranel McCoy and Devil Anse Hatfield had fought for the South in an aggressive guerrilla band called the Logan Wildcats. Then in 1878 an angry dispute between the Hatfields and McCoys over a stolen hog was settled in court, but left bitter feelings.

The feud began in full on election day, on August 7, 1882, when Devil Anse's brother Ellison Hatfield got into a brawl with Tolbert McCoy and two of his brothers. During those times, election days were celebrated with rowdy carousing, horse racing, gambling, arguing, and whiskey guzzling. One witness said the day reeked with "strife and ambition." An argument over claims that a Hatfield owed fifty cents for a fiddle escalated into a fight when Ellison proclaimed, "I am the best damn man in the county." Tolbert exploded, screaming, "I am hell on earth!" and, with knife in hand, charged Ellison. A handsome, powerful war hero who had once served under Robert E. Lee, Ellison would probably have killed Tolbert had Tolbert's two brothers not jumped into the fray: Bud with a knife, and Pharmer with a gun, critically injuring Elllison.

When Ellison died, Devil Anse took sudden revenge. Hatfield's

> "Anse Hatfield had a lot of, shall we say, testosterone-impaired sons—high levels of it."
> —John Alexander Williams, professor of history, Appalachian State University

> "The Civil War accustomed people in Appalachia to use violence to settle grievances, and that lasted until the era of state police and automobiles. There were two or three generations of extraordinary violence, extraordinary by national and regional standards. It took place on the edge of places, the edge of counties, the edge of states, where in the pre-automobile era, the arm of the law didn't quite reach."
> —John Alexander Williams

"[Ellison] was about six foot six—a big man, raw-boned. He was with Lee at Appomattox when they surrendered. The [McCoys] stabbed [Ellison] twenty-seven times and shot him three times. When they killed Uncle Ellison, that set it off there. Drinkin', one of them owed the other one a half-dollar or a dollar. That was money then for a fiddle. And they jumped him over it. They killed him [and] . . . he . . . died within three days."

—*Jack Hatfield, grandson of "Devil" Anse Hatfield*

Ellison Hatfield
(Photographer unknown,
Courtesy of the West Virginia
State Archives)

vigilante posse brought the three McCoy boys from Kentucky back to West Virginia, where they were tied to a pawpaw bush and gunned down.

Complicating matters between the Hatfields and McCoys was a healthy dose of lust and tainted love, which eventually obliterated the bloodlines that the feuds had drawn: A Lothario of sorts, Johnse Hatfield wooed a gullible McCoy woman, Roseanna McCoy, in 1881.

On New Year's Day in 1888, Johnse and a gang of Hatfields led a drunken raid on Ranel McCoy's cabin, in which there were only women and children. The Hatfields burned down the cabin, killing two adult children (Alifair and Calvin) and beating Ranel's wife, "Aunt" Sally McCoy, as she tried to save her daughter, who lay dying in the snow.

A notorious Kentucky gunman named Bad Frank Phillips led a series of McCoy retribution raids into West Virginia. In a fierce battle at Grapevine Creek, Phillips took nine Hatfield prisoners. Soon after, he captured the heart of Johnse Hatfield's wife, Nancy, as well.

Seven Hatfields were charged for the New Year's Day killings. Most received prison terms, but to appease the McCoys, someone had to be hanged. Thus, a retarded boy named Ellison Mounts received the death sentence and was executed on February 18, 1889.

Some twenty years after the feud had ended, Devil Anse Hatfield finally found salvation. In 1911, at age seventy-three, he was baptized in Main Island Creek, which, according to one newspaper account, "sizzled" when Devil Anse was immersed. The preacher, Uncle Dyke Garrett, proclaimed, "I have baptized the Devil!" From that time on they say Anse Hatfield only "sipped a little whiskey from the lid of a jar." Ranel McCoy, who also survived the feud, went on to operate a ferryboat in Pikeville, Kentucky. Johnse Hatfield, sentenced to life for the New Year's raid, was pardoned after he saved a guard's life during a prison brawl. He went on to work for U.S. Steel.

The feud between the Hatfields and McCoys was over a little

"Johnse Hatfield is sleeping with Roseanna McCoy? Johnse Hatfield slept with everybody. . . . "
—*John Alexander Williams*

"The Tombstone"
(Archie L. Musick, courtesy of Judy P. Byers, Archives of the West Virginia Folklife Center, Fairmont State)

"Uncle Johnse wears them cellophane collars and goes to them dances. He's a ladies' man—they call him the Romeo of the family. They say he's just a good-time fella. Well, Johnse took [Roseanna McCoy] home and wanted to marry her and got her pregnant, and about a month later he married her first cousin. That's rubbing salt in the wound, isn't it? That caused hard feelings, too."
—*Jack Hatfield*

"The day she met Johnse, she ran off with him. Roseanna had the baby down the creek here. It was a little girl; she called it Sarie Elizabeth. The baby got the measles, and they buried the baby up on the hill back of the cabin. Roseanna prostrated herself on the baby's grave, and you'd go looking for her and she'd be up there next to the baby's grave, crying. In the meantime, Johnse married her first cousin Nancy. *Aww, that hurt!* I believe she grieved herself to death."

—McCoy descendant Jimmy Wolford

"[Frank Phillips] was pretty rowdy. [He'd] get drunk [and] make them other drunks dance for him while he was shooting under their feet."
—Jack Hatfield

Anse Hatfield reportedly found religion in 1911.
(Photographer unknown, Courtesy of the West Virginia State Archives)

more than a decade after it had begun. Ever since, the Hatfields and McCoys have gathered each year to commemorate old times and compete in a tug-of-war on the banks of the Tug Fork. In 2003, the families announced that they had signed a peace treaty; today, they are far more interested in creating a tourist attraction in their little part of Appalachia than they are in feuding.

APPALACHIAN MYTHS AND THE LEGACY OF COAL

RONALD L. LEWIS

The most commonplace knowledge about Appalachia is rooted in myths constructed by popular fiction writers at the turn of the twentieth century. Ironically, at precisely the same time that Appalachia was being fictionalized as a "place where time stood still," the region was, in fact, undergoing a dramatic industrial transition. Coal was its centerpiece, and even a cursory history of the industry dispels these misconceptions, now so entrenched in American popular culture.

One of the most enduring myths is that Appalachia is a poor region because the economic growth that elevated America to a world power simply bypassed the region. The truth is that Appalachia was at the leading edge of this industrial expansion. Industrial society advanced into the mountains behind armies of native and immigrant laborers who laid the tracks for four major railroad systems. The first to cut its way through the mountains was the Baltimore and Ohio Railroad, which reached the Ohio River at Wheeling, Virginia (later West Virginia), in 1852. Then, in 1873, the Chesapeake & Ohio Railroad invaded the formerly inaccessible New River Gorge country, laying the iron rails linking Richmond, Virginia, and Huntington, West Virginia. The coalfields of southern West Virginia and then southwest Virginia were connected to the national markets by the Norfolk and Western Railroad when it linked the port of Norfolk, Virginia, with the Ohio River at Huntington, West Virginia, in 1893. While the C&O and the N&W were penetrating central Appalachia from the east, the Louisville and Nashville

Miners were a fearless breed of men.
(Photographer unknown, West Virginia State Archives, Coal Life Project)

Railroad penetrated the coalfields of eastern Kentucky from the west. By the end of World War I, the entire region was integrated by an elaborate web of rails.

Railroads carried away coal, but they also returned with manufactured products, such as dry goods, household furnishings, farm supplies, and other items people purchased from mail-order catalogs. The railroad connected local communities to the national markets and, as elsewhere in rural America, exerted a profound influence on the standard of living. They were the lines of communication that made available newspapers, the telegraph, and the telephone, while at the same time integrating Appalachians into the national culture and identity.

Train operators were forced to build their own facilities in this

"My grandfather worked fifty-five years in the coal mines. He was under a fall three times. Once he was trapped three days; his buddy got his arm caught and Grandpa got his knife out and cut the fellow's arm off to keep him alive. You were just like a donkey or a horse to them in the coal mines. If you didn't like it—I guess that's where the expression 'you can lump it' came from.

"There was no safety, and there was no money, and everything had to be spent in that coal camp at the company store, so everything was just turned right back over. When [musician] Merle Travis sang, 'I owe my soul to the company store,' Merle knew what he was talking about."

—*West Virginia resident Jimmy Wolford*

Underground in the mines, men of various ethnic groups all worked together. (Photographer unknown, West Virginia State Archives, Coal Life Project)

remote section of the mountains, and the unincorporated company town became one of the defining features of life in the Appalachian coalfields. The very nature of the coal company town militated against the development of those civic ideals associated with American democracy. The company not only built the mine but also became the miners' landlord, offered police and fire protection, erected the churches and stores, and provided the utilities and other services that towns required. Of course, there were great differences among company towns, ranging from crude coal camps thrown up on "gob piles" to model towns with all the modern conveniences and a benevolent owner/operator. All of them, however, were privately owned entities, not sovereign political jurisdictions, and the operators who owned them exerted extraordinary influence. Organized into operator associations, they collectively manipulated state legislation, the judiciary, and public policy to their own advantage, often with little regard for the public at large.

Another myth is that Appalachia is home to a static, homogeneous folk culture descended from British stock. This was the case until the late nineteenth century, when the Appalachian coalfields became a cauldron of cultural exchange. A scarcity of labor in the region required that the coal companies import a large portion of the workforce. Consequently, the population of the central Appalachian Plateau exploded between 1880 and 1920, from fewer than 200,000 in 1870 to more than 1.2 million in 1920. The reaction of native Appalachians to industrialization was mixed. Some Appalachian farmers were hesitant to trade their independence for dependency on wage labor, but many others showed little reluctance in moving to the proliferating mine towns. Undoubtedly, this ambivalence was keenest among women who engaged in a variety of farm work but who found no employment opportunities in the mine camps, other than the endless cycle of cooking and cleaning. Central Appalachia's preindustrial African-American population was relatively small, approximately 14,360 in 1870, but their numbers had swelled to 108,872 by 1930 when the in-migration ended.

In the coalfields, native whites and African Americans who relocated from other southern regions encountered a bewildering array of newly arrived European immigrants. As the immigrants poured into an industrializing America during the late nineteenth century, the number of immigrant miners in the region grew correspondingly, between 1880 and 1920, to at least one quarter of the Appalachian mining population, and much higher in some locations. These immigrants, representing nearly all European nations, either were transported from Ellis Island by labor recruiters or followed family and friends who had immigrated earlier.

Native whites, African Americans, and foreign immigrants lived

"[During a coal strike, labor organizer] Mother Jones walked up to this machine-gun nest and gave the soldiers the devil, pushed the gun aside, and said, 'You harm a hair on these boys' heads and I'll call God Almighty after you!' She could stand up and face down the hired guards and the coal operators and stand up in front of thousands of people and give 'em hell in a speech and say, 'When I die and go to heaven, I am going to tell God Almighty about West Virginia!'"
—*University of West Virginia scholar Ronald L. Lewis*

Coal was at the center of Appalachia's culture. (Photographer unknown, West Virginia State Archives, Coal Life Project)

and worked in the company towns in sections designated, for example, as "Colored Town," "Hunky Hollow," or "Little Italy." Generally, discrimination was exhibited by the kinds of jobs available to each group, but once underground, the men worked together. Even on the surface, however, the rigid lines of segregation often became blurred as the miners came to focus on their common economic interests through the United Mine Workers of America, the one organization in which they exerted some measure of democratic expression and control.

As coal mining boomed, so, too, did the grievances of the miners in this most hazardous of all American occupations. In addition to being riled by the knowledge that wages in Appalachian mines were fixed well below what companies paid miners above the Ohio River, miners were rankled by the poor working conditions, some of which were life threatening. Just how threatening is revealed by the tens of thousands of miners who have lost their lives in Appalachian coal mines. Most of them died one by one in roof falls, but it was the frequent explosions that attracted the press and captured the nation's imagination.

Immigrants made up a majority of the dead in many of these disasters. The worst disaster in American mining history, which

Kentucky coal mining brothers, 1992
(© Shelby Lee Adams)

"Ghosts of Mine Horses"
(Archie L. Musick, courtesy of
Judy P. Byers, from the
Archives of the West Virginia
Folklife Center, Fairmont State)

occurred at Monongah, West Virginia, on December 6, 1907, killed at least 362 men and boys. Along with the 74 white Americans and 11 African Americans who died in the explosion were 15 Austrians, 52 Hungarians, 31 Russians, 171 Italians, and 5 Turks. Three were never identified. Reflective of the diversity of cultures as well as nationalities, the victims were buried in segregated cemeteries, in ground consecrated by the Roman Catholic priest and the Russian Orthodox priest, as well as various Protestant ministers.

The history of the struggle to unionize the coal industry in Appalachia eloquently contradicts another persistent myth that Appalachians were too individualistic and fatalistic to organize themselves for collective action. Coal operators were unrelenting in their hostility toward the United Mine Workers of America, and they used every means at their disposal to destroy the union. The long campaign to establish a union occasionally exploded into what became known as the "mine wars" because of the scale of violence involved. The most legendary of these mine wars occurred in West Virginia in 1912–13, in 1919–21, and again in 1928–31. The Battle for Blair Mountain in 1921 pitted thousands of armed miners against company police, the National Guard, and even the fledgling U.S. Army Air Corps. The Harlan County, Kentucky, mine war was fought on and off during the 1930s. In all of these protracted conflicts, the coal companies prevailed because sympathetic local, state, and federal governments intervened on the company's side to break organized labor.

Union organizers in the Appalachian coalfields were frustrated in their efforts until the Wagner Act of 1935. This piece of New Deal legislation granted workers the legal right to organize into labor unions, and almost overnight the Appalachian coalfields became organized. The coal industry burgeoned during World War II, and the postwar expansion of the Appalachian coal industry peaked in the early 1950s, with the employment of approximately five hundred thousand people. The last half of the century was marked by an increasing reliance on machines to mine coal, a trend that dramatically reduced costs. More machines meant fewer miners, however, and their numbers dropped precipitously to a mere fraction of the once-mighty workforce they had been.

Finally, the myth that Appalachians are so attached to the mountains that they prefer being poor at home rather than relocating to find a better life should have been shattered by the great out-migration of coal mining families in the last half of the twentieth century when jobs disappeared. More than a million Appalachians left the region between 1940 and 1960, heading for urban factory jobs in Midwestern cities. In the 1980s, their destinations shifted toward booming southern cities, particularly Charlotte, North Carolina. With at least 1.5 million migrating out of Appalachia, it is difficult to see how the myth of irrational immobility can persist.

Although the coal industry provided high-paying jobs for decades, the shift to high technology and cheaper production methods has left some bitter legacies. The displacement of families who joined the diaspora to the urban industrial centers and the chronic unemployment and poverty synonymous with Appalachia spawned the War on Poverty in the 1960s, prompting the federal government to create the Appalachian Regional Commission (ARC) to help rebuild the area's economy.

Who Will Remember

Who will remember the coal miner's widow
These long long years he's been in the ground
Who will remember all of her hard times
Will anybody walk with her the road she's going down

Who will remember all the coal dust dreams
Given up in darkness in the Pocahontas seam
Who will remember have we ever met
Will it be your neighbor who covers all our bets

Who will remember Coalwood and Keystone
Where the ghosts of miners in the quiet dusk still moan
Who will remember who will light the lamps
In these and a hundred other spirit haunted camps

Who will remember the passion and the pain
Of being ground into the dust for a rich man's gain
Who will remember speak to his name
Will it be your neighbor who says never again

Who will remember the hopes that filled this life
A woman for her family a husband for his wife
Who will remember or should we all forget
All of God's dear children who in these coal camps met
—*Connie Townsend and David Parker*

*Underground in the mines: the
most hazardous of all American
occupations*
(Photographer unknown,
West Virginia State Archives,
Coal Life Project)

Moreover, mining has inflicted heavy damage on the environment. Many streams run orange from acid mine drainage, while
mountaintop removal, which uses giant earth-moving machines to
get at the coal by pushing the tops of mountains into the valleys,
threatens to alter the physical landscape forever. This method produces coal more cheaply, but most independent analysts agree that
the environmental and social costs will saddle subsequent generations with extraordinary social and financial burdens.

The persistence of a mythical Appalachia bypassed by progress
and fatalistically clinging to a homogeneous folk culture notwith-
standing, a century ago the region was transformed into an indus-

trial society by the coal industry. Like other industrial regions, such as the "rust belt," today central Appalachia suffers from postindustrial problems, precipitated again by the coal industry. Now that the jobs are disappearing, it is difficult to predict how long residents will continue to tolerate the growing magnitude of problems generated by its most important industry.

MOONSHINE ON THE MOUNTAIN

TOM ROBERTSON

Whiskey making was always part of frontier life in Appalachia, as it was in most of rural America. There was virtually no commercial distribution in the mountains, and homemade whiskey was often safer to drink than unprocessed water. Even preachers sometimes accepted home-brewed spirits in lieu of a cash tithe for spiritual guidance. When money was scarce, whiskey was like money—an important trading commodity. In the early years on the frontier, Americans imbibed on the average more than seven gallons of pure alcohol each year—almost four times as much alcohol per capita as they drink now.

Whiskey production was unfettered until after the American

Stereotyped images of hillbillies with the ever-present jug of moonshine helped perpetuate the idea that mountaineers and "white lightnin'" went together like biscuits and gravy. (Holly George-Warren Collection)

Revolution, when George Washington's administration decided to help solve the young nation's financial woes by taxing whiskey. In the Appalachian Mountains, where U.S. currency was rare and whiskey was money, mountain men who had fought the English now turned on the new U.S. government. Beginning in 1794, during what would come to be called the Whiskey Rebellion, mountaineers refused to pay the tax on alcohol. Tax collectors, or "revenuers," were tarred and feathered, shot at, and chased out; in western Carolina, one revenuer had his nose ground off on a grinding wheel. Secretary of the Treasury Alexander Hamilton wanted to hang a few of the angry rebels, but the government eventually backed off and dropped the tax, at least temporarily.

Moonshiner Jesse Estep, Harlan County, Kentucky, 1986
(© Shelby Lee Adams)

The mountain people continued their old whiskey ways. Although a few fermented recipes called for wheat, berries, or potatoes, the most and best whiskey came from corn: Monongahela rye, or "white lightning," took your breath away like the kick of a mule. In isolated mountain areas, where the roads were bad and farmland sparse, turning fruit or corn into whiskey made good economic sense: It increased the value and reduced the weight of produce. After all, it was a lot easier and more profitable to carry a few jugs or barrels of whiskey than wagonloads of corn.

"In the late nineteenth century, 75 percent of all the Internal Revenue officers in the United States were stationed in the southern mountains, trying to enforce the liquor tax."

—Dr. Gordon B. McKinney,
Director, Appalachian
Center, Berea College,
Berea, Kentucky

The era of Prohibition, from 1920 to 1933, took moonshine to the broader American market, one that went far beyond hollow, ridge, or county line. In the 1920s, Appalachia became a land of saints and sinners, exploiters and exploited. Dodging federal revenuers, bootleggers hauled white lightning down backwoods rutted mountain roads to sate the outlawed thirst of the neighborhood and the nation. By the time Prohibition ended, the Great Depression had set in, and for some mountain residents, moonshine became a way to survive hard times. It was a part of mountain life.

Since then, however, with law-enforcement crackdowns in the most remote counties, and the ever-increasing availability of liquor in stores and restaurants, moonshine has been relegated to a few renegades on the fringe of society. The economic sense that moonshine once made is now gone. Even in a state like Kentucky, where most counties are "dry," it is generally cheaper and safer to drive across the county line to select one's alcohol of choice. Though homemade white lightning is still produced in a few remote mountain stills and enjoyed by some old mountaineers, it is no longer a socially or economically relevant factor in Appalachian life . . . though the myth lives on.

Ballad of Thunder Road

Adding to the lore of moonshine in the 1950s was the song and film "Ballad of Thunder Road," written by actor Robert Mitchum, who also starred in the movie. According to Mitchum's daughter, Petrine, her father had wanted Elvis Presley for the lead, but he was unavailable, so Mitchum took it on himself. Mitchum's concept, apparently, was inspired by the legendary booze-runner Junior Johnson, who hailed from the Appalachian Mountains of North Carolina. Johnson's souped-up engine and daredevil driving style gave birth to the sport of stock car racing, which first became popular in the South.   Today, NASCAR racing has become hugely popular all over the country. The song "Ballad of Thunder Road" also became a phenomenon, with Mitchum recording it twice in 1957, and again in the late 1960s, for a country & western album he cut in Nashville with legendary guitarist Harold Bradley and other session greats. Bluegrass duo Jim and Jessie are among the many artists who've covered the song.

One drop'll make a rabbit whup a bulldog
One drop'll make a cat chase a wild hog—
Make a bull frog spit in a black snake's face—
And make a hard-shell preacher fall from grace
And the lamb will lay down with the lion
After drinkin' this old moonshine

—An old mountain ballad

THE BRISTOL SESSIONS

CHARLES WOLFE

Illustration by R. Crumb
(Courtesy of Yazoo/Shanachie
Records)

The story of the Bristol Sessions, the landmark recordings done in a makeshift studio in Appalachia's Bristol, Tennessee, is the story of the beginnings of the country music recording industry. The types of material recorded over several days in July and August 1927 illustrate the kinds of songs being played and sung by rural folks of the day. It's been seventy-five years since those early country music sides were cut in Appalachia, and their impact is still reverberating in today's popular bluegrass, country-folk, and gospel fields.

In the early 1920s the fledgling record business had fallen on hard times, thanks to the introduction of household radios: After all, why should people pay seventy-five cents for a record when they could tune in to the radio and get music for free? When popular music sales dropped dramatically in mainstream America, record companies sought new, untapped markets for their wares. One of the first they discovered was an African-American market for blues music, beginning with Mamie Smith's "Crazy Blues" in 1920.

In the summer of 1923 talent scout Ralph Peer, who worked for the General Phonograph Company in New York, made a trip to Atlanta and purely by accident recorded an old-time fiddler. This record, "The Little Old Log Cabin in the Lane," credited to Fiddlin' John Carson, sold very well. The lesson that Peer and his colleagues learned was that they could sell records of "hillbilly music" to Southern mountaineers as easily as they could market blues discs to blacks. After a few tentative attempts to record mountaineer songs like "Wreck of the Old 97" with New York–based studio singers such as Vernon Dalhart, the companies tried bringing a few artists north from Virginia to record. It was hard to coax these musicians to leave their homes, however.

When in 1927 the Western Electric Company invented a new carbon microphone that increased the mobility for recording outside a studio, the decision was made to go to where the hillbilly musicians were. With recording equipment stashed in the back of his 1920 touring car, Ralph Peer, now working for the Victor Recording Company, started making the rounds of Southern towns, looking for prospective recording artists. He started out in Memphis, then Atlanta, before giving Bristol a try. Why he chose Bristol is an endlessly debatable question. Possibly, the main reason was he had working for him in Bristol a man named Cecil McLister, a local Victrola dealer who was a great fan of old-time music. McLister knew the Carter Family, of nearby Clinch Mountain, and a lot of other good musicians in the area and had probably told Peer about them.

Ralph Peer
(Photographer unknown,
Charles Wolfe Collection)

Going into the sessions, which began July 25, 1927, the big star was undoubtedly Ernest "Pop" Stoneman, the founder of country's first dynasty, the Stoneman Family. Working from his base in nearby Galax, Virginia, by mid-1927 Stoneman had recorded more than any other Southern artist—more than one hundred sides for various companies, including OKeh and Victor, in New York and New Jersey. A versatile instrumentalist and fine singer, he had a nose for good songs and got them from both printed and oral sources. The second number recorded at the sessions, Stoneman's "Tell Mother I Will Meet

Her," came from a 1903 songbook compiled by Georgia publisher John B. Vaughan. "Are You Washed in the Blood"—sung by Stoneman; his wife, Hatsie; his brother-in-law; sister-in-law Irma Frost; and other Galax friends—is a gospel standard by Elisha Hoffman, dating from 1878, while "The Resurrection" came from a Pentecostal songbook of the same era.

Stoneman also called upon traditional Appalachian folksongs for his repertoire: "Skip to My Lou" and a delightful duet with his wife, "The Mountain's Courtship," which is often called "Old Greybeard," though Stoneman titled it "No Sir" in his own manuscript version. Only recently discovered in the Victor vaults, "Midnight on the Stormy Deep" (sung as a duet between Stoneman and his sister-in-law) was a traditional ballad, later popularized by the Blue Sky Boys. "Old Time Corn Shuckin'" featured most of the Galax area musicians Stoneman brought with him to the sessions, who were billed as Ernest Stoneman and His Dixie Mountaineers. That recording marked Victor's entry into the genre of rural comedy. A few months earlier, Columbia had issued a skit by the Georgia band the Skillet Lickers about a fiddling contest and had seen it become a bestseller. Peer had asked Stoneman to write a similar one, and, fresh from a real corn shucking on a Virginia farm, he obliged. The very first record issued from the session, it was rushed out less than a month later.

Peer was fascinated with what he called "holy roller" music and went out of his way to record it when he could. On the second day of the session, July 26, Peer interrupted his Stoneman recordings to devote the entire day to a session with a Pentecostal group from Gray, Kentucky (near Corbin), led by preacher/singer Ernest Phipps. "I Want to Go Where Jesus Is," the first of a number of sides Phipps would make for Peer and Victor, captures the performers' fervent holiness church style so rarely heard on commercial recordings of the time.

On July 28 Peer recorded Charles and Paul Johnson, a well-known vaudeville team from nearby Happy Valley. By 1926, the Johnsons were living in Johnson City and had already traveled to New York to record for Victor. "Pot Licker Blues" is a harmonica piece featuring Charles backing a musician known only as "El" Wassom. Wassom was a Johnson City resident, and probably black, but little else is known of him, save that he backed the Johnsons on one of their longer sides. Both "The Jealous Sweetheart" and a minstrel number called "A Passing Policeman" feature Paul on steel and vocals and Charles on guitar. On the latter ballad, a third person, possibly El Wassom, plays the thin bars of bone or wood that were holdovers from the minstrel show days of Stephen Foster. Also known as "The Little Lost Child," "A Passing Policeman" had been a hit in 1894 on Broadway, when it was written by music composer Edward Marks and pianist Joe Storr. The Johnsons later dropped out of music.

The same day the Johnsons recorded, a remarkable singer/songwriter of protest and gospel music from Princeton, West Virginia, came forth. Peer had earlier heard of Blind Alfred Reed's topical ballad "The Wreck of the Virginian" and, mindful of the appeal of train wreck songs, asked him to come in; Reed also did his own piece, "Walking in the Way with Jesus." Reed would record again, writing such songs as "How Can a Poor Man Stand Such Times and Live," revised in the 1970s by Ry Cooder.

An equally distinctive gospel singer was preacher Alfred Karnes, from Corbin, Kentucky. Attracted by local newspaper stories about the recording sessions, Karnes drove over the mountains to Bristol, bringing with him his rare Gibson harp-guitar, with its

"When I was small, my mother had a few recordings, mainly Jimmie Rodgers and the original Carter Family—'Keep on the Sunnyside.' I knew most of the stuff the Carter Family had ever done. I got all [their] recordings, and later the Carters got to doing some national radio stuff and I'd listen to them every chance I'd get. They had a catalog of good songs that just suited me fine. It was really something that broadened my knowledge of playing and my enjoyment of music. Never in my wildest dreams did I imagine I'd get to record with Maybelle Carter one day. She was a jewel of a lady. When I got to know her, she was just like homefolks. I don't think she ever knew she was the tremendous star she was. I met her when Lester [Flatt] and I were together. She was in Nashville, and we got to playing some dates. I really enjoyed playing that stuff that Maybelle had played before me, and it was a happy thing to get to be with her, hear her sing and play along with her. I felt our audience was the same as hers, so we started using her on our local television show on Saturday afternoons. Then she'd go play some dates with us, and, boy, I soon learned that people still remembered the old Carter Family and especially Maybelle Carter."

—North Carolina–born musician Earl Scruggs

three sets of strings. He played it on "I Am Bound for the Promised Land," with old words welded to the driving melody of "Don't Let Your Deal Go Down"; on Dion De Marbello's 1887 standard "When They Ring Those Golden Bells"; and on Fanny Crosby's 1899 gospel hymn "To the Work." Karnes' lively gospel songs were some of the best-selling records from the session, and in 1928 Peer called him back for more. Karnes brought with him another superb traditional singer, B. P. (Frank) Shelton, a Corbin barber who had supposedly met Karnes while an inmate in a prison where Karnes preached. Their "O Molly Dear," with its stark, modal sound, is one of the outstanding examples of traditional Southern music recorded in the twentieth century: The lyrics, better known as "East Virginia Blues," have helped define the concept of mountain blues.

Throughout that July weekend, Peer continued to audition groups that came out of the nearby mountains. On Monday, August 1, he recorded two fiddle bands. One was a Hillsville, Virginia, duo composed of banjo player/singer J. P. Nessor and fiddler Norman Edmonds, who recorded a tune called "Black-Eyed Susie." Edmonds would go on to become a widely known and recorded old-time fiddler in the 1950s and 1960s.

From Coeburn, Virginia, came the Bull Mountain Moonshiners, headed by fiddler Charles McReynolds, the grandfather of the great bluegrass brother-duo Jim and Jesse. The Moonshiners' "Johnny Goodwin," their sole record issued, is a delightful and intricate reading of the old fiddle tune "The Girl He Left Behind." After supper, from 6:30 to 9:30, Peer recorded a third Virginia group, an act he initially identified as "Mr. and Mrs. Carter from Maces Springs." They were A.P. and Sara, a middle-aged couple who'd been married some twelve years and were both fond of old songs, and Sara's cousin

"When I think of Appalachian music, I hear joy, but I hear a lot of sorrow. That sorrow started coming into those mountains after the first- and second-generation musicians came in here missing their homeland, missing their families who were thousands of miles away in Ireland and Scotland, who they'll never see again on this side of the earth. So I think there was a high lonesome pining sort of sound that came into the music after the Irish and Scottish immigrants came into Appalachia."

—Cordell, Kentucky–born
musician Ricky Skaggs

Maybelle, barely eighteen, who had shyly asked A.P., before they had left home, whether or not she should bring her guitar.

"They wander in," Peer later recalled. "He's dressed in overalls, and the women are country women from way back there. They look like hillbillies. But as soon as I heard Sara's voice, that was it. I knew it was going to be wonderful." They began with a song Sara and Maybelle had both known since childhood, "Bury Me Under the Weeping

A rare photograph of (from left) *Maybelle, A.P., and Sara Carter visiting Washington, D.C.* (Photographer unknown, Charles Wolfe Collection)

Willow," a nineteenth-century ballad widely known in the mountains. They then moved to "Little Log Cabin by the Sea" and "Poor Orphan Child," two songs A.P. had learned from an old gospel songbook used at the local church, where he had sung in the choir. Sara and A.P. sang them as duets. All three voices returned for "The Storms Are on the Ocean," a lyric derived from an old Scot ballad. The next morning, the session continued, but recently discovered Victor files show that, for some reason, A.P. was not present for the last two recordings. Sara, accompanied only by her autoharp and Maybelle's guitar, did two solos: "Wandering Boy," which she had known all her life, and "Single Girl," a song she had learned from a boy in Russell County in about 1905 that, she felt, "ripped off" the session. The Carters didn't know it then, but they had just started a long career, one in which A.P. would serve as frontman and manager, leaving the two women to carry most of the musical burden.

August 2 and 3 saw more local talent. From Alcoa, Tennessee, came John "Lennie" Wells' Alcoa Quartet, then the favorite singing group to perform at gospel conventions or funerals in west

JIMMIE RODGERS

Illustration by R. Crumb
(Courtesy of Yazoo/Shanachie
Records)

Tennessee. "I'm Redeemed," sung unaccompanied from a hymnal known as a "seven-shape rose book," was their favorite. The group had also recorded earlier and later appeared with a young Roy Acuff on Knoxville radio. Another veteran was a harmonica player named Henry Whitner, whose "Fox Chase" had been recorded in 1924 for OKeh and had established the piece as a standard. Peer felt an electrical recording of the novelty would give it a new sales appeal, and he was right. From Meadows of Dan, Virginia, came the Shelor Family—actually the Shelor-Blackard family—with their unusual instrumentation of piano, banjo, and two fiddles. Their recording of "Billy Grimes, the Rover," an old English music hall song that was sung in America before 1850, featured vocalist Joe Blackard, who had been visited by famed Appalachian folksong collector Cecil Sharp in 1918. The group also contributed "Sandy River Belle," a popular fiddle tune, upon which Joe Blackard sang a wordless second verse—an archaic Irish technique called "diddling."

Wednesday night was given over to the band of Mr. and Mrs. James Baker, cousins of the Carters, from nearby Falls Branch, who did a driving version of "The Newmarket Wreck," about an accident near Morristown, Tennessee, in 1904. While the Bakers were recording, the members of the band slated to record the following morning, Thursday, August 4, had been arguing among themselves. Called the Tennessee Ramblers since their formation in 1923, they were led by Claude and Jack Grant, with Jack Pierce on the fiddle. Since March 1927, the trio had teamed up with a young Mississippi singer skillful at yodeling and with a flair for promotion; his name was Jimmie Rodgers. Working regularly at a mountain resort in Asheville, North Carolina, the Ramblers serendipitously discovered Peer's Bristol Sessions while visiting Pierce's mother, who ran a boarding house just across the street from the studio. After successfully auditioning for Peer and promising to return with older, more downhome songs than their typical repertoire, the band and Rodgers quarreled over how their record was to be credited—and split up. As a result, the Ramblers quickly recruited a banjo player to replace Rodgers and recorded "The Longest Train I Ever Saw," a version of the blues tune "In the Pines." It was to be the start of a long recording career for the band members.

At two that afternoon, young Rodgers appeared alone for his session, accompanied by his Martin guitar. Disappointed with Rodgers' fairly new pop songs, Peer asked him to sing older ones that sounded old-timey but could be copyrighted. Rodgers came up with his version of the World War I song "The Soldier's Sweetheart," sung to the tune of the Irish ballad "Where the River Shannon Flows." After four takes, Peer approved it. To display his yodeling, Rodgers did "Sleep, Baby, Sleep," a vaudeville song from the 1860s that had already been recorded several times by other singers. "I thought his yodel alone might spell success," Peer recalled in a classic understatement. Rodgers would go on to become the biggest early star of country music, before his premature death in 1933 from tuberculosis.

The Bristol Sessions concluded on the following day, August 5, with a pair of sides by a fiddle band called the West Virginia Coon Hunters and the thirty-member Tennessee Mountaineers, who cut the 1886 hymn "Standing on the Promises." Among the latter, composed of a church group, was A. P. Carter's brother-in-law Roy Hobbs, in whose home the Carters had stayed when they recorded three days earlier.

After the session, Peer packed up the heavy wax masters for shipment back to New York and moved on to Charlotte, North

Carolina. About two months later, on October 7, Bristol papers carried advertising for the first real batch of the records to be issued. "New Southern Series," trumpeted the ad, and people rushed to their local furniture stores to hear their friends' and neighbors' new records. Validating the popularity of their mountain music, this grassroots audience was ushering in a new era in American music. Country music—the moniker Peer bestowed upon hillbilly music—was about to go into high gear.

THE STORY OF MY FAMILY: THE CARTER FAMILY

Rita Forrester

A.P., Sara, and Maybelle Carter performed as the Carter Family. A.P. and Sara were man and wife; Maybelle married A. P. Carter's brother Ezra. Maybelle (Addington) and Sara (Dougherty) were first cousins. A.P. and Ezra Carter grew up in Maces Springs, Virginia; Sara and Maybelle grew up in Nickelsville, Virginia. These communities lie on opposite sides of Clinch Mountain, in the southwestern tip of the state, close to where Tennessee and Kentucky join Virginia.

A.P. met Sara while selling fruit trees. He traveled on foot across Clinch Mountain from Maces Springs to Nickelsville, near Copper Creek. Sara was living with her aunt and uncle, Melinda and Milburn Nickels (Aunt Nick & Uncle Mill). She had come to live with them when she was only a few years old, after her mother had died. A.P. said that when he walked onto the Nickels farm, he came upon the most beautiful girl he had ever seen, singing "Engine 143." No one knows if he sold Uncle Mill any fruit trees. A.P. did say that Sara tried to sell him a set of dishes, and he told her he would buy the entire set if she came with them. Whether he actually bought any dishes is also unknown, but he did marry Sara a few years later.

Both young couples moved to Maces Springs near A.P. and Ezra's parents, Bob and Mollie Carter. Bob was a farmer; Mollie, who was one-quarter Cherokee Indian, was a midwife. A.P. was the eldest of eight children, and Mollie always said that he was

Historians believe that the young woman holding the banjo is possibly a cousin of Mollie Carter. (Photographer unknown, Charles Wolfe Collection)

From left: *A.P. and Sara Carter with their daughter Janette* (Photographer unknown, Charles Wolfe Collection)

"marked" by lightning, because when she was pregnant with A.P., she was picking apples one day and a storm blew in. Lightning played all around her feet and frightened her, thus marking A.P., whose hands shook all his life in a sort of tremor. In fact, they never stopped shaking until just before he died. Mollie removed A.P. from public school after only a few years because she didn't want the other children making fun of him. Despite his limited education, A.P. was an inquisitive, intelligent young man who had an interest in almost anything he came in contact with. He was intrigued by so many things that he often had difficulty focusing on just one. In addition to selling fruit trees, A.P. was a farmer and a carpenter who owned various saw mills over the years. Ezra farmed and later went to work for the railroad carrying mail. A.P. and Sara had three children: Gladys, Janette, and Joe. Maybelle and Ezra had three, also: Helen, June, and Anita.

Sara played the banjo and the autoharp, which is the instrument she was playing when A.P. first saw her. Maybelle and A.P. played guitar. Although Maybelle came to play the autoharp later, she didn't play it when they first recorded. Part of the unique nature of the group may be the upbringing they had. A.P. and Ezra grew up in a deeply religious home in which the church was a central part of their everyday lives. Sara and Maybelle also grew up in religious households. Their families, however, routinely danced at home and went to dances for entertainment. Bootlegging was a common vocation for many of Sara and Maybelle's family members. Virtually every mountain family was poor then, and jobs were very scarce.

The Carters went to the Victor recording session in Bristol in August of 1927 as a result of an ad A.P. saw in the paper while logging in Kingsport, Tennessee. The family had been playing in churches and schools prior to responding to Ralph Peer's ad. A.P. was determined they audition, but Sara and Maybelle were reluctant. A.P. and Sara now had three children, and their youngest, Joe, was a baby who was still nursing. Maybelle was eight months pregnant with her first child, Helen, at the time. After much persuasion and a promise to Ezra that he would hoe out a corn patch for the use of his car, A.P. got the ladies to Bristol. They had three flat tires on the trip there.

At the first session, they recorded a total of six songs. Although they never saw him at the 1927 sessions, Jimmie Rodgers also recorded then. He has come to be known as the Father of Country Music, and the Carters are known as the First Family of Country Music. The Carters went on to record more than three hundred songs during the course of their career. As a result of A.P.'s lifelong efforts to collect and write songs, the foundation was laid for coun-

After the Carter Family split up, Maybelle began touring with her daughters as Mother Maybelle Carter and the Carter Sisters. This publicity picture of the group was included in a souvenir packet available for purchase at the Old Dominion Barn Dance in the 1940s.
(Photographer unknown, Holly George-Warren Collection)

try music as we know it today. But for his efforts, many songs would have been forever lost or never composed. A.P.'s insistence that their music programs be "morally good" set the tone for the industry. His songs told a story, and they revolved around church and family. It's difficult to pick up a country anthology CD that doesn't contain music by the Carter Family. Almost everyone who's ever played an acoustic guitar knows who Maybelle Carter is, and they've probably played "Wildwood Flower" at least a few hundred times. Reportedly, Mick Jagger sang the Carter Family song "Will the Circle Be Unbroken" at his mother's funeral, say-ing later it felt like the right thing to do. Many Carter songs evoke memories of family events or milestones. Johnny Cash once said that no matter where his show performed throughout the world, everyone knew the words to the Carter Family songs, regardless of the language of the country they happened to be in.

A.P., Sara, and Maybelle took their children on the road with them from the beginning of their career. Janette, Joe, June, Helen, and Anita all performed from the time they were children. Janette was sixteen and Anita was only six when they traveled to Del Rio, Texas, to record on XERA in Mexico. Anita traveled so much that she said for most of her young life she thought guitar cases were made to sleep in. The second generation of the Carter Family has worked a lifetime in music just as their parents did. Janette played on all the border radio recordings that make up the bulk of recorded material available by the Carter Family today. She followed her father on many song-collecting trips because she had such an excellent memory. After the Carter Family quit performing in the 1940s, Maybelle took Helen, June, and Anita on the road. They performed with several radio shows and later on at the Grand Ole Opry. June married Johnny Cash after they met at the Opry, and the group toured the world with the Johnny Cash Show.

Janette's lifelong adoration of her father resulted in the creation of the Carter Family Memorial Music Center in Hiltons, Virginia. (The community of Maces Springs is now known as Hiltons.) A.P. had asked Janette shortly before his death in 1960 to see that his work live on. Her creation of the music center was the fulfillment of that promise. The center has presented programs of acoustic-only old-time and bluegrass music every Saturday since 1976. Music programs originally began in August 1974, in the one-room A. P. Carter Store, and moved in 1976 to the newly built Carter Fold music theater. At that time, the A. P. Carter Store was converted into a museum. A.P. had run the country grocery in the 1940s and 1950s, after the family left Texas. Saturday shows and an annual two-day music and crafts festival each August attract visitors from all over the world. It's not unusual for crowds watching the Saturday shows to overflow the indoor seating, spilling out onto the hillside. The Johnny Cash Show performed many times at the center. Marty Stuart, Waylon Jennings, Tom T. Hall, Ricky Skaggs, and many others have taken the stage there as well. Most of the performances are scheduled, but sometimes audiences are surprised by their visits. The center has been featured in numerous documentaries, a Johnny Cash Christmas special, and several features for television.

"After high school, I went on the road with my dad and the Carter Family. On the bus, we'd sing lots of old country songs. Dad gave me a list of one hundred I should know. 'The Banks of the Ohio,' one of June's favorite Carter Family songs, was the first song I learned to play on guitar. Helen and June taught it to me. Helen was a great guitar player—she had learned from Maybelle. When I learned to play, I thought that was the one and only way you play guitar. The technique Maybelle developed came to be called the Carter Scratch: You pick the bass notes with your thumb while playing rhythm on the higher strings. I don't do it very well, but Helen and Maybelle had it down.

"Maybelle was great to be around. Her Autoharp was so much a part of her. Every night backstage, June and Helen were showing me songs. It was like a lost world. I couldn't believe how much I loved these songs. Not only loved them, but knew them—it was like discovering part of my own body."

—*Rosanne Cash*

A 1950s publicity picture of Mother Maybelle (front) *and the Carter Sisters,* (from left) *June, Anita, and Helen*
(Photographer unknown, Charles Wolfe Collection)

Unfortunately, A.P. died before he fully realized what a monumental musical legacy he had left behind. Sara and Maybelle lived to see the induction of the Carter Family into the Country Music Hall of Fame in 1971. The work and music of the Carter Family is known throughout the world today. How proud A.P. would be if he knew!

FALLING IN LOVE
WITH THE CARTERS

JOHNNY CASH

When I was a boy growing up in Arkansas, my mother played the guitar and sang songs to me and taught me my first song. Every night I would listen to the radio, and the first time I heard the Carter Family was listening to them on the radio from Del Rio, Texas, singing the songs of the Appalachian Mountains, like "My Clinch Mountain Home." Those fine old songs have sustained me all these years and made a lasting impression on me. It's like old-home week hearing these songs again coming from the younger people who have just recently discovered them as treasures. I also found in those songs a beautiful treasure.

There's a common thread that runs through the Carter Family songs and other folk music from the Appalachians: The basic emotions we all know and find joy in or suffer from in our lifetime—joy, sorrow, sickness, health, death, love, hate, leaving, staying—all of these feelings were in the songs that were there before the so-called new songs that come out today.

Maybelle inspired me with her guitar playing when I first started playing in the air force. I tried to play some of the licks that Mother

Johnny Cash and June Carter Cash
(Ray Witherell/Holly George-Warren Collection)

Maybelle Carter was playing on the guitar—she was an inspiration for me.

When I took the Carter Family on the road with me in the early sixties, it was because I loved their music—and, actually, I had my eye on that girl in the middle—called June. And I knew if I could get her working with her family and on my show, she'd stay. So she did. She stayed and kept her family working close until we got very close together and she became my love, and then she became my wife. And that was in 1968.

In 1969, I had been doing my weekly TV show, and I had this idea of a historic reunion to bring Sara and Maybelle together for one last project. They had been separated for many, many years and not working together. So I brought Sara back from California to go on TV with me, and Maybelle was already there. It was easy to pick up the old thrill and sing those songs again. A great inspiration to young people, they did a historic reunion record.

Country music has always been family music: mother, father, daughters, and sons. If they had the talent, a whole family onstage singing those songs was a surefire winner. Of course, the Carter Family had that talent. They were a great inspiration to me and countless other musicians and fans.

Part Three

BOOM OR BUST

Wetzel County, West Virginia, 2000
(Van Slider)

The best way to understand Appalachia is to listen to its people. Appalachians are master storytellers. They can sit on a porch or at the kitchen table and artfully demonstrate the oral tradition of preserving history. Appalachians have a remarkable knack for recollecting years gone by. They can call up important incidents, crotchety neighbors, births and deaths, Saturday nights, the family dog, even an old pair of shoes, with the detail of a poet.

Of course, it's nearly impossible to listen to anything or any-

{ *Garrett County, Maryland*
{ (Van Slider)

one in Appalachia for very long without running headfirst into music. In Appalachia, music has always been used for more than social expression and getting people onto the dance floor. The songs of Appalachia carry more than the emotions of the region. They live and breathe like the people who wrote them. They carry the unofficial history of the region in their melodies and lyrics. An Appalachian song can reveal more about any hill or holler than can a bookload of facts.

In "Discoveries of the People: An Introduction to the Music of Appalachia," Paul Burch, a singer/songwriter deeply influenced by the music from the hills, presents a personalized account of its history. To Burch, like so many others, Appalachian music seems to have sprung up from the ground and taken root wherever there is a story to tell and a feeling to express. In many cases, the songs of Appalachia are nothing less than American folk music at its finest.

In this section you'll also take a journey through the heart of Appalachia with a few prominent West Virginians as well as common folk who represent mountaineers' grit and resolve.

Senator Robert Byrd, whose family is something of an Appalachian institution, and Congressman Alan B. Mollohan, who, like Byrd, represents the state of West Virginia in Washington, D.C., examine Appalachia, but from different points of view. Byrd's narrative is personal—an oral history with a hint of nostalgia, as he recalls growing up in West Virginia. Mollohan's essay, more formal in nature, tells the story of the Appalachian Regional Commission, praising its efforts to cut poverty in the region.

The setting for Martha Hume's essay is Kentucky—like West Virginia, a state whose soul is inextricably Appalachian. With Hume as our guide, we go back in time to 1902, when her hometown of Stearns, Kentucky, was founded, and meet her family, whose history mirrors the history of Appalachia in the twentieth century. David Giffels places the Ohio city of Akron, the Goodyear Rubber Company, and Route 21 into the Appalachian story. The section kicks off with "A Hillbilly Timeline," which shows when and how these stereotypical caricatures of Appalachian people found their way into our national lexicon.

A HILLBILLY TIMELINE

HOLLY GEORGE-WARREN

According to J. W. Williamson, author of the excellent book *Hillbillyland: What the Movies Did to the Mountains & What the Mountains Did to the Movies,* the term "hillbilly" "was no doubt in common parlance throughout the latter half of the nineteenth century." Following are the dates that mark pop-culture events that further popularized both the term and the stereotypical caricature of the hillbilly.

(Holly George-Warren Collection)

1900: "Hillbilly" appears in print for the first time, in the *New York Journal:* "A Hill Billie is a free and untrammeled white citizen of Alabama, who lives in the hills, has no means to speak of, dresses as he can, talks as he pleases, drinks whiskey when he gets it, and fires off his revolver as the fancy takes him."

1904: The year after the silent film *The Great Train Robbery* is released, the "flicker" *The Moonshiner* is issued by Biograph.

1910: The stage play *The Cub,* starring Douglas Fairbanks and satirizing feuding mountaineers, opens on Broadway.

1910–1916: Nickelodeons feature approximately three hundred different flickers about moonshining or mountain feuds.

1915: "Hillbilly" appears in a movie title for the first time, via the two-reeler *Billie–The Hill Billie; Harper's Monthly Magazine* publishes a

(Holly George-Warren
Collection)

travel article by William Aspenwall Bradley entitled "Hobnobbing with Hillbillies."

1923: The first musical group to use "hillbilly" in their name, Galax, Virginia, string band Al Hopkins and the Hill Billies, come up with their moniker after a recording session in New York: When asked their name, Hopkins answered, "We're nothin' but a bunch of hillbillies. . . . Call us anything."

1925: The term "hillbilly record" is a new category added to the OKeh Records catalog by A&R man Ralph Peer, after his recording of Fiddlin' John Carson's "Hill Billie Blues" sells half a million copies.

1926: The stereotypically depicted east Kentucky hillbilly is portrayed for the first time in a film, *Rainbow Riley,* which is based on *The Cub.*

1929: Hillbilly music is introduced to national movie audiences when Al Hopkins and the Hill Billies are featured in a short subject that runs with Al Jolson's *The Singing Fool.*

1930: Montgomery Ward begins offering "hillbilly records" in its mail-order catalog.

1934: Al Capp's *Li'l Abner* comic strip and Billy DeBeck's comic *Snuffy Smith* debut; cartoonist Paul Webb introduces his signature hillbilly characters, the Mountain Boys, in *Esquire.*

1935: The first animated cartoon short with "hillbilly" in the title—"Hill Billys"—is released by Walter Lanz; other hillbilly-themed cartoons follow, with such stars as Porky and Petunia Pig ("Naughty Neighbors," 1939) and Betty Boop ("Musical Mountaineers," 1939).

1942: A hillbilly character named Yosef is introduced in the year-book of Appalachian State University, in Boone, North Carolina; Yosef soon becomes the college's mascot.

1949: The film *Ma and Pa Kettle* is released; several sequels follow.

1950: Little Jimmy Dickens' "Hillbilly Fever" hits Number Three on the C&W chart, then still known as the hillbilly chart.

1951: The Lou Costello vehicle *Comin' 'Round the Mountain,* inspired by a collection of 1938 Paul Webb Mountain Boys cartoons, is released.

1953: Andy Griffith releases the comedy album *What It Was Was Football,* which becomes very popular, introducing his North Carolina mountain accent and colloquialisms to a wide audience.

1958: *Thunder Road,* starring Robert Mitchum, is released.

1959: The musical movie *Li'l Abner* is released.

1960: Sheriff Andy Taylor of Mayberry, played by Andy Griffith, is introduced on *The Danny Thomas Show; The Andy Griffith Show* debuts later that year.

1962: *The Beverly Hillbillies* debuts on CBS, where it runs for nine seasons, totaling 274 episodes.

1963: *Petticoat Junction* debuts on television, where it runs in prime time until 1970.

1965: *Green Acres* debuts on television, where it runs in prime time until 1971.

1969: *Hee-Haw* debuts on television, where it runs until 1994.

XXX "The Mountain Boys" COCKTAIL NAPKINS by PAUL WEBB

(Holly George-Warren Collection)

(Holly George-Warren Collection)

1971: The film *Deliverance,* directed by John Boorman and based on the novel by James Dickey, is released.

1973: The film *The Last American Hero,* starring Jeff Bridges as mountain booze-runner Junior Johnson and based on an *Esquire* profile by Tom Wolfe, is released.

1975: *The Dukes of Hazzard* debuts on television.

1977: The film *Smokey and the Bandit,* starring Burt Reynolds, is released.

1980: The film *Coal Miner's Daughter,* starring Sissy Spacek as Loretta Lynn, is released.

1986: Steve Earle's single "Hillbilly Highway" makes the country Top Forty.

1987: Dwight Yoakam's second album, *Hillbilly Deluxe,* makes him a star.

1990: Marty Stuart's "Hillbilly Rock" hits Number Eight on the country chart.

1993: The feature film *The Beverly Hillbillies,* directed by Penelope Spheeris, is released.

2000: The Coen Brothers film *O Brother, Where Art Thou?* introduces old-timey Appalachian music to the masses; the soundtrack album sweeps the 2001 Grammys in February 2002.

Pocahontas County, West Virginia, 1986.
(Van Slider)

Spencer, West Virginia, 1978
(Chuck Conner)

Tyler County, West Virginia,
1986
(Van Slider)

Wetzel County, West Virginia
(Van Slider)

The Josephs' porch, 1994
(© Shelby Lee Adams)

Grandparents eating watermelon,
1974
(© Shelby Lee Adams)

Wetzel County, West Virginia,
2001
(Van Slider)

Barbour County, West Virginia,
1999
(Van Slider)

The rim of Blackwater Falls
State Park near Davis, West
Virginia, 1999
(Van Slider)

The Fall of Lucifer
(Gary Carden/photographed by
Marian Steinert)

Adam and Lilith
(Gary Carden/photographed by
Marian Steinert)

Jacob's Ladder
(Gary Carden/photographed by
Marian Steinert)

*Blackwater River, Canaan
Valley, West Virginia, 2002*
(Karl Badgley)

Dryfork, West Virginia, 2001
(Karl Badgley)

Mountain, West Virginia, 1991
(Van Slider)

Hazard, Kentucky, 1964
(Jim Marshall)

Tyler County, West Virginia,
1994
(Van Slider)

Tucker County, West Virginia, 2003
(Karl Badgley)

Mineral County, West Virginia,
1995
(Van Slider)

DISCOVERIES OF THE PEOPLE: AN INTRODUCTION TO THE MUSIC OF APPALACHIA

PAUL BURCH

When I was six years old, my family moved to just outside Washington, D.C., into a 1920s farmhouse formerly owned by Arthur Godfrey, a self-ordained talent scout who was one of television's early stars. At the time, northern Virginia was a paradise of deep woods, clean streams, rolling hills, horse farms, petting zoos, wild raccoons, and foxes.

Back then, D.C. had a music scene that was the best-kept secret in the country. While San Francisco, Los Angeles, Detroit, and Memphis got all the attention and the hits, Washington was home to bluegrass, rhythm & blues, rock & roll, jazz, and string-band music.

Although my parents took me to numerous shows (I have vague memories of Les McCann, Gram Parsons, and Roberta Flack), for me, no trip to D.C. was complete without going to the Smithsonian's Museum of History and Technology (now the Museum of American History), where the basement gift shop had a collection of records featuring the sound of train engines revving, bird calls, and Native American dances. I loved records and anything that had to do with sound. But the ones that I was most interested in were on a label called Folkways. There, I found the *Anthology of American Folk Music,* compiled by someone named Harry Smith; a record with so many songs by different artists had to hold a lot of surprises.

Fiddlin' John Carson and his daughter, Moonshine Kate (Photographer unknown, Charles Wolfe Collection)

"I'm just glad I lived to see the world changed by music."
—Archivist Harry Smith, compiler of the Anthology of American Folk Music

Bill Monroe (right) *first played professionally in a group with his brothers; as the Monroe Brothers, Charlie* (left) *played guitar and sang, while Bill played mandolin.*
(Photographer unknown, Charles Wolfe Collection)

Tom Dula

The original version of "Tom Dooley," "Tom Dula" was written about Dula's January 1866 murder of Laura Foster in western North Carolina. Tom Davenport is thought to be the ballad's author. After it was recorded as "Tom Dooley" by the Kingston Trio in 1959, it took Appalachian folk music to the top of the charts. These are the original lyrics:

Hang down your head Tom Dula,
   hang down your head and cry;
You killed poor Laura Foster and
   now you're bound to die.
You met her on the hillside, God
   Almighty knows;
You met her on the hillside and
   there you hid her clothes.
You met her on the hillside there
   to be your wife;
You met her on the hillside and
   there you took her life.

For a dreamy, music-obsessed child like me, living on a farm with creaky barns peppered with snake skins, baby mice, discarded car parts, and horses that would occasionally break out of their fences and stand guard for me at the bus stop, the sound of fiddles, banjos, and high, strange voices blended perfectly with my surroundings. The anthology was the kind of record that I dreamed should exist, one with fantastic voices and stories. As Isaac Bashevis Singer wrote of his own dream storybook, "It was a book I both wanted to find and to one day write." To me, then—and now—the best songs on that revered collection came from America's enchanted forest, a place that I discovered was at my backdoor: Appalachia.

Appalachia is the Eden of American folklore that few know well but all speak of with a sense of awe and undisguised ignorance. Though the land has been pitted with "the world's largest shovel" (as so eloquently sung by Kentucky native John Prine in "Paradise"), politicized by the Great Society, parodied by *The Andy Griffith Show,* and filmed in Technicolor by Hollywood, Appalachia is still, for American musicians, a kind of fountain of youth we always go back to, the old home place to a group of artists who represent the quintessence of American independence, fortitude, genius, and madness.

From Virginia came A. P. Carter, the creator of the American folksong folio. Leading the Carter Family, he became the Johnny Appleseed of country music: writing, collecting, copyrighting, and broadcasting American song across the nation before wandering off the pages of history, a mystery to everyone who knew him. From Kentucky came Bill Monroe, who grew up cross-eyed, lonely, and shy, but who, when given the mandolin as a kind of punishment by his older brothers (who took up fiddle and guitar) turned the ladies'

Canaan Valley, West Virginia,
circa 2000
(Chuck Conner)

parlor instrument into the musical equivalent of Babe Ruth's bat, playing faster and singing higher than anyone, while leading a band still unmatched in virtuosity. Monroe (not without controversy) single-handedly formalized every strand of string-band music, mixed in blues and jazz, and created its current living form, bluegrass. From West Virginia came Roscoe Holcomb, whose long face and skinny frame is incongruous with his piercing, aching voice. From Virginia came Dock Boggs, a mystery for many record collectors; until the early sixties, many of them concocted outrageous theories of the

"Now you've heard all these rambunctious fiddle tunes—well, the men would sit out back in the shadows and drink moonshine and chew tobacco, and they had dirty lyrics to all these old fiddle tunes. Of course, they never made it into the public domain because of our prudent nature."

—*Olive Hill, Kentucky–born musician Tom T. Hall*

Fiddlin' John Carson (left) *and Gil Tanner* (right) *were two of Georgia's most famous fiddlers of the 1920s. Taken in 1922, this photo predates Carson's first recording by one year.* (Photographer unknown, Charles Wolfe Collection)

"I got a television set for the kids. One night I was a-settin' looking at some foolishness when three fellers stepped out with guitar and banjer and went to singing 'Tom Dooley,' and they clowned and hip-swinged. I began to feel sort of sick, like I'd lost a loved one. . . .

"Tears came into my eyes, yes. I went out and bawled on the ridge, looking toward old Wilkes, the land of Tom Dooley. I looked up across the mountains and said, 'Lord, couldn't they leave me the good memories?'"

—*Frank Proffitt, the North Carolina musician whose "Tom Dula" was converted into "Tom Dooley" by the Kingston Trio*

kind of life that was lived behind a voice that seemed neither black nor white, northern nor southern, dead nor alive.

The preservation of this music was largely accidental. Recordists like RCA Victor's Ralph Peer, H. C. Spier in Mississippi (Charlie Patton, Skip James, Tommy Johnson), Art Satherly, and many others were only seeking out music that would sell, unlike the goal of musicologists John and Alan Lomax and later Frank Warner (the latter of whom recorded "Tom Dula" by singer Frank Proffitt), preservation of folk music by the record men was a by-product of what was a purely commercial enterprise.

The surprise success of recordings by Texas fiddler Eck Robertson (whose "Sally Goodin" is still exciting), Georgia's Fiddlin' John Carson, Grayson and Whitter, and Pop Stoneman ("The Sinking of the Titantic") in the early twenties convinced field reps that folk music from the hills could sell as well to rural white audiences as had blues records by Mamie Smith and Blind Lemon Jefferson in the "race market," composed of black music fans.

Ironically, much of the audience for this music was leaving the old home place even as record-company carpetbaggers were trying to preserve it. As rural residents moved to urban areas, seeking jobs in manufacturing, the affordability of radio sets and the ascension of a handful of high-wattage stations such as the Sears-Roebuck-owned WLS (World's Largest Store) in Chicago, WSB in Atlanta, and WSM in Nashville meant that this new workforce could tune in to the old home place and hear the music of their youth (whether real or imagined). It wasn't long before radio stations realized that their new audience members were also sitting ducks for live music with a touch of advertising, delivered with sincerity by their favorite artists.

Mountain music was also getting national attention from an unlikely source. Henry Ford, chagrined at the deterioration of morals during the Jazz Age, sponsored nationwide fiddle contests, imploring his ever-growing workforce to take up traditional music and preserve it from the anti-American and subversive sounds of jazz and Tin Pan Alley.

But, as is often the way in American culture, everything influences everybody, and jazz, Tin Pan Alley, blues, pop, and ragtime eventually found their way into Appalachian music as well. The confluence of radio, the record industry, and inventions like the electronic microphone (which vastly improved the fidelity of recordings) and portable recording equipment made it possible to capture untainted folk music at the source, if only for a brief moment. Peer and others like him were looking for original songs both for their audience and for themselves, since publishing rights were one of the few perks of the low-paying and travel-heavy job of recording. But finding truly original songs and musicians soon became difficult. Modern technology meant that successful records were quickly imitated. Originality also became harder to come by as the popularity of artists such as Jimmie Rodgers and his disciples (among them Gene Autry and Ernest Tubb) spread across the country. Religious fundamentalism, manifested in many ways throughout the region, beginning as far back as the 1850s, caused many musicians to question whether a life of performing was morally and spiritually right. A number of the *Anthology*'s musicians were such a mystery to collectors because not only had they stopped

This early country group used mason jars as part of their sound and took advantage of radio's need for live performances on the air. (Photographer unknown, Charles Wolfe Collection)

"'Writing out the ballit' for our family songs was rarely done. All of us—Mom, Dad, and all thirteen children—could write, but these old songs and their music were in our heads, or hearts, or somewhere part of us, and we never needed to write them down. They were there, like games and rhymes and riddles, like churning-chants and baby-bouncers and gingerbread stack cake recipes, to be employed and enjoyed when the time came for them. Nobody got scholarly about them, and I have a feeling that's why they have been genuinely popular all these years."
—*Jean Ritchie, Appalachian folksinger and dulcimer player, 1961*

"There are some good white blues singers: Roscoe Holcomb and Dock Boggs, to mention two. I guess you couldn't find two men who sound so unlike Negroes or look so definitely 'unhip.' Maybe that's why their way of singing the blues sounds so real and true. [Their] singing is stamped with [their] life and experiences."
—*African-American critic Julius Lester, 1964*

Roy Acuff (with fiddle) *was one of the Opry's first big stars. Note the NBC microphone in this 1940 photograph.* (Photographer unknown, Charles Wolfe Collection)

Illustration by R. Crumb (Courtesy of Yazoo/Shanachie Records)

making records during the Depression but many had put down their instruments for good shortly after recording.

The Grand Ole Opry grew in prominence in the 1930s and with it came a new kind of music, despite the Depression and the near collapse of the record industry. Many of the small labels (Lonesome Ace, Silvertone, Black Patty) that specialized in rural music went out of business, while others (OKeh, Brunswick, Paramount) were absorbed into larger corporations. As the Opry developed star personalities like Roy Acuff, Eddy Arnold, Ernest Tubb, and Bill Monroe, the starkly original performers (mostly amateur) who had brief recording careers quickly found that being a professional musician had taken on a new definition. Country artists such as Acuff began appearing in films, as well as on records and national radio, while "old-fashioned" string bands and medicine shows increasingly lost popularity, considered part of a quaint, turn-of-the-century America.

Today we can listen to fiddlers and banjo pickers on the

Anthology and imagine that we are dipping our feet in a stream that runs back to the days of moonshiners, all-night dancing, and ancient tunes. In reality, the ballads, blues, hymns, reels, and dance calls were a haphazard blend of traditional tunes from the British Isles, work songs, and even professional Tin Pan Alley songwriting. In the hands of the region's greatest musicians, though, none bear any resemblance to the timbre or timing of their origins. Lyrics are often somber and desperate. The modal melodies seem to end abruptly, resuming on the singer's whim or mood. Still, these songs are our lexicon, and it is the music of Appalachia from the twenties and thirties that is celebrated as the essence of American values of home and tradition while it is simultaneously derided by contemporary country radio as backwoods, ignorant noise. In reality the music of Appalachia has been a rich source of exploitation just as the land has been. In that way, it is as American as it can get. Sometimes the exploitation has been for the better, as in the case of the *Anthology of American Folk Music,* which greatly inspired the folk revival of the fifties and sixties. But with revival came adaptation and commercialization.

In a letter to *Billboard* in the mid-1940s, Fred Rose, mentor to Hank Williams and, with Roy Acuff, founder of the Acuff-Rose publishing empire, sensed folk music would be exploited without being appreciated: "We pride ourselves in being a very intelligent people and good Americans, but are we? . . . We read all kinds of books that will give us an understanding of foreign folklore, but what do we say and do about our own good ol' American folklore? We call it 'hillbilly' music, and sometimes we're ashamed to call it music."

Indeed, the music of Appalachia is demanding and difficult. It sings of death, murder, revelation, insanity, desolation, and the

Early twentieth-century Appalachian families relied on their musical abilities to entertain themselves. It wasn't unusual for each member of the family to learn to play an instrument, often ordered through a mail-order catalog, such as Sears-Roebuck. Sometimes instruments were passed down from one generation to the next, just as songs were. (Photographer unknown, Mari-Lynn Evans Collection)

"It's all born out of the blues, out of hard times. It's all born out of people telling their stories—not so much to be hit records, and that's the purity of it. People are drawn to the fact that it's honest. The majority of our country music, our bluegrass music, is roots music, all born out of those old fiddle tunes."
—*Musician Vince Gill*

Bible. It is rhythmic and joyful. As Americans, we claim it as evidence of our uniqueness and our tradition, and yet it is private music, too. Over the years as they have been discovered, anthologized, and absorbed into history, the voices on these records come to sound even more stark and unsettled, as if they have been buried alive.

An early publicity photo of the Stanley Brothers, with Ralph on banjo and brother Carter on guitar (Photographer unknown, Charles Wolfe Collection)

DANVILLE GIRL

I went down to the railroad yard,
Watch that train come by,
Knew the train would roll that day,
But I did not know what time

I did not know what time, boys,
Did not know what time
Knew the train would roll that day
But I did not know what time

Good morning Mister Railroad Man,
What time does your train roll by?
Nine-sixteen and two-forty-four,
Twenty-five minutes 'til five

At nine-sixteen, two-forty-four,
Twenty-five minutes 'til five
Thank you Mister Railroad Man,
I wanna watch your train roll by

Standing on the platform,
Smoking a big cigar,
Waitin' for some old freight train
That carries an empty car

I rode her down to Danville Town,
Got stuck on a Danville girl,
Bet your life she was a pearl,
She wore that Danville curl

She wore her hat on the back of her head
Like high-tone people all do,

Very next train come down that track,
I bid that girl adieu

I bid that girl adieu, poor boys,
I bid that girl adieu,
The very next train come down that track,
I bid that girl adieu

An early cast picture of the
Grand Ole Opry, circa 1928
(Photographer unknown,
Charles Wolfe Collection)

A WEST VIRGINIA LIFE

Senator Robert C. Byrd

My mother died in the flu epidemic of 1918 when I was a year-old baby. My father was a furniture maker who earned about three or four dollars a week, and I had three brothers and a sister. Before she passed on, Mother told Father to give me to the Byrds, whose son had died of scarlet fever. My adoptive dad worked in the mines and lived in Algonquin, where he paid $1,800 for a farm up Wolf

North Fork Valley, West Virginia
(Jonathan Jessup)

Creek Hollow. Though he never had much education, he could play music and had a great memory—he memorized entire chapters of the Bible. Those days up Wolf Creek Hollow did more to influence my outlook than anything in my life. We were poor, and there was no electricity and no running water—we had a spring house for that. We had a horse named George, two or three pigs, and Mom would put butter in the spring house in summer. I'd lie on the ground and taste water. I had God-fearing parents, but they didn't wear their religion on their sleeves and make a big hoop-de-doo about it. They would tell me Bible stories, and every night my mom would pray on her knees. We children respected our elders, were taught by the Bible to honor our father and mother. The people who raised me taught me to be thankful for what God had given me and to strive for more—that this was a country where a person could go as far as he wanted to go if he had the ambition and the drive and the get-up-and-go!

We lived near Sotesbury, a typical mining town owned by the

coal company. It took an interest in the employees and encouraged them to keep their yards clean. The miners worked all day, from dark until dark, for two dollars a day, paid in company scrip. I went through high school at Wolf Creek in a two-room school. I used to memorize my history lesson by kerosene light. During the Great Depression, we never missed anything since we had no refrigerator or car or things like that anyway. We had horses and buggies. In those times, things moved about as fast as a worm crawls. The houses were little more than shacks, and there was no running water; there were pumps at the community hydrant. There was a creek, a dirt road, coal dust, and slate. My dad liked to have pigs, so each fall he would buy pigs, and my job was to slop the hogs. We'd save scraps, and after school I'd gather the scraps and, in large buckets, mix them with grain and go feed the hogs. In November, when hog-cutting time came around, I would shoot the hogs with a .22 rifle and slit their throats. We'd help each other and salt down the shoulders and hams and bacon. We'd give some ribs or something to elderly ladies. My dad would give me one of those hogs, and I would sell it and keep the money. We shopped at the company store.

We would go to the square dance in Mercer County on Saturday nights. The square dances were something I always looked forward to; I liked to play the fiddle. The principal's wife taught me to play classical music on the violin. She didn't want to hear me playing by ear, but nevertheless I liked to play by ear. I took six years of violin lessons, and Dad took me to Beckley and bought me a violin for twenty-five dollars. I heard Mr. James, my future wife's father, play the fiddle, and when I lived over in the country up Wolf Creek Hollow, we used to go to molasses makings, and there was a left-handed fiddler, Hiram Reed, there. I always enjoyed hearing him play. I used to listen to my favorite fiddlers, and I would write the

A West Virginia hog butchering, a ritual that was part of Senator Byrd's childhood
(Photographer unknown, Mari-Lynn Evans Collection)

Many a young West Virginia woman either played fiddle or taught violin lessons. (Photographer unknown, Mari-Lynn Evans Collection)

Fiddlers competed among themselves and entertained their communities. (Photographer unknown, Charles Wolfe Collection)

music down. I had had the good fortune to have been given lessons, and I was able to write the music on the sheets. Then I would play it back, and after playing it a few times, I could put the sheets aside because it just flowed by rote. Sometimes I would add my own notes. My future wife was a good square dancer. Many nights I'd play music all over—we'd usually have a banjo picker and a guitar player, and sometimes we'd have a stand-up-bass player with us.

There was something about that mountain music that came from the British Isles, from Ireland and Scotland. You could hear in the haunting strains of the music that those people had lived during hard times. They toiled. They earned their bread by the sweat of their brow. And playing music was a time for relaxation. They gave vent to their emotions, their love stories, their stories about their future life: the old hymns with such as lyrics as "on Jordan's stormy banks I stand, he cast a wishful eye, to Canaan's fair and happy land, where my possessions lie. . . ." Those were the kind of songs that Thomas Jefferson probably played his fiddle to. They were handed down, the reels and the jigs and the airs. There's an inner strength that comes from that music. I found that this was a side of our life that rounded out something that was missing. Even when I became majority leader—with all the pressures of being majority leader—I could go home at night and play the fiddle and have my grandchildren gather around me and just forget all about the cares of the world. The tensions went away. Back then, there was the other sad side of life. We had so many disasters—the Silver Bridge disaster at Point Pleasant, the Buffalo Creek disaster in Logan County. We've had floods, we've had droughts, we've had explosions—the explosion at Monongah in Marion County on December 6, 1907, snuffed out thirty-six lives. Time after time, we've seen these disasters occur in West Virginia. And the people who have lived through them have come out stronger—these are strong people in West Virginia.

When a coal miner was killed, we'd carry that coal miner's heavy coffin down those steep hillsides. I saw the sorrows that came to the homes of the coal miners. They are great people—a different breed. They'll go into a coal mine after an explosion, knowing there could be another ignition of gas that could snuff out their lives, yet they'll go, hoping there'll be a group of miners huddled in back of a piece of canvas somewhere in the mine waiting to be rescued. They go. I've been at the pit of a mine during an explosion, seen the faces of the mothers, the sisters, the wives, and the little children— there they were waiting.

I remember when the unions came into the mining areas. The coal miners went off and met in secret, then it became more open. It became lawful for them to be able to bargain collectively concerning their own working conditions and their own wages. There was a spirit of hope that was just everywhere. We knew there was a better day coming for the coal miners. The coal miners would march for miles for union leader John L. Lewis Day, or Labor Day. I would go with them. My dad would get in line. It was a new day! A new time! And I'd carry with me my fiddle and go to those labor events, and they'd give me a place on the program, and I'd play some tunes. Those miners would love to hear me play "Old Joe Clark" and "Arkansas Traveler" and "Turkey in the Straw."

I graduated high school in 1934 and got a job at W. P. Meyers

The interior of a coal camp kitchen and dining hall, restored and opened for tourists, Cass, West Virginia
(© Mary Almond)

Little Jimmy Dickens
(Photographer unknown,
Charles Wolfe Collection)

"We were very poor, but we didn't know that. We thought everybody in the world lived like we lived. During the Great Depression, people would come by where my grandmother lived and stop for a drink of water—like a man and his wife and three or four children all walkin', not going any place in particular, just lookin' for work. It was a tough, tough time for coal mining people.

"[After leaving home], I went back and I looked up and it was evening time and I saw this one little light bulb hanging down on the front porch and I thought, Boy, they've gone uptown on me now! My grandmother was afraid of electricity—she was scared to death of it, and in this little old house where they lived, they had one little light bulb hanging down out of the ceiling. Later on, my uncles got them a refrigerator, and that was the height of her glory, boy!"
        —*Bolt, West Virginia–born musician Little Jimmy Dickens*

Store in Stotesbury, where I made fifty dollars a month. It was a four-mile walk to get there, but I was glad to have a job. It was a company store, and I was the produce boy, but I watched the meat cutters and learned meat cutting. I found a manual and studied at night, training myself to be a meat cutter. I became the head meat cutter and was paid $110 a month. As time went on, I married, and my wife and I have been married for sixty-three years. The willingness to work long hours—and not gripe about the work, but to work all the harder, to overcome—helped to spur me on to better work. I wanted to be a James Madison, the hero of American history whom I had studied.

When FDR became president, it did something to the country—there was a new spirit that moved across the land. A New Deal! You saw his picture in every coal miner's home, no matter how humble that coal miner's home. There were pictures of Franklin Roosevelt and John L. Lewis on the wall. I remember when I was a boy, I sold the *Cincinnati Post,* saved up seven dollars, and put that seven dollars in the bank in Mercer County. When the bank went under, I lost my seven dollars and I've never seen my seven dollars since. But along came Roosevelt, and working with a Democratic congress, he passed laws that provided Federal Deposit Insurance, so that no more would a little boy put seven dollars in the bank and see it vanish. It was things like that that made an impression on me.

When Social Security came, the mine workers felt they could die with some dignity. I remember the old county poor farm in Raleigh County; we used to pass by there and see the old folks sitting in their rocking chairs on the porch. By establishing the Social Security Act, Roosevelt took all that away. We called it the "old-age pension" in the early days. My dad and my mom were able to draw Social Security. When my dad died, he didn't owe any man a dime.

A train makes its way through Hinton, West Virginia.
(© Mary Almond)

It was an era in which there was a new creation, new sidewalks, buildings, and schools. Even today, in some of the towns in West Virginia, one can walk on the sidewalk and see inscribed in the cement WPA 1933 or whatever it was. The WPA gave us a sense of community, a sense that we weren't alone, we weren't going to just be left there to die, that there was going to be some future.

Then the war years brought an awakening that things would never be the same again. I began working as a welder, and my wife and I got us a little fabricated house in Baltimore, where I worked in the shipyards. We'd get on the train that came through southern West Virginia at Prince and go through Hinton, White Sulphur Springs, Covington, Clifton Forge, Lexington, on into Washington, and get to that big station at about two in the morning and change trains for Baltimore. The trains were filled with sailors and soldiers, many of them lying in the aisles, which were crowded with men

"We couldn't pay any rent because we didn't have any money. The winters were very bad, and at times, when I was a five-year-old going to bed at night, I'd just hope I wouldn't wake up in the morning. Our bathtub was a washtub in the kitchen by the coal stove. About once a week they'd fill it up with water from the coal stove and we would each take a bath. We were so poor we didn't know when the Depression came."

—*West Virginia resident Ken Evans*

going off to war. As a welder, I earned more money than I had ever earned up to that time. We were building Victory Ships and Liberty Ships in Baltimore. Things were buzzing, humming. The streetcars were filled, and more people were being employed; women whose husbands were soldiers and sailors were going into the shipyards. We had our two daughters in Baltimore and later lived in Tampa, Florida, where I worked in the shipyard.

At the end of the war in 1945, we went home to West Virginia, where I took back my old job as a meat cutter. I worked at the Carolina Supermarket in southern Raleigh County. I started college in 1948, then went on to law school in Washington, D.C., at American University. When I ran for Congress in 1952, there were 125,000 coal miners in West Virginia; today there are about 20,000.

Mining became highly mechanized, and as it did, the miners left West Virginia because they no longer had a job. They moved to Ohio, Michigan, and other states, mostly in the north and east. There began a transition. We had the old core industries—glass, pottery, chemicals, coal, steel, timbering, gas, and oil. These were the smokestack industries, and most of these industries were owned by out-of-state people who were not West Virginians, for the most part. This transition began, and we could all see it coming. As I gained seniority as a member of the House of Representatives and later as a senator, I was able to work myself into a position where I could help more and more with funding new infrastructure in West Virginia. That was what we needed. When I went down to the House as a delegate in 1947, we only had four miles of divided four-lane highway. Well, along came the Appalachian Regional Commission, and in 1965 members of

The remains of an abandoned timber company's facilities, West Virginia
(© Mary Almond)

the commission and the governors of the states agreed to construct a vast network of corridors to connect with the interstate highways. I was in the Senate when President Eisenhower started the interstate highway system, and I had voted for that. I knew we needed to rebuild our infrastructure. We'd have to have better water and sewage facilities, and roads so that the people could get to work, go to schools, to the hospitals, to the child care facilities. And we needed safer highways. And so for decades I worked to get better roads. The *Saturday Evening Post*, on February 6, 1950, said, "West Virginia's highway system is decades behind that of its neighbors." Not years behind, decades! Those words are seared into my mind. And having traveled those roads at all hours of the day and night, I knew what these coal miners and the people of West Virginia had to deal with when it came to driving in that terrain. And I knew what businesses and industries would have to contend with in coming into the state and in expanding. So we've had this transition going on for these many years; it has taken time. While we are still very supportive of the old core industries—coal, steel, chemicals, oil, and gas—we have to understand that we need to reach out further. And in order to keep young people in West Virginia—and that's where they should stay, because it's the best state in the union—we have to have new industries, high-tech industries. Therefore, by building up the infrastructure, by making it possible for industries to have water, for communities to have sanitary sewage disposal, by having research labs, by bringing to West Virginia federal agencies such as the FBI, NASA, the Bureau of Prisons, and the Bureau of Alcohol, Tobacco, and Firearms, and the Internal Revenue Service, we bring in employers who will not be here today and gone tomorrow. So I've done what I could to bring agencies into the state.

Some say West Virginia is a kind of hard-luck state. We've suf-

"We had a little one-room cabin us kids helped build 'cause Daddy would let us go get the clay and gather up the straw. We was barefoot so we could just mix it up with our feet—you know, like they make wine. I remember back when Daddy worked on the WPA, he got his first check, and Mommy got a yard of material. That was my first store-bought-material dress. 'Cause the rest of it was always feedsack, and Mommy was [part Cherokee] Indian, so she would dye the feed sacks different colors.

"Mommy . . . would carry the little twins down the road a mile to the oldest daughter—their oldest sister, who had just had a baby (she was sixteen)—and they would nurse. I said, 'Mommy, how long did they live?' And she said they were six months old when they died. The little boy died one day, and the next day the little girl died, 'cause I'm sure they starved to death. I said, 'Mommy, what did you do with them?' She said, 'We just dug a little hole and wrapped 'em up in some old rags and buried 'em.

"John L. Lewis was the big deal over at the mines, so Daddy had his picture up, and he had great big fuzzy eyebrows. I asked Mommy who it was, and she said, 'John L. Lewis—your daddy was working for a dollar a day in the mines, and he came in and he was with the union, and now they'll make more money.' Daddy got off the WPA and got a job back in mines. I was eleven years old when I tasted my first ice cream."
—*Butcher Holler, Kentucky–born musician Loretta Lynn*

The majestic mountains of West Virginia are appropriate symbols of the strength of the state's people.
(Jonathan Jessup)

"The impact of WW II on Appalachia is almost beyond calculation. It had a tremendously big impact. First of all, young men and women of the mountains entered the armed forces in much larger proportion than other Americans did. Breathit County in east Kentucky is the only county in the United States not to have had selective service enforced during the Second World War. That was because there were so many volunteers."

—*Gordon McKinney*

One of the newer paved roads winding through the mountains of West Virginia
(© Mary Almond)

fered with one another. We've been isolated by these mountains. We've had to fend for ourselves. We've been looked down upon, laughed at, scorned, made fun of, called hillbillies, but we're determined to believe in ourselves, and we know we can do anything others can. We can do anything we want to do. We have the brains here that are like the brains in New York City or in any of the great cities of this country. And the people here have something else: steadfast faith. They're used to hard times, and they can go through them again. When we hear politicians talk about family values, this is where you find them. This is where our forefathers came and hewed the forest and carved out a living in the rivers and the mountains. Here, where the mountains meet the sky, the men and women who come from these mountains are so much like the mountains.

BLUE KENTUCKY GIRL

MARTHA HUME

I grew up in the curvy Kentucky hollows of a geological formation called the Cumberland Plateau, named long ago for some English duke of Cumberland. The plateau is made of sandstone ravines and rock arches carved by the Cumberland River and high cliffs overlooking the forest that carpets the hills with hardwood, evergreen, rhododendron, and tulip poplars. It is beautiful.

Author Martha Hume surveys the forest surrounding her hometown. (Stephanie Chernikowski)

Beneath it all lies coal. The people who lived there when I was born had come to get the coal, supplanting the sparse population of backwoodsmen and women who hunted, grew small gardens, and sold some timber. My particular town was called Stearns, Kentucky, after the Stearns family who owned it.

Stearns was a new town, founded in 1902 at a railroad crossing then called Hemlock. Attracted by the virgin timber, Michigan lumberman Justus S. Stearns sent land agents to buy thirty thousand acres of it. To get the timber off the land, he built a railroad through terrain that was so rough it is reported to have cost fifty-thousand dollars a mile to build the first ten miles. To prepare the lumber for market, he built a huge electric-powered sawmill, said to have been the first in the world of its kind. To accommodate all the people it took to run the Stearns Lumber Company, he built a town and named it after himself. Mr. Stearns populated his town with hired executives from his home state and from cities in the North.

Shortly after the timber operation was under way and losing money, Mr. Stearns realized that coal would be his real treasure.

A hand, a star, and a tree—but no name—mark this pioneer grave in Honeybee, Kentucky, near Stearns.
(Stephanie Chernikowski)

The first coal came out in 1904, and plans were to have everything stripped out and sold within forty years; both the town and the company were intended to be self-liquidating. Consequently, the first new citizens of Stearns probably saw themselves as colonials, come to make a killing and retire back home. The native population, most of whose lives had changed little in the past hundred years, likely thought they, too, would get rich. They sold their land, along with its mineral rights and access to those minerals, and then they went to work for the Stearns Coal & Lumber Company. Some cut timber and worked in the sawmill. Others built houses, offices, and stores. Some became railroad men and road builders. Some became clerks and timekeepers. Many became coal miners. The miners lived in even more temporary towns, called camps, at the mouths of the mines. The camps were to be abandoned when the coal was gone. So were the coal miners.

The only bump in the road to progress came in 1908, when a union man barricaded himself in the town hotel on Christmas Day and called on the workers to join him in a stand against the company. This situation was resolved by burning the hotel to the ground with the union man in it. The site became the location of the Stearns mansion, and a new hotel was built into the side of the hill across from the house. There was no more trouble from the unions for many years.

World War I turned Stearns into a boom town. By the end of the war, the town had a company headquarters, a post office, a school, a bank, its own money—called scrip—a dry goods store, a grocery store, a pool hall, a barbershop, a confectionery, a movie theater, and a golf course. It had electricity, telephones, running water, and steam heat. In 1922, a reporter from the Louisville *Courier Journal* wrote:

> Twenty years ago the high plateau which bears the town of Stearns was the center of a vast and roaring wilderness. Nothing but the calls of animals and the soughing of wind through the pines disturbed its quiet serenity. Today, it is the industrial heart of McCreary County, through which flows a million tons of coal from summer to summer.
>
> There are new noises, the noises of civilization. After all, what is the difference between savagery and civilization than differences in noises? Supplant the howls of wild animals with the heavy breathing of steam locomotives, the thud and the clink of coal-loading, the hum of a power plant and a sawmill, and you have in capsule form the whole history of McCreary County development.
>
> In Stearns itself, the noises are more complex and illuminating. For here, on this high, rocky shelf, may be detected more subtle noises; those made by women gossiping over bridge tables, by the contact of golf balls against wood and iron, by water running into shiny porcelain tubs, and by telephone bells. Indeed, it is all the gentle cacophony and euphony identified with twentieth-century manners.

Stearns old-timer, circa 1980
(Stephanie Chernikowski)

The coal-company towns that sprouted all over east Kentucky around the turn of the century were of two kinds. The first were rural slums—basic, utilitarian groups of flimsy frame houses and stores that had neither running water nor electricity. The second type, fewer in number, were "model towns." Stearns was one of these. The paternalistic owners of these towns provided all the modern conveniences. The children were educated, the citizenry was entertained, and the employees were presumed to be happy. And many were.

The catch was that the town was captive. The company owned

Churches of all denominations dot the hills of McCreary County.
(Stephanie Chernikowski)

everything, including the law, and the citizens were confined to a distinct class structure. At the top were the Stearnses, of course, along with their close business partners and their families. Then came the high-ranking company factotums. Together, these groups made up what my mama called the Official Family. Virtually every member of this group came from faraway towns and cities. Next in rank were white-collar workers—store managers, bookkeepers, bankers, mining engineers. These employees were also drawn from other towns, but more of them were from the surrounding region. The fourth tier consisted of industrial supervisors—the mine superintendents, the sawmill bosses, the construction chiefs. Some of these were local people—"natives." Finally came the laborers themselves, nearly all of them natives. What was left of the original population of the county who did not work for Stearns survived by subsistence farming or trading and did not participate in the life of the community, although they resented it a great deal.

Stearns was the chance of a lifetime for my mama and daddy. Both had grown up impoverished in long-established rural settlements in Tennessee and Kentucky, respectively, where everyone was closely related and family position was strictly defined—staying home meant one's future would be limited to one's past. In Stearns, however, no one knew or cared about the past. All that mattered was one's position with the company. Thus, with a little education, one could start at the middle of the social ladder fairly easily. Daddy, Whitman Hume, had a college degree from the University of Kentucky, in Lexington, and came to Stearns in 1927 to teach school and coach the basketball team. Mama, Hattie Carter, was a graduate of a business college in Knoxville, Tennessee. She flew from Harlan to Stearns that same year, in an open biplane piloted by her friend Estelle's boyfriend, and took up a job as a secretary with the company. Being single, both Mama and Daddy boarded at the Hotel Stearns, where they were assigned to the same table at dinner and fell in love.

The Hotel Stearns, the town's social center, was the perfect place to shed one's agricultural origins. Married men ate there when wives were out of town, and the company entertained VIPs there. There was a card game in the lobby almost every night. There were dances, traveling salesmen, single men, and single women. Couples formed. Better yet, if these couples were presentable at all, they would eventually be invited to dinner parties in the homes of company officials. Stearns was isolated, and the town was not big enough to allow hostesses to be overexclusive—otherwise they would have had no guests. But these hostesses did not come from the rural South. They came from cities like Cincinnati, Ohio, and they had sterling silver and real bone china. The ladies wore evening gowns and the gentlemen smoked manufactured cigarettes and knew how to dance the fox-trot.

Daddy was invited to these parties because he was a college-educated professional who was fine company and whose first basketball team made it to the state tournament—no small thing in Kentucky. Mama, the secretary, was invited because she dated Whitman Hume.

They had to learn everything, of course: table manners, party manners, dancing, polite conversation, clothes, golf, and bridge—especially bridge. Daddy made friends easily, and he became the protégé of Mr. W. A. Kinne, the very first resident of Stearns and a high company official. Mr. Kinne had a car, and he let Daddy drive him on trips into the country to buy land for the Stearnses and up to Lexington to see basketball games. Mama made friends with young married women and with other single women at the Hotel Stearns. Enormously impressed with the social life of the town and ambitious to be part of it, she became a student of manners. She learned proper Southern cooking from Mrs. Neat Sublette, the town's premier housekeeper. She learned about china and silver patterns at dinner parties. She learned how to dress and groom herself from Miss Gloria Bradley, the ex-mistress of the second Mr. Stearns and the current love of the third, who also lived at the Hotel Stearns.

Like everything else in Stearns, tolerance for sin depended on one's connections. The town abetted the third Mr. Stearns' romance with his father's ex-paramour because Bob, as he was called, was destined to be the next big boss, and he intended to marry Gloria Bradley as soon as his father, R.L., was dead. Also tolerated were adulterous affairs between husbands and wives of company officials. Less tolerated were affairs between natives and company executives, or worse, between executives' wives and natives. The worst crime of all was to steal from the company. Those who were caught doing this lost not only their jobs, but their homes and their social positions. These people had to leave town for good.

Mama and Daddy kept their noses clean and hewed to the company's laws. After taking the basketball team to the state tournament, Daddy became popular to the point that he was asked to edit the *McCreary County Record*, a four-page newspaper the company owned. This put him in the thick of things, so he soon knew everyone in the county. He continued to teach school and bought a Model T Ford, and he and Mama were married in Lexington in

1929. Mama stayed on with the company, and they continued to live at the hotel for two more years while they paid off the car and the $149 Daddy had borrowed when he was in college.

In 1932 they were rewarded with a little house on the Brick Hill. They didn't get to buy the house—no one in Stearns owned houses except the Stearnses—but they did get to rent it. Houses were assigned according to the family's rank in the company. The best, with steam heat and large lawns, were on Front Ridge, a street that ran across the top of the level ridge above company headquarters. The next best were on a sloping, unnamed street that ran perpendicular to Front Ridge. This road merged with the highway that ran through town and formed Brick Hill, where the houses had smaller lawns and coal furnaces. A fourth group lined the road to the schoolhouse, and others crowded onto the tops of ridges above the sawmill. All—in fact, every building in town and in the mining camps down the railroad line—were white with green trim except for the Stearns home, which had blue trim. I don't know if anyone ever tried to paint their house a different color; if so, they didn't succeed. There was no rebellion in Stearns—it's very difficult to rebel against the source of your home and livelihood when it's the only house and job available in what is otherwise a wilderness.

After the coal company left, the people of Stearns did what they could to earn money. This combination bus station/motel/tombstone store is one solution.
(Stephanie Chernikowski)

Stearns was still in business when I was born in 1947 because another world war had saved the company. Bob, the third Mr. Stearns, now married to his father's mistress, had taken over the business and the big house with the blue trim on Front Ridge. He was the last Stearns to live there, for he and Gloria had no children, and there were no other men in the immediate family. Unlike his father, Bob Stearns was solitary. He had few interests outside of his wife, business, drinking, and playing cards. He and Gloria isolated themselves at home and became a mystery to most people in town. Mama said one of the Front Ridge ladies blackmailed Gloria Stearns, but if that is true, Mrs. Stearns must have paid, for there was never a whisper about her past transgressions when she lived at the Hotel Stearns. On the other hand, there was blessed little talk about any other company official either, even though every single one of them had at least one adulterous affair. Years later, when Mama cataloged all the liaisons for me, I was shocked. Growing up there, I addressed these venerated elders as "ma'am" and "sir." Although the Stearns family had taken the profits for itself, retiring company officials were comfortably situated, especially given the condition of everyone else in Appalachia. By that time there had come to be a kind of aristocracy in Stearns, with membership determined by one's position, place of residence, and length of service with the company. It was only a temporary system, since Mr. Stearns still owned everything, but it mattered to Mama and, I suspect, to Daddy as well.

They had achieved quite a bit of status by the time they brought me home to the rented house on Brick Hill in November of 1947. Daddy's school had educated a generation of children and was working on the next. Mama's new position as clerk of the draft board gave her the power to send one's firstborn son to the military. Consequently, she was feared and even hated. Meanwhile, Daddy, now called Prof Hume, was regarded with affection and respect because his school was producing high school graduates, many of whom entered college and went on to become prosperous citizens—always somewhere else besides Stearns, for even though the company was doing well, it could no longer grow. The timber was almost gone, and the best veins of coal were exhausted. I grew up in a town that was in its death throes.

"Budded on earth to bloom in heaven,"
Honeybee, Kentucky
(Stephanie Chernikowski)

The most obvious sign was in the breakdown of the housing assignment system. In 1953, my family was allowed to move into Mr. Kinne's house on Front Ridge itself, next door to the Hotel Stearns and right across the road from the Stearnses themselves. Not long after, the owner of a strip-mining company not affiliated with Stearns was allowed to live in a company house in a respectable location. The Stearns Coal & Lumber Company was no longer hiring executives, and it needed to fill the empty space. Another sign was the lack of children. I was a late-life child, and my older brother and sister had both gone off to college. There was only one other child my age on Front Ridge and only three or four more in the town itself. Increasingly, Daddy's students were the children of unemployed coal miners. As the mines closed one by one, miners were faced with the choice of trying to subsist on the small parcels of land their families had not sold to the company or joining the Appalachian diaspora to factories in the North. Many of those who stayed sank rapidly into destitution. My parents started buying shoes for needy children so they wouldn't have to go barefoot to school. One night after dark, a schoolmate of mine came to our door to beg for food. Mama had me fill the child's sack. Even though Mama and Daddy made only ten thousand dollars a year between them, we had become rich in relation to those around us.

All was going according to plan. The timber was cut, the coal was almost gone. All that was left was the enduring beautiful land, which was gradually being reclaimed by nature. On days when there was no school and Mama and Daddy were working at the draft board and the newspaper, I took to wandering the town alone. All the streets ran along the tops of hills; the fastest way to get from one to another was to run downhill through the forested hollow and up the other side to the road. The hollows had been left mostly undisturbed. There were

Doctors were scarce in Stearns. The front row of tombstones in this McCreary County cemetery all belong to children from one family.
(Stephanie Chernikowski)

shallow sandstone caves to explore and paths that led to springs that fed pools where tadpoles thrived in the summer. There were wildflowers and snakes to collect. Sometimes the woods were so thick that being in them was like being submerged in a deep green ocean.

Surfacing, I walked along the roads and visited all the company executives along Front Ridge, sometimes bringing them flowers from the woods. Old people now, they were always happy to tell stories to the only little girl in town. I was too intimidated to visit Bob and Gloria Stearns, but their house was so big that I could sneak into it undetected, and I did so occasionally, when the coast looked very clear. Once, in their basement recreation room, I found a table spread with seashells and preserved sea horses that Mrs. Stearns was assembling into a picture. East Kentucky was impossibly far from the blue Atlantic, and the desiccated sea horses held an almost pornographic fascination for me. I wanted to steal one, but that would have been like stealing from God, so I returned to look at them as often as I could, until one day the shells were gone. Not long after, I heard that Mr. Stearns had died, and I didn't go back into the big house for many years.

By that time, Stearns was being dismantled. It fell to Bob Gable, the last of Mr. Stearns' nephews, to close what remained of the mines and the sawmill. He sold the stores and the houses to the highest bidder, who was not always the person who worked or lived in them. My mama and daddy couldn't afford to buy the house they had rented on Front Ridge; like the families of the coal miners Daddy had educated, they had to leave and go north, and it was not too long before Daddy was dead. The people who did buy houses in Stearns immediately painted them every color under the sun except green or white, but there are still no jobs and life is

Small churches and passionate preachers not only promise salvation from this vale of tears; they also provide an emotional outlet for a taciturn and God-fearing people.
(Stephanie Chernikowski)

rough. The land itself is now a national park, returning to its wild self, only slightly constrained by the government that tries to manage it.

I left, too. I went even farther north, to New York City, thinking that there I could find as many seahorses as my heart desired but learning, finally, that blue dreams are dangerous to a creature from the green world. I live as near to that world as I can now, as near as it will allow me to come. People have not been kind to the green sea, and we must make amends.

—Excerpted from *Missing Scarlett,*
a work in progress

The many ghosts of Appalachia will never lack for places to live. (Archie L. Musick, courtesy of Judy P. Byers, from the Archives of the West Virginia Folklife Center, Fairmont State)

READIN', WRITIN', AND ROUTE 21:
THE ROAD FROM
WEST VIRGINIA TO OHIO

David Giffels

Spencer, West Virginia, is a town of just under three thousand, the seat of Roane County, population fifteen thousand. Its social hub is the White Oak Restaurant, the kind of place where gravy is a given and toothpicks provide entrée to lazy conversation. The main street is called Main Street. There isn't quite enough action to fill an entire week, so much of the town just takes off Thursday afternoons to go fishing. It is also a place with an oddly intense connection to the "Rubber Capital of the World"—Akron, Ohio.

Route 21 led thousands of West Virginians to Ohio.
(Paul Tople, from *Wheels of Fortune,* courtesy of the University of Akron Press)

For a visiting stranger from Ohio, the subject of Akron quickly becomes the ultimate icebreaker. The pharmacist at Staats Drugstore lived in Akron when his dad worked at Goodyear Aircraft. One of his coworkers was born and raised there. The city clerk used to live in Peninsula, north of Akron. The newspaper publisher's wife was born in Akron. The co-owner of a local funeral home has been there lots of times—in the hearse, to pick up those whose final wish was to be buried at home, in tiny Spencer, West Virginia.

The local newspaper, *The Times Record,* has 930 out-of-state subscribers. Of those, 151 are in Akron and its suburbs. Compare that with 13 in Cleveland, 8 in Columbus, and 2 in Toledo. It's hard to find people in Spencer who've never lived in the Rubber City.

During the boom years of the rubber industry—the first two decades of the last century, and then during World War II—people came to Akron in droves from Appalachia: western West Virginia, eastern Kentucky, eastern Tennessee, western Pennsylvania, and southern Ohio. They came from places where coal mines had tapped out, farmland had soured, and oil wells had dried up to a place where well-paying jobs were as plentiful as crab apples in September.

During the early 1900s, a few brave souls from Spencer first made the journey up old Route 21 to Akron; in those days, it took seven hours. They had heard about a new kind of work in the rubber factories there. They quickly found that the jobs were plentiful and the money was good. So, one weekend when they went home to visit, they told their friends and family about the boomtown up north. Word spread quickly, as it does so well in Spencer. The grapevine was flourishing, but Akron wanted to fertilize it. This ad appeared on April 20, 1903, in Roane County's *Weekly Bulletin:*

> *Wanted. Strong active men for automobile and bicycle tire making and press work. Mill men and laborers. Steady work and good pay. Apply at Falor St. gate. The Diamond Rubber Co. Akron, Ohio.*

The same newspaper, in 1909, began running an "Akron, Ohio Items" column and estimated that there were six hundred Roane County natives in Akron. The pipeline flowed freely. Some went to Akron and stayed. Others left in the winter and returned to their farms in the spring. And most, whether they stayed or not, came home to visit as often as they could. Every Friday night, the roads out of Akron were filled with cars bearing West Virginia plates. Folks would head for the hills, cure their homesickness, and drive back in time for work on Monday.

In fact, Ray C. Bliss, former head of the Summit County

Republican Party, is said to have arranged for the rubber plants' annual weeklong cleaning to take place as Akron held its 1935 mayoral election. The cleaning would close the plants, and Bliss banked on the West Virginians, primarily Democrats, eschewing polling places for their home state on the days off. He supposedly watched with delight from a hillside south of Akron as the heavy traffic flow confirmed his plan had worked. And the GOP candidate, Lee D. Schroy, won handily.

Appalachians in Akron, joined by immigrants from other places, found their niches. By 1920, there were more people in Akron who were born in other states or abroad than in Ohio. Foreign immigrants—the greatest numbers from Hungary, Austria, Italy, Russia, and Germany—peppered the stew. There were ethnic neighborhoods: North Hill for the Italians, Barberton for the Hungarians, Lakemore and Rittman for the West Virginians.

Employees at Goodyear comprised a melting pot of nationalities. (Paul Tople, from *Wheels of Fortune,* courtesy of the University of Akron Press)

According to historian George Knepper, the hill folks from states surrounding Ohio easily are Akron's largest ethnic group: "They had all the same characteristics: speech patterns, consorting with one another in common organizational groups, going to the same types of churches, looking for the same types of recreation, living in compact communities for mutual support because that is all they could afford. Well, that happened in Akron in a very, very big way." Phillip Obermiller, an expert on Appalachian culture who teaches at the University of Cincinnati, agrees that West Virginians and Pennsylvanians were drawn to Akron because "it was close. They could go back home and visit if they needed; those industrial jobs were plentiful; and the collateral construction jobs and service jobs were also there." Migration from Appalachia occurred mostly along family lines, Obermiller points out. "Word of mouth generally traveled back and forth. . . . If they were hiring at one factory, folks back in the region soon knew about it."

In 1910, according to U.S. Census figures, West Virginia natives accounted for 2,075 of Akron's 69,000 people. By 1920, Akron's West Virginia population had soared to 13,527. The city's total population was 208,435. Excluding West Virginia cities, Akron, in 1920, had more West Virginians than any other U.S. city of 50,000 or more. The number of West Virginians living in Akron grew to 18,902 in 1930, before declining to 15,071 in 1940. Even with the shrinkage, Akron by then had more West Virginia natives than any other U.S. city of more than 100,000. Although Pennsylvania provided the largest number of migrants—22,963 lived in Akron in 1920—West Virginians made the strongest impression on the bustling industrial city. They had to deal with the jokes that are inevitable for outsiders. The Appalachians were teased, sometimes cruelly, called "snakes" and "hillbillies."

Women found work in the tire plants, too. (Paul Tople, from *Wheels of Fortune,* courtesy of the University of Akron Press)

The jokes are well-worn:

What's the capital of West Virginia? Akron.

What are the three "R"s in a West Virginia education? Readin', 'ritin', and Route 21 to Akron.

Did you hear that the governor of West Virginia resigned? He got recalled to Goodyear.

Fact is, the West Virginians simply stood out more than the Pennsylvanians. There was the accent, for one thing. The distinctive twang that turned "Akron" into "Ack-ern" and "Firestone" into "Farstone" quickly established itself in Akron's growing Tower of Babel.

"Oh, West Virginians! Oh, Jesus, yes! Hillbilly—hillbilly language," exclaims Olympia Mangli, a Greek immigrant who waited on lots of West Virginians when she worked at restaurants near the rubber plants. "I didn't understand them at first. Of course, nobody understood me either. Everybody's got an accent."

The rubber companies did their part to help the migration along.

Betty Dunlevy, who worked in the personnel department at General Tire during World War II, recalls that recruiters would head south into the hills in a bus looking for potential workers. When they found one, they would take a little tag with the name of the rubber company and hook it through the prospect's buttonhole. At the Akron Greyhound station, company representatives would round up prospective workers according to the name on the tag. Others were even more direct, delivering new employees straight to the factory doors.

As recruits to the rubber army, West Virginians were attractive for a number of reasons. They were thought to be hardworking, strapping farmhands who could handle the physical labor of tire building. These newcomers, more often than not, found themselves at the bottom of a clearly defined ladder at the rubber factories. Many had to start in the hot, black, stinking environment called the mill room, or in the tire-curing area, better known as the Pit.

Obermiller says that the management believed Southerners would be less prone to communism than European recruits and that Appalachians, with their strongly independent spirit, would be less likely to unionize. He points to the success of the mountaineer-intensive United Mine Workers, however, to shoot down the second theory.

Once West Virginians came to Akron, they made their mark by celebrating their culture with exuberance, gathering to sing and play

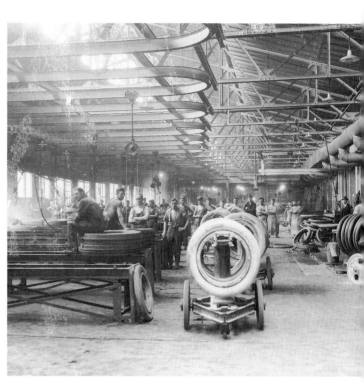

Workers take a break from the grueling job of manufacturing tires. (Paul Tople, from *Wheels of Fortune,* courtesy of the University of Akron Press)

The job of "rubber reclamation" was smelly, dirty, and dangerous—requiring brute strength. (Paul Tople, from *Wheels of Fortune,* courtesy of the University of Akron Press)

mountain songs, maintaining their farming lifestyle with gardens, never losing pride in their roots and their religious traditions.

Some were Baptist, some were Pentecostal, some were "shouting Methodists." Different strains with one thing in common: The Southern religious folks celebrated with a fervor Akron had never seen. And no one shepherded them with more skill than Dallas Billington. Billington, the son of a Kentucky farmer, born in a log house, sensed a spiritual yearning in all these transplanted Southerners when he arrived in Akron in the 1920s to take a job at Goodyear. "Akron," he once said, "is the wickedest place this side of hell."

Akron probably was no worse than any other industrial city its size during the Prohibition era, but the morals of its citizens did become relaxed to a shocking extent. Authorities looked the other way when laws on drinking, gambling, drugs, and prostitution were flouted. Women of good reputation avoided the Grand Opera House, which featured midnight burlesque shows. High rollers hung out at the Buchtel and Windsor hotels, among Akron's finest. So Billington started preaching. His first sermon, at Akron's Furnace Street Mission in 1929, was delivered to a shabby gathering of drunks and whores. They were the people who needed him.

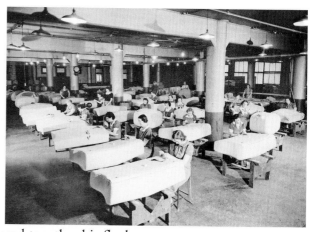

Women joined the labor force in huge numbers during World War II. (Paul Tople, from Wheels of Fortune, *courtesy of the University of Akron Press)*

Soon he started holding revivals in churches and tents—wherever he could find a place. When a tent wasn't big enough, he arranged to use part of Rimer Grade School. But that wasn't big enough, either. So he gathered together his flock and built what would soon earn a reputation as one of the largest Baptist churches in the country: Akron Baptist Temple, dedicated on Easter Sunday, 1938. The temple, on Manchester Road in Akron, had pews to seat 2,600 worshipers, and on some Sundays, even *that* wasn't big enough. (The church has been rebuilt twice and now seats more than 4,000 people.) The worshipers, most of them transplanted Southerners, came to hear this big man with a big voice and an even bigger message. Dallas Billington, six feet tall, with a square jaw, black hair, and black eyeglasses, bore a passing resemblance to Clark Kent. As a preacher, he was more like Superman, fully capable of slugging it out in prayer. He was hauled into court one time for disorderly conduct: His preaching, projected through a loudspeaker, was too loud for the neighbors.

Church singers, 1996
(© Shelby Lee Adams)

Billington was a talented evangelist with the foresight to take his message beyond the church walls and onto the airwaves. During the 1940s, 1950s, and 1960s, Akron Baptist Temple's services were broadcast across North America. But it all began in Akron, in 1932, when Billington started broadcasting his ministry over radio station WJW (an acronym, he said, for "Watch Jesus Win"). From the first day, the phone at the station rang as Akron residents called to say this was the evangelist for them. Old-time religion had found its place in Akron.

For people away from home, in a strange place with strange temptations, Billington and others like him provided comfort and direction. While the distance was only a couple hundred miles, Akron was a far, far piece from West Virginia.

MY WEST VIRGINIA

CONGRESSMAN ALAN B. MOLLOHAN

Held together by the mountains that look so strong but make it weak,
Appalachia sweeps northward from the isolated dog-trot cabins of
Alabama to the bleak coalfields of Pennsylvania. The name, borrowed
from the Appalachian Mountain system, was coined by the federal
government to describe a most depressed area. . . .

—"The Mountains of Poverty,"
The New York Times Magazine, 1964

It was the 1960s, and millions of Americans were shocked to find that economic prosperity had somehow bypassed a long strip of the eastern United States. But there was the proof, in haunting pictures and stories such as that from which the above passage is an excerpt.

The wealth of the Appalachians—including its colorful history, rich culture, and resilient people—was virtually ignored by the media of the day. To be honest, the snub probably didn't matter. The stark photographs of ramshackle homes, populated by struggling families, were too overpowering. They seared a perception in the public mind: This was a place of utter poverty, and in desperate need of outside help.

It was, of course, stereotyping of a highly diverse region; even *The New York Times Magazine* writer acknowledged Appalachia's "pockets of prosperity." Yet, at the core, the stories told an inarguable truth: Much of the region was lagging behind, and its people were suffering the effects.

But why? In my home state of West Virginia, one of thirteen states served by today's Appalachian Regional Commission (ARC)

New River Bridge, West Virginia
(© Mary Almond)

West Virginia byway
(© Mary Almond)

"When Daddy would come home from the mines, he would be just covered with black soot. Mother and Daddy didn't let on to us kids how tough it was and what hard times they were having. I do know my dad did not ever want any of the kids working in the coal mines. I do know that."

—*Pikeville, Kentucky–born musician Patty Loveless*

and the only one fully within ARC's coverage area, answering that question has required us to confront hard truths about our past. Certainly the topography of West Virginia—aptly nicknamed "the Mountain State"—had long hindered the flow of people and commerce. If nature had challenged us in this respect, however, it blessed us in another: with abundant deposits that made our state a natural resource and industrial power. West Virginia coal mines, oil and gas fields, timber stands, and manufacturing plants helped to build America. They also provided a good, dependable livelihood for generations of our families. As these industries prospered, so did we.

Unfortunately, we were not thoughtful stewards of what nature bestowed. Outside ownership of our resources was more the rule than the exception, so few profits were reinvested to diversify our economy. Instead, West Virginia's entire infrastructure, everything from its

The remains of the West Virginia Pulp and Paper Mill and its drying kilns, after two fires, one in 1978 and then another in 1982, totally destroyed it. During its peak, somewhere between 1908 and 1922, the mill employed between 2,500 and 3,000 men, working eleven-hour shifts. All that is left are ivy-covered foundations and twisted remains.
(© Mary Almond)

labor supply to its banking system, grew around an immense yet narrow industrial sector. This left our communities ill prepared for normal downturns in the business cycle—let alone for fundamental changes caused by technological advances, increased overseas competition, and greater environmental sensitivities.

We paid a heavy price for our lack of strategic planning. We paid it in the form of lost resources, lost profits, lost opportunity, and most painful of all, lost people.

Four decades have passed since President Kennedy laid the

"When I came to this creek, the hills were still full of game. Now you can't hear the quail call anywhere. See that chimney? Used to be a house. A slide just pushed it away—a dozer came around the mountain one day and started rolling boulders down the hill. Any man comes in here with a bulldozer will leave in a box.

"Strip mining is completely destroying this country—destroying it completely. Absolutely makes me mad—and I don't deny it—plenty mad—it makes me mad to hear a bulldozer in the hills—mad enough to shoot 'em if I was up there. I'm gonna fight . . . they'll have to kill me afore they go through."
—*West Virginia resident Uncle Dan Gibson*

groundwork and President Johnson mobilized the government for the War on Poverty. Some observers point to the region's continuing struggles and claim that poverty won. I do not believe that the facts support this conclusion.

As ARC accurately notes, poverty rates in the Appalachians have been cut in half. Educational attainment has sharply improved. New roads have opened our communities to increased economic development. And while much work remains, life is better for many of the citizens across our region. Those isolated "pockets of prosperity" referenced in *The New York Times Magazine* forty years ago are increasing in number.

In the congressional district that I serve, for example, we point with pride to our success in diversifying the economy through information technology, aerospace, and government service activities. They are opening a world of opportunities to the people of northern West Virginia. Likewise, many of our neighbors have achieved success in developing sectors that are built on the unique strengths of their own areas.

Federal grants and loans, largely courtesy of ARC and the U.S. Economic Development Administration, have significantly contributed to this progress. So have the private investments leveraged by those federal dollars. And the people of Appalachia have no greater friend than Senator Robert C. Byrd, dean of our West Virginia Congressional Delegation, whose faithful advocacy of the region has been a powerful influence for half a century.

The War on Poverty has not been lost. Nor has it yet been won. It is an ongoing battle and must be continually waged until every family–in Appalachia and across our country–has access to the sanitary housing, quality education, and decent employment opportunities that befit the wealthiest nation on Earth.

Part Four

MEMORIES: KEEPING THE SPIRIT IN THE MODERN WORLD

Canaan Valley, West Virginia
(Jonathan Jessup)

The history of Appalachia has been a history of struggle. In the region's earliest years, European settlers wrestled with the land, turning it from frontier to farmland. During the colonial period, the Cherokee, Choctaw, and other Indian nations fought a losing war to preserve their homeland. Later, the Civil War saw brothers battling brothers to preserve a way of life. The fight against poverty was ongoing in the late nineteenth and twentieth centuries. And

Davis, West Virginia, 2003
(Karl Badgley)

with the arrival in Appalachia of big-business coal came a battle for rights and a fair wage. Worker against management meant bloody blows were thrown on each side.

By the second half of the last century, the fight to preserve the integrity of the land—namely, to stop the ravaging ways of strip mining and more recently the destructiveness of "mountaintop removal"—was followed by an attempt to keep the Appalachian way of life intact in the face of modernity. And then, finally, came the battle with the media's distorted depiction of Appalachia as well as efforts to destroy stereotypes that perpetuated the image of Appalachians as barefooted hillbillies.

This section contains essays that define some of Appalachia's most recent struggles as well as the role religion has played in them and in the personal pursuit of salvation. Gary Carden's vignette, "The Trunk in the Attic," has no particular Appalachian address but serves as a small reminder that we all have trunks in the attic where our most precious memories are preserved. Vivian Stockman's "Killing Our Hills: The Devastation of Mountaintop Removal" and Julia Bonds' "Fighting for My Appalachia Home" reveal the passion of two Appalachians in their quest to save the land. The ecology of Appalachia has been in peril ever since the search for easier and cheaper ways to extract coal from the earth led to strip mining and mountaintop removal. The essays of both Stockman and Bonds detail the fight between what's right economically versus what's right ecologically.

Like in so many other regions throughout America, religion has provided hope and spiritual nourishment over the years for many of Appalachia's people. Whether it was the fear of God or the love of God or a combination of both, Appalachians searched for salvation and redemption in a world that often seemed all too corrupt and sinful. How they praised God and sought to bring religion into their lives was spread across the Christian spectrum of worship. Howard Dorgan, in his essay, "Religion in Appalachia: Examples of the Diversity," presents an overview of the many offshoots of the

Protestant faith, from all versions of Baptists to followers of the various types of Pentecostal worship.

In "The Jolo Church of the Lord Jesus," Shannon Bell describes the most radical practice of Christianity in Appalachia—perhaps in all of America: serpent handling. To outsiders, serpent handling as a religious ritual takes the blind belief in salvation to its extreme. In some pockets of Appalachia, however, those who embrace this tradition do so with zeal and unwavering confidence and see it as the most effective test of faith.

The section illustrates Appalachia's singular artistic contributions with an excerpt from novelist Lee Smith's vibrant tale of life in the Virginia Blue Ridge entitled "Black Mountain Breakdown"; author Tony Earley's essay on the unique dialect in his native western North Carolina entitled "The Quare Gene"; and photographer Shelby Lee Adams' "The Picture Man," in which he shares his thoughts on growing up in a Kentucky holler and capturing his neighbors on film. Edwin Sweeney's short essay, "Full Circle," describes the simple beauty of an Appalachian funeral; while the musician Jason Ringenberg's piece, "This Train Passes Through but Doesn't Stop," is a fitting final testament to Appalachia and all the things that make this region one of the most original and intriguing in all of America.

THE TRUNK IN THE ATTIC

GARY CARDEN

The attic in the house that my grandfather built was never finished. The windows were papered over with newsprint, and most of the floor was exposed joists. In summer, during warm twilight, it was filled with the drone of groggy wasps that flew through the dim light like lost pilots searching for a landing strip. In winter, wind-driven snow filtered through the eaves and settled across the rope bed, the stacks of *Farmer's Almanacs*, and my grandmother's dried leather britches. The old trunk, a strange white and yellow assemblage, was set against a brick chimney that rose through the roof like a red tree.

When I was a child, the attic had all the allure of an exotic land, and on rainy days I went there to explore Africa and Mars. Sometimes I read. Usually I opened the trunk. The leather straps, brass hinges, and formidable locks were purely decorative. I always raised the lid in slow inches so that my grandmother would not hear the squeak, although she usually did.

The trunk contained all that was left of my father. Cushioned in little padded compartments were his cuff links, ornate belt buckles, and a collection of porkpie hats. Dozens of picks made of amber, wood, and ivory glittered in the dim light. A photograph album held hundreds of pictures, many of my father holding a guitar, mandolin, or banjo, and always smiling. His nickname was "Happy." The mandolin nestled at the bottom of the trunk smelled of rose oil. When I lifted it, it glowed, all buffed wood and polish.

Always, I would pluck a string, and a single note, bright as a

Going Back to the House
The white clapboard saltbox is covered
with powder-blue aluminum siding, and the
dirt-and-gravel driveway is all blacktop now.
A glassed-in porch covers the cement patio
I helped my father build when I was ten.
In the back yard, the tulip poplar I planted
(carried home from camp in a Maxwell House
coffee can), now stands sixty feet. I can see
my brother poking his head out from behind
the giant pin oak, just like the day we were
playing Cain and Abel and I hit him between
the eyes with a stone from my slingshot.
When I look up at the attic bedroom window,
I can see myself climbing down the side
of the house on a rope. I'm running away again

firefly in the darkness, would hang in the air with the droning wasps. I came to feel that the wavering note was as close as I would ever come to hearing my father speak. Then I would hear my grandmother below, "What are you doing up there?"

I would answer, "Nothing."

And she would say, "Not in that trunk, are you?"

I would assure her that I wasn't. I realize now that it was a game that we played. Certainly she knew that the mandolin was in my lap.

"Come down now and do your homework."

I would bury the mandolin, close the lid, and retrace my steps, emerging in the bright, sunlit kitchen where my grandmother stoked the fire in the old Home Comfort stove.

As the years went by, I began to put my own objects in the trunk, each with a story to tell. When Toby, my favorite dog, became rabid and had to be shot, I buried him in the cornfield. The following year, my grandfather's plow turned up Toby's skull, delicate as an eggshell. I wrapped it in an old shirt and put it in the trunk along with the hood ornament from a wrecked '53 Chevrolet, a gaudy pin that I bought for a cheerleader and never had the nerve to give her, a bicuspid I lost in a fight, and a tarnished Saint Christopher medal. Each object triggered memories. I could pick them up and hold them to the light and hear Toby's bark and see the little mole on the cheerleader's neck.

After my grandparents died and I moved away to teach, the old house sheltered a series of families. Other women cooked on the Home Comfort, and on rainy days other children explored the attic. A few token items found their way to me: pictures of stern relatives and my smiling father.

The trunk and the mandolin vanished. However, one of my

(Gary Carden/photographed by Marian Steinert)

before my father gets home and
  whips me
for damn near blinding my brother.
  Out front,
the wild cherry and the tupelo
  remain.
I can see my father, standing in the
  doorway
in just a T-shirt, paint pants and
  bare feet.
He's holding a string of Christmas
  lights
and he's yelling at me as I trudge
  through
the snow, as I fade into the night,
beyond the halos of street lamps.
He's just smacked me again for
  acting a fool
so I'm running away from home for
  the third
time in a week. And now, there he
  is, silhouetted
in the doorway; my mother peek-
  ing out from
behind him, his voice pleading,
  "Johnny,
  come back! Come back!"
                    —John Sokol

Holy van, Kentucky, 1995
(© Shelby Lee Adams)

most pleasant, recurring dreams is of the trunk in the attic. Again I can raise the lid, unwrap the mandolin, and pluck the string that resonates in the darkness. In a sense I still have the trunk, and figuratively, I continue to place objects in it. I am talking about memory, of course—a writer's (and a storyteller's) most valuable tool. I continue to store faces, moments, and emotions, which, like Wordsworth's injunction, can be "recollected in tranquility." Lifting the lid, I reach down through layers of pain and joy, mandolins and memories.

We all have a trunk in the attic, I guess. Perhaps you have forgotten yours; however, like a faithful servant, it is there, waiting. All it takes is a moment of quiet introspection and you are lifting the lid, sifting through layers and layers of memories.

Unlike my original trunk in the attic, this trunk is bottomless.

BLACK MOUNTAIN BREAKDOWN

LEE SMITH

The lightning bugs come up from the mossy ground along the river-bank, first one, then two together, then more, hesitant at first, from the darkness gathered there already in the brush beneath the trees. Crystal sits and watches, holds her breath, the Mason jar beside her knee; if she looks down, she can't even see it now. She touches it with her finger and feels the glass with the letters raised and indecipherable in the dimness, so they could be anything, any words at all. They could be French. Suddenly out of the scrub grass at her knees comes rising a small, pale, flickering light, sickly underneath yellowish green, fairy light. It is so close she can breathe on it and see the whirring, tiny wings. Crystal doesn't move. She could catch it, but she doesn't. Only her eyes move to follow the flight, erratic at first, as if blown by wind although there is no wind in the hot damp of early June on the riverbank, then up into the dark branches, away and gone. Crystal can barely see the river on down the bank, barely hear it. She looks across the riverbed now to the railroad track cut into the mountain which goes straight up on the other side, almost perpendicular, impenetrable, too steep for houses or even trails: Black Mountain. Its rocky top makes a jagged black hump across the sky, and it is surprisingly light that far up in the sky; but the river bottom lies deep in the mountain's shadow, and even in Crystal's yard and in Agnes' yard next door and on Highway 460 in front of the house it is dark. Cars have their lights on.

"You get any yet?"

Kentucky girls, 1994
(© Shelby Lee Adams)

Crystal jumps, even though she knows it's only Agnes, and standing up, she knocks over her jar and has to bend down to get it.

"Come on," Agnes says. "I've been waiting for you over at the house. I thought that was what she said, after supper at my house. What are you doing out here anyway?" Even now, at twelve, Agnes has a flat and nasal, curious voice.

Nikki and Bobbie Jo, 2001
(© Shelby Lee Adams)

"I'm coming," Crystal says, pulling beggar-lice off the back of her shorts. She hates to leave the river. Beside it in the dark, she can think it is like her daddy told her it used to be, not flat and dried out and little, but big and full of water. The Levisa River. With huge log rafts on it floating down through the mountains in spring and early summer to the sawmills in Catlettsburg, Kentucky. Sometimes men rode those logs all the way, Daddy said. In the 1920s. Just sitting and floating, the trip would take days, watching the land coming at you on either side like a dream, the green trees hanging into the water, not ever knowing what would be around the bend. Seeing animals, too. Daddy said these hills were full of animals then, all kinds. Maybe see a panther. And the water would be clear with fish in it. You could see straight to the bottom. Now the water is black because they wash coal into it upriver, at the Island Creek tipple at Vansant. And the coal dust sinks to the bottom and covers the rocks, so they are black, too. The *real* black rock, the one Daddy said they named the town for, doesn't even exist anymore. It used to hang way out over a swimming hole near Hoot Owl, and everybody jumped from it and two people drowned in that hole. But when the Norfolk and Western came through in the thirties and built the railroad, they blasted the rock into little bitty pieces, and it fell into the river and was gone. Probably you could find a piece of it now, in the river by Hoot Owl, if you knew where to look.

"I'm going on." Agnes is mad. "I don't like it out here."

"Why not?" Crystal asks. She turns her head toward the yard and Agnes and sees that Agnes already has got a bunch of lightning bugs in her jar. Captive and pulsing, they cast a soft irregular glow like the twinkle lights last winter on her aunts' Christmas tree.

"Booger man might get us," Agnes says scornfully. She is not scared of any booger man herself, but she knows Crystal is, or anyway she used to be. "I've got better things to do than stand out here in some old trees and get a cold." Agnes sounds like Lorene, Crystal's mother.

Agnes goes up the bank and Crystal follows, still picking off beggar-lice because she knows how mad her mother will get if she comes in with them all over her shorts.

At the edge of the backyards Crystal can see their neighborhood

Shelby's porch, 1994
(© Shelby Lee Adams)

all stretched out along the road. Lights shine at the back of every house, in the kitchen where the women are finishing up. Sometimes the black shadow of a woman's head crosses a kitchen window for a minute and then vanishes. Agnes' mama's shadow stays firmly there in her lighted square. That's where their sink is, by the window. In the front rooms, the televisions are on and the men are watching TV or reading the paper, tired. And sometimes she wishes she lived in one of these other houses, where probably some of the men have gone to sleep already, stretched out in reclining chairs. The Varney boys, Horn and Daris, who are older, have got a big light on in their driveway and they are out there working on a car. That's what they do all the time. Their yard is full of parts of cars. Still, they are good boys: Horn was the quarterback last year at Black Rock High, and they are Eagle Scouts. Crystal would like to have the Varney boys for brothers, grease-stained and open and grinning all the time. Not like her own, Jules, who is so old she doesn't even know him; he's just thin and furious when he's home, which is almost never now, off teaching in a college; or Sykes, plain ornery, her mother says, always up to something, so they sent him off to military school at Union Springs, and that didn't do any good at all except to make him more secretive about what he's up to. Tomorrow he's going to summer school at VPI. Idly, Crystal wonders where he is now. His window is dark. But she doesn't really care. The way he treats her daddy, she will be glad when he's gone for good.

"Get that one," Agnes says. "Go on."

Crystal catches it and puts it in her jar and screws the top back on. It looks lonesome in there by itself, so she catches another one and then another one and some more, and by then they are in Agnes' backyard by the clothesline, close enough to hear Jubal Thacker's daddy picking his guitar on his back porch beyond the

George's porch
(© Shelby Lee Adams)

Thackers' garden. He's doing "Wildwood Flower," Crystal realizes as she goes up the steps, doing it slow, with the music floating out soft and a little bit sad in the June night across the backyards.

I will laugh, I will sing, and my heart will be gay.

Now Agnes and Crystal go out into the front yard and catch lightning bugs until they are tired of it and the jars are full, and then they sit together on the porch swing and put the jars on the little table before them, fantastic lanterns, while beyond the climbing clematis vine on the porch posts and beyond the little yard the traffic goes by on the road. They rock the swing. They sit out here a lot, because of the way things are over at Crystal's house.

If they want to talk they have to talk loud, over the noise of the traffic, because the road is not far from the front of these houses although the backyards are sizable, big enough for gardens, vast for children. And there is a lot of traffic: 460 is the only real road that runs through these mountains, going from Richlands, Virginia, up into the Black Rock area, following first the Dismal River and then the Levisa, winding and climbing up and then back down into Pikeville, Kentucky. There are other roads going up the hollers, some paved and some not, depending on how many people live up them. Houses everywhere are close to the road because anything resembling flat land is so hard to come by, must be bulldozed out and created.

Crystal sees the map of this county in her mind; she has studied it in school. A ragged diamond shape. Heavily inhabited where it is inhabited, with people piled up all along the creeks while whole mountains and mountainsides go empty and wild. Crystal rocks and thinks about the wild places, how it would be there. They say that the first man who ever settled in this county was a trapper named Stigner who lived in a big hollow tree up near the bend of Slate Creek. Of course it would not have been Slate Creek *then*, Crystal reminds herself. There was no coal and so there would have been no slate, either, just a big creek without a name and a hollow tree there, cut out by lightning perhaps.

Crystal wonders who the people are in all these cars and trucks and where in the world they are going. The traffic puts her in a kind of trance. She watches it sometimes for hours. Sometimes the same cars go up and down, up and down, until she wonders what they're looking for. Sometimes she sees a car from out of state. Now all she can see is their lights, flashing out into the night when they come around the curve by the Esso station, then beamed again on the road through their neighborhood, headed downtown. A lot of times cars rattle when they hit the hole in the road in front of Agnes' house. Now something clanks on the side of the road.

"What's that?" Crystal says.

"Beer can," says Agnes.

Crystal stretches. She was almost asleep in the swing. Summer rolls out in front of her as far as that road goes; fall, and junior high school seem far, far away. Already this summer Crystal has read *Scaramouche*. Right now she is reading *Quo Vadis*.

"Who's that?" Agnes asks. Agnes can't see very well in the dark, but Crystal has cat eyes. A couple walks up the side of the road toward the Esso station, holding hands.

"Pearl Deskins," Crystal whispers, "and some boy."

"Who is it?"

"I don't know," Crystal whispers back. "I can't see him real good, but I probably wouldn't know him anyway. He looks a whole lot older to me."

The traffic has slacked off now, and for a minute no car comes. Pearl Deskins and the boy are like shadows without bodies, walking. They stop to light cigarettes and when the match flares up, Crystal sees momentarily Pearl's thin, feral face, black eyes, her red mouth.

"I wish you'd look at that!" Agnes says. *"Smoking!"*

All up and down the bottom it is dark except for the lights from an occasional car or truck on the road and the arc lights at the Esso station, which will be open all night, catering to truckers and men on

Brittany, 2001
(© Shelby Lee Adams)

the graveyard shift in the mines. If you go back up the road away from the town of Black Rock toward Richlands, after five or six miles you leave the Levisa River bottom and go into the Dismal River bottom and start climbing, following 460 up until you reach the bend of Dismal where the coke ovens are, nearly eight hundred of them, roaring and sending up smoke and red fire into the night. The coke ovens stretch in irregular lines along the Dismal River and then up the steep slopes, too, above the railroad track, and the sight of them is awesome, as vast and red and terrible as hell itself. The trees on the mountains around the coke ovens have long since died, their blackened shapes like ghosts of trees on the blackened hills. This is where the high school students come to make out, parked along the old mine road off 460, above the bend, where they have the best view. . . .

Crystal lies flat on her back in her bed, while the jar of lightning bugs blinks softly on her dresser. Crystal listens to all the creaking sounds of her house, [her father] Grant's low rattling snore from downstairs, her mother clicking bottles together, then flushing the toilet, then the bedsprings creaking, a truck now and then on the road, the frogs singing rivets up from the river, loud and full through her open window, which faces the river and Black Mountain out to the back. *Come into my parlor, said the spider to the fly*. Crystal shivers and pulls the sheet up tight to her chin. *It's the prettiest little parlor that you ever did spy.* The jar of lightning bugs casts a soft, weird, flickering light on the wallpaper and Crystal watches it until she falls asleep.

–Excerpted from the novel
Black Mountain Breakdown by Lee Smith
(G.P. Putnam's Sons, 1980)

KILLING OUR HILLS:
THE DEVASTATION
OF MOUNTAINTOP REMOVAL

Vivian Stockman

This hollow is like so many others—a twisted, narrow ribbon of fertile bottomland separating the steep, convoluted mountains of southern West Virginia. Here, as in all these valleys, it's easy to see that this sheltering, isolating landscape molded the culture of the Appalachian folk as they made a living off what they could harvest both from above and below the ground.

A rock-strewn stream meanders through the hollow. Minnows dart in and out of the shade cast by elderberry bushes, scrubby willows, and a trio of sycamores, their upper trunks nearly all white. Come autumn, a woman will pick the elderberries for a cobbler made from a recipe given to her mother by her grandmother. Each of them grew up in this hollow, sharing with the birds the berries from these same bushes.

A pickerel frog, perhaps startled by a muskrat, springs in a graceful arc from the bank, landing in the cold water with barely a splash. The flutelike trill of a wood thrush floats out from the branches of a stream-bank dogwood that, in

Babcock, West Virginia
(© Mary Almond)

Dryfork, West Virginia, 2002
(Karl Badgley)

response to its prime edge habitat, spreads wider and taller than its woodland counterparts.

A tidy farmhouse sits alongside a little brook that flows into the bigger stream. Here, it's just a few yards before the gardens and clipped lawn surrounding the house give way to dense thickets of hazelnut, blackberry, and blooming multiflora rose, marking the dark edge of the woods. A deer bounds into this maze and disappears within seconds. Now, in late May, the landscape is utterly dominated by a breeze-tossed wall in many shades of green—the leaves from scores of tree varieties, each rooted in the immeasurably ancient soil of the Appalachian Mountains. The tree-covered slopes rise hundreds of feet above the hollow, so that only a sliver of perfect azure sky, complete with cotton candy clouds, is visible from the old home place.

Inside the woods, life expresses itself in myriad ways—this is the mixed mesophytic forest, home to one of the most richly diverse plant communities of all temperate climates on Earth. A recent rain shower has tumbled the last tulip tree flowers to the forest floor. Earthy soil scents mingle with the light, fruity aroma of the blossoms. The heart-shaped leaves of the wood violet tell of wildflowers missed, while a late bluet sways in the slightest breeze. Sunlight dapples the yellow-green fronds of maidenhair ferns as they bob on delicate black stalks below a towering white oak. Velvety emerald green moss and scaly gray-green lichen carpet a sandstone boulder that serves as a resting perch for anyone making her way through the forest.

Fern-filled forestland,
West Virginia
(Andy Sabol)

The diversity of the woods shapes the activities of local people's lives. In early spring, folks gather ramps and greens for tonics—an internal spring cleaning. Molly moochers, or morels, reward the sharp-eyed person who knows the exact moment in spring when rainfall will sprout these delicacies from the damp soil. The seasons,

Sheep grazing at a
West Virginia farm
(© Mary Almond)

The Sorrow of Birds

Mourning doves coo in the eaves
and a woodpecker stutters
for a grub on the telephone pole
outside your window. Wrens
chatter on the wire while sparrows
and chickadees shiver in the dead
bushes. A woman across the street
is sweeping away the quilt
of snow
some starlings stitched
on her porch,
and in the field beside her house,
a dozen crows scream
from treetops
as young boys fling something
frozen
and flat—like a black
frisbee—back
and forth, across the white ground.

—John Sokol

Tyler and Maranda, 2001
(© Shelby Lee Adams)

too, dictate when one should scramble about the steep woods, hunting herbs like black cohosh and ginseng, both for personal medicines and for some cash income. To flavor mugs of aromatic tea, locals pluck wintergreen that creeps along the forest floor and dig the roots of sassafras saplings. They harvest fallen trees and fell hardwoods for firewood and lumber. In the fall, black walnut and hickories feed animals of the two- and four-legged varieties. Some of those quadrapeds fall to the hunter's gun, providing protein for families throughout the winter. After the first freeze, people shake the persimmon tree for its custardlike fruits that dangle with an offer of sweet sustenance. So the woods cycle through the seasons, from stark winter to lush summer jungle.

Back down in the hollow, people resting on the front porch mark the onset of a spring evening by the increased nattering of a catbird mimicking its cousins. As twilight fades into night, the whip-poor-will, named for its song, begins its repetitive call.

Up until a few years ago, such was the beauty, serenity, and bounty of this hollow. Now the whip-poor-will's cry no longer heralds dusk, and few people continue to live within this landscape's seasonal rhythms. Some days the remaining folks can still hear the melodious songs of the ever-dwindling number of birds, the bubbling of the brooks, and the whisperings of the leaves. Other days, when the wind blows differently, the blasts and mechanical rumblings and beeps of nearby destruction shatter the soundscape. The din draws ever closer—a noisy foreboding of the annihilation heading this way.

Profit-crazed coal companies that practice mountaintop-removal/valley-fill coal mining are coming to claim this hollow, despite the objections of the people who want to stay on the land they love—people who, so far, have resisted the buyout offers. Long ago, their ancestors, deceived by the slick talk of company reps, signed away their rights to the coal deposits beneath their land. Of course, those ancestors could never have conceived of mountaintop removal.

For more than a century, the coal has been mined from the ground beneath these hills and hollows. For many families living here, the mining jobs provided cash that helped buy what the land could not offer. That cash came with a toll, as tens of thousands of miners died from accidents, or from black lung disease, or from battling the companies in order to establish unions. The coal industry promised prosperity, but the wealth was mostly whisked out of state. To this day, the majority of West Virginians have very little monetary wealth compared to folks in other states.

Sadly, now the area's most important natural wealth—the forests, the streams, and the culture—is being devastated so that companies can get more coal, more quickly and more cheaply, with far fewer miners. The moonscapes—the biological deserts—that are the aftermath of mountaintop removal have come to southern West Virginia, eastern Kentucky, and, to a limited degree, portions of Virginia and Tennessee.

New River Gorge, West Virginia
(Van Slider)

To get to the multiple, thin layers of low-sulfur coal that underlie these mountains, coal companies first raze the verdant forests, scraping away the topsoil and its priceless bank of seeds. In a mad dash to get to the coal, the trees are usually shoved out of the way, not even harvested as lumber. The understory herbs like ginseng and goldenseal are trashed with an arrogant disregard for their current worth, let alone their value to future generations.

Up to eight hundred feet of denuded mountaintop and the underlying rock is then systematically blown up. The explosives used can register anywhere from ten to one hundred times the strength of the explosion that tore open the Oklahoma City Federal Building. The blasts send health-endangering, silica-laden dust into the air. The shock waves can travel miles from the site, sometimes ferociously rattling the foundations of homes as well as people's nerves. The blasting has affected groundwater, drying up wells or ruining the taste and color of the water. "Fly rock," more aptly named fly *boulder,* can occasionally rain off the blasting sites, endangering residents' homes and lives.

A ravaged West Virginia landscape: The towering dragline (center) *is dwarfed by the size of the mountaintop-removal operation; 2003.*
(© Vivian Stockman)

The layers of coal are then scooped out by giant draglines, up to twenty stories tall. Behemoth dump trucks cart hundreds of millions of tons of "overburden"–the former mountaintops–to the narrow, adjacent valleys. The trucks dump the rubble over the sides, filling the valleys and burying the headwater streams, which scientists say provide habitat for an unusually high diversity of aquatic organisms. These critters act as the biological engines that drive the life downstream. Across Appalachia, according to a draft environmental impact statement on mountaintop removal, valley fills already have buried forever 724 miles of streams and have negatively impacted a total of 1,200 stream miles. Some aquatic biologists argue that the figure is much greater, and that the destruction is more harmful than most people realize. Selenium is just one toxic metal that has been found in high concentrations in the water seeping from valley fills.

Already, mountaintop removal has claimed nearly four hundred thousand acres of forested mountains. Entire communities, built long ago in hollows the companies now desire for valley fills, have been bought out. For other communities, mountaintop removal grinds ever closer, and worries about the blasting damages become almost routine, as even bigger problems claim attention. Every time it rains, folks who live close to this greed-crazed form of mining get scared. Really scared.

Government studies have shown that valley fills can dramatically worsen floods associated with heavy summer thunderstorms. Residents really didn't need these studies to back up their experience—thousands of acres of bulldozed forests, blown-up mountains, and rubble-filled valleys just don't handle rain like intact ecosystems do. In southern West Virginia, flooding in 2001 and 2002 killed fifteen people, destroyed thousands of homes, and damaged thousands more. Recovery efforts so far have topped $150 million. Residents blame mountaintop removal and virtually unregulated logging for making the floods far worse than they would have been without these disturbances.

Floods don't just come off valley fills. Mountaintop removal generates huge amounts of waste. While the solid waste becomes the fills, the liquid waste, created when coal is washed and processed for market, is stored in massive slurry impoundments that loom above communities. These lakes of slurry contain water contaminated with a black, toxic brew of carcinogenic chemicals—used to wash the coal—as well as particles laden with all the heavy metals found in coal, including arsenic and mercury. Several times a year, water plant operators are forced to shut down drinking water intake valves as upstream waters are blackened by spills from coal-processing plants and sludge impoundments.

In 2000, the floor of one coal-sludge impoundment near Inez, Kentucky, partially broke through into an abandoned underground

Marfork Coal's (a Massey Energy subsidiary) Brushy Fork coal-slurry impoundment, which, at its final stage, will hold billions of gallons of coal waste sludge. The impoundment lies partially over old undergound mines and is upstream from the town of Whitesville, West Virginia; 2003.
(© Vivian Stockman)

mine. More than three hundred million gallons of sludge spewed into people's yards, in some places up to fifteen feet deep, and fouled seventy-five miles of waterways. Several similar impoundments still sit above schools and towns. People believe it's a matter of "when" not "if" for the next disaster. They fearfully wonder if this time someone will be killed.

For years, while coal companies have had their way with the coalfields, both state and federal regulators have failed to enforce mining laws that would rein in some of the worst abuses. Many politicians, secure in the coal industry's pocket, have ignored requests for help. Feeling under siege, people mourn the loss of their home places. They question the wisdom of those who can rationalize such devastation as necessary for meeting the nation's "cheap" energy needs.

And they turn to each other for answers. With the help of West Virginia environmental groups like Coal River Mountain Watch, the Applachian Center for the Economy and the Environment, Ohio Valley Environmental Coalition, and West Virginia Highlands Conservancy, as well as Kentuckians for the Commonwealth, people are rising up to demand an end to this ecocidal form of coal mining. They organize, educate, litigate, and strategize to save what is left of the central Appalachian forest—and they are making strides to save this land and its people.

FIGHTING FOR MY APPALACHIAN HOME

JULIA BONDS

As a child growing up the daughter of a coal miner in southern West Virginia, I felt nurtured and protected by my family and the ancient mountains that were our home. I was protected from an outside world I later discovered considered me an ignorant hillbilly. It has taken a lifetime to fit together the pieces of the puzzle: The people who exploited Appalachia, such as the coal and land barons, stereotyped us to justify the treatment of my people, to make us the "national sacrifice zone" for America's cheap energy. We are the unwanted bastard children of America.

Bear Rocks, Grant County,
West Virginia, 2002
(Karl Badgley)

It took the sturdiest, hardiest people to settle the steep, mountainous region that I call home, which is a testament to the men and women of central Appalachia. Then came the great "land grab," when coal and land barons came to steal, cheat, and murder—to confiscate our land and take natural resources and their revenue out of the state to their homes for their own well-dressed children and their well-kept mansions. Appalachian women stood strong. We watched our mates and our young male children, some as young as ten, slave away in the masters' mines beside their fathers. They died like flies from inhuman and unsafe working conditions, leaving many widows to raise their families as best they could. We endured! These masters put us in shanties to live, and when my people cried out for justice, the coal barons evicted our families. We set up tents and we endured the agony of watching our children freeze to death; many, many of our children died in the mine wars. We survived Bull Moose Specials, so-called guards and security agents hired by coal companies to shoot into our tents and murder our men, women, and children. Appalachian women stood strong and faced the beast that invaded our land. We stood and fought beside our men for basic human rights. We finally won a union that guaranteed us better wages and safer working conditions, but coal mining remained a dangerous job that maimed our men, shortened their lives, broke their bodies and spirits, and blackened their lungs.

Train tracks near Cass, West Virginia
(© Mary Almond)

Born in 1952, I barely remember twice-weekly, nighttime foraging excursions: My mother and older sisters would sometimes take me to forage for coal that had fallen off the train along the tracks in our hollow. We did this so our family would not freeze. Work stoppage was still frequent in the coalfields; the union helped, but the inhuman treatment from the coal companies continued. The women walked picket lines and went to jail with the men. Through the storytelling of my mother and the community elders, I came to realize that all this coal was *ours:* These companies had stolen our coal, our land, our heritage, and our humanity!

Strengthened by stories of hardship, strife, Mother Jones, and other brave women who fought back by merely living and staying put in our homeland, we stood strong, we endured.

Now we have come almost full circle with those who would erase the last of my people—my history, my heritage, and my children's future. Today, we fight the final battle: Appalachia's last stand! Four

"My mother would get up at four or five in the morning before gettin' us off to school. I remember her walking out to the coal house, which was just a little old house where you could keep the coal dry from the snow. She would fill up her buckets and bring the buckets of coal back and build a fire in the coal fireplaces before she would get any of us out of bed, to try and at least have one or two rooms warm for us before we got up."
—*Pikeville, Kentucky–born musician Patty Loveless*

Mountaintop-removal/valley-fill coal mining in southern West Virginia, 2003
(© Vivian Stockman)

"Mommy was the one in our family who hunted. Ya'll are gonna holler when I say 'possum,' but that was Daddy's favorite dish. They would cook it and take it out of the oven and put it in a bread pan 'cause possum is very greasy. She would put sweet potatoes in the pan. And put sage all over 'em and that was Daddy's favorite dish.

"Anything that moved, Mommy got it. She could shoot good. There wasn't no better. I could shoot good, too, and [my husband] Doolittle hated that. We'd go over behind the little schoolhouse. 'Let's practice us a little shootin',' he'd say. We'd get there on good terms, but coming back he wouldn't speak to me. I didn't know you wasn't supposed to hit the bull's eye. I hit that baby and he didn't! And he'd get mad and wouldn't talk to me on the way back."

—*Butcher Holler, Kentucky–born musician Loretta Lynn*

men and a dragline are taking *all* that we have left. A highly destructive mining practice called mountaintop removal is steadily ravaging the Appalachian mountain range and forcing neighboring communities, some of whose residents have lived in the region for generations, to abandon their homes.

In 2001, my family became the last to evacuate our hometown of Marfork Hollow, where six generations of my family had lived. Marfork has been virtually destroyed by mountaintop-removal mining, which involves blasting off entire mountains' tops so that huge machines can mine thin seams of coal. Mountaintop-removal mining completely annihilates streams and forests, causing extensive flooding and blast damage to homes. The pollution from mining and the toxic chemicals used in the preparation of coal for market have been linked to rising asthma rates and other serious respiratory ailments, particularly among children (including my grandson). Residents who live near the mining-blast zones also suffer from traumatic stress disorder. Slurry dams thick with heavy metallic elements such as arsenic, mercury, and lead routinely overflow into watersheds, contaminating drinking water and driving toxic sludge into residents' backyards. As a result, thousands of local residents have been driven out of their homes.

Mountaintop-removal mining also has been catastrophic for Appalachia's waterways. Coal companies routinely dump tons of mountaintop debris into nearby valleys and streams. Today, more than one thousand miles of Appalachian headwater streams have been completely buried, and three hundred thousand acres of the world's most diverse temperate hardwood forests have been obliterated by so-called valley fill.

This devastating mountaintop removal has become *mountaineer* removal, eliminating our culture, heritage, home, communities, children's future, streams, forests, and the beloved mountains. These mountains sustain us, offering hunting, fishing, medicinal herbs, berries, food, and abundant water. We didn't and wouldn't need anything if only these mountains and hollows stayed intact. These mountains give us *freedom*. We are part of these mountains and they are part of us: We are one. We are connected to this ancient, reverent land, and the women of Appalachia, again, stand strong, and like the ironweeds, our roots run deep—*try and move us!*

I have been asked many times, "Why are the women of Appalachia leading this battle to fight mountaintop removal?" I can only suggest that the answer is our strength—from our mothers and grandmothers have been handed down the nurturing instincts to protect our children, their future, our homes, our culture. We will fight to protect our land with our last breath. This is God's land, and He leads us.

Old Home Place

It's been ten long years since I left
  my home
In the hollow where I was born
Where the cool fall nights make the
  wood smoke rise
And the foxhunter blows his horn

I fell in love with a girl from the
  town
I thought that she would be true
I ran away to Charlottesville
And worked in a sawmill or two

What have they done to the old
home place
Why did they tear it down
And why did I leave the plow in
  the field
And look for a job in the town

Well my girl she ran off with
  somebody else
The taverns took all my pay
And here I stand where the old
  home stood
Before they took it away

Now the geese they fly south and
  the cold wind blows
As I stand here and hang my head
I've lost my love I've lost my home
And now I wish that I was dead
    —Connie Townsend and David
                Parker

Caanan Valley State Park, Tucker County, West Virginia, 2002
(Karl Badgley)

RELIGION IN APPALACHIA: EXAMPLES OF THE DIVERSITY

HOWARD DORGAN

Colly Creek Regular Primitive Baptist Church, Colly Creek, Letcher County, Kentucky (© Howard Dorgan)

Appalachia may be one of the most religiously diverse regions in America. Here, Baptist subsets alone can number into the seventies or eighties, depending on how narrowly the divisions are drawn. "Old Baptists"—who trace their origins directly to the first colonial members of this faith to arrive in Appalachia and who now preserve a wide range of eighteenth- and nineteenth-century worship traditions—have splintered into an array of denominations and sub-denominations. In addition, Pentecostals and Holiness-Pentecostals challenge the Baptists with their own lengthy continuum of persuasions, particularly the small independent congregations that gather in homes, abandoned storefronts, or backcountry wood-frame structures, displaying cryptic titles such as the Foursquare Holiness-Pentecostal Church of Miracles, Signs, and Wonders. In short, these mountains are home to a complex patchwork of Christian faiths that give Appalachia a wonderfully rich and varied religious face.

The region's Old Baptist, or Old-Time Baptist, denominations include, as examples, Old Missionary Baptists, Old Regular Baptists, Old School Primitive Baptists, Regular Baptists, Regular Primitive Baptists, Separate Baptists, Union Baptists, and United Baptists. These groups receive attention from outside observers because they preserve such eighteenth- and nineteenth-century traditions as feet-washing, lined singing, restrictions against within-the-church musical instruments, living water baptisms, chanted or sung impromptu preaching, Pauline gender mandates, and a host of other worship and polity practices dating back to colonial times or earlier.

"Feet-washing," or "foot-washing," as the practice is most frequently referenced in this region, is observed by these faithful Christians as a church "ordinance," following Christ's command "do as I have done" that concludes the account of the first feet-washing in the Christian tradition (John 13:4–15); therefore once a year, at the close of their annual Communion Service, each fellowship washes feet, usually the most emotionally charged rite of the year.

*Samaria Church of Old Regular
Baptist of Jesus Christ,
near Wolfit, Kentucky*
(© Howard Dorgan)

"Lined singing" was first practiced in seventeenth-century England by the Westminster Assembly of Baptists, and this style of hymnody became popular when Baptists first migrated west of the

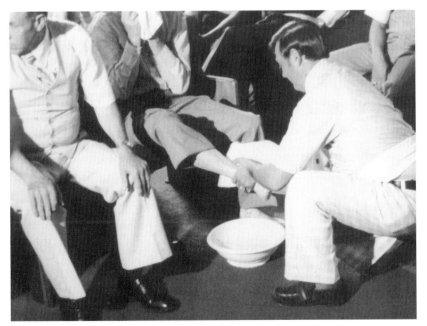

*A foot-washing service at
Mt. Pinon Missionary Baptist
Church, Deep Gap,
North Carolina, circa 1981*
(© Howard Dorgan)

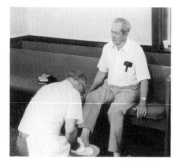

A foot-washing at Mt. Pleasant Primitive Baptist Universalist Church in Greenbrier County, West Virginia, near the small community of Trout
(© Howard Dorgan)

Alleghenies, where congregations had few hymnals and may not have been able to read the ones they did have. This singing mode required a "liner" to chant out the lyrics, usually one couplet at a time, followed by the congregation's repetition of the line with a largely atonal sound that can be very slow and dirgelike. Still these fellowships love their lined hymns and during contemporary times have been extremely reluctant to yield to what they call note book singing, either by the use of shaped notes or otherwise.

Living water baptism, also occasionally referenced as natural water baptism, labels the mode of emersion practiced in creeks, rivers, ponds, lakes, and other "natural" bodies of water, and its practice suggests that artificial baptisteries, especially those built inside a church, violate the traditions that grew from the River Jordan experience of Christ and John the Baptist. A poignant scene viewed frequently in these mountains is that of an aging and frail woman being led down to the frigid water of an Appalachian creek, having refused to accept, even at that late age, a form of emersion less severe in its effect upon her physical being.

The traditional preaching style required for the pulpits of Old-Time Baptist churches emerges from extemporized rhetoric, with the preacher thus shunning the use of any notes, manuscript, or memorization, the assumption being that unprepared exhorting gives God a chance to speak through the exhorter, while prepared-ahead-of-time sermons are more likely to be only man speaking. In addition, the highly rhythmic (chanted or sung) oral performance suggests to mountain congregations that the speaker is "carried out" or "blessed," having therefore been possessed by the divine Spirit.

A list of the smaller Old Baptist subdenominations includes such colorful and provocative titles as Duck River Baptists, Landmark Missionary Baptists, Landmark Regular Baptists, New

Baptism in the Dismal River, Buchanan County, Virginia, by the Primitive Baptist Universalists
(© Howard Dorgan)

Hope Baptists, Six Principle Baptists, Two-Seed-in-the-Spirit Predestinarian Baptists, Truevine Baptists, and Universalist Regular Primitive Baptists. The Primitive Baptists of Appalachia can be cited as an excellent example of difficulty in cataloging the region's Old Baptists. The tendency in both scholarly and nonscholarly writing is to sweep all Primitives together, presuming that they possess a high degree of uniformity in doctrine as well as in practice. For example, even the broadest categorizations of Appalachian Primitives must include at least four generic types: the single-predestination Primitives, the double-predestination Primitives, the progressive Primitives, and the Universalist Primitives, the rarest of the lot. Also, each category contains additional divisions.

Preaching at the Regular Primitive Baptist Washing annual meeting, Hale Church Creek, Buchanan County, Virginia, 1996
(© Howard Dorgan)

Single-predestination Primitives accept the Calvinistic doctrine of election, which proclaims Christ's atonement for Adamic sin to be limited only to those individuals—identified before the beginning of time—whom God chose for his church. Double-predestination Primitives take this deterministic theology one step further, charging that God not only predestined the elect but also all conditions of the human experience. Progressive Primitives occasionally circumscribe predestination and adopt one or more of a number of practices that the more traditional Primitives don't permit: paid preachers (either by fixed salaries or special collections), Sunday schools, radio ministries and other forms of religious outreach, communion services that do not include feet-washing, or baptismal fonts within the church.

Universalist Primitives are indigenous to Appalachia, and their doctrine of absolute and universal determinism applies not only to Adamic sin but also to Christ's atonement for that sin: "For as in Adam all die, even so in Christ shall all be made alive" (I Cor. 15:22). Thus their doctrine proclaims an afterlife consisting only of

Hooterville, Kentucky, 1991
(© Shelby Lee Adams)

Gracie serpent handling, 1990
(© Shelby Lee Adams)

Heaven; Hell becomes a factor solely of the temporal world, with all sin being punished in the here and now. Consequently, after Resurrection, all of God's children are ensconced in a heaven somewhat reminiscent of Eden, absent the garden motif, to spend the remainder of eternity in communion with their creator. Even Satan—thought of by many Universalist Primitives as natural man constantly warring against spiritual man—is relegated to the terrestrial world. The most diminutive of the four generic Primitive groups, Universalist Primitives are composed of only four small associations, with churches located in limited areas of east Tennessee, eastern Kentucky, southwestern Virginia, and southern West Virginia. Four out-migrant fellowships exist, though, three in Ohio and one in Pennsylvania. These are churches that were established outside of traditional Appalachian regions when hard times in the coalfields of central Appalachia drove Kentucky, Virginia, or West Virginia workers to move into Midwestern regions in search of employment, usually carrying their mountain faiths with them. Initially, such wanderers from the region had found it impossible to find an Old Regular Baptist church in Ohio, Indiana, Illinois, or points north, east, or west.

Old-Time Baptists are handed competition in this diversity picture by the immense variability within the Pentecostal and Holiness-Pentecostal movements. It would be difficult—if not impossible—to determine a champion in this particular diversity match, however, since churches of both faiths are difficult to canvas. Such membership tallies work well with mainline churches, but not so successfully with either wholly independent congregations or often minuscule associations that round out the various divisions of Old-Time Baptists. Larger denominations are eager to have their statistics recorded, while these reclusive congregations or associations are not. In many cases, the Holiness-Pentecostals don't even know their numbers.

Several larger Pentecostal divisions in Appalachia maintain very detailed records of their statistics: Assemblies of God; Church of God, Cleveland, Tennessee; Church of God, Mountain Assembly; Church of God of Prophecy; International Church of the Foursquare Gospel; International Pentecostal Church of Christ; International Pentecostal Holiness Church; Open Bible Standard Churches; and Pentecostal Church of God. The small and largely independent Holiness-Pentecostal congregations are often fragile, and transient fellowships may not stay in one place for a significant length of time. Usually organized by self-proclaimed preachers, these fellowships promote a variety of doctrines and practices. They are primarily Pentecostal in tradition, even though the term "holiness" is included in the title. Their identifying conventions include the practice of glossolalia (speaking in tongues), the use of healing exercises (laying on of hands and anointing with oil), and a range of other behaviors that worshipers believe are induced when one becomes possessed by the Holy Spirit. Such possessions include "perishing in the Spirit"—swooning and falling backward onto the floor or the ground, and sometimes remaining there for a considerable length of time; "the jerks"—spasmodic shudders or tremors that may conclude in a prolonged swoon; "running in the Spirit"—either running in place, which is generally associated with an attempt to get away from spiritual tension, or running in circles, perhaps in the church, which is typically interpreted as celebrational; "dancing in the Spirit"—with feet and leg movements often resembling mountain clogging or other forms of step dance; and "twirling in the Spirit"—which may continue until the worshiper collapses.

The *Holiness* side of this Holiness-Pentecostal fusion originated

"The country is run mad after preaching. Here is a new sect called Cumberland Presbyterians, and between these, the Baptists, and the Methodists, the woods resound. As they have no churches, they preach out of doors mostly. Preacher Burges . . . of Virginia is the finest public speaker in the union . . . a monstrous fine preacher . . . redoubled his strength, spit in his hands, and smote them together 'til the forest resounded. . . . Young women, after tumbling to the ground and kicking some times, would spring nearly a yard from the ground, sometimes crying out 'glory, glory' as loud as their strength would admit . . . yelling and screaming like wild beasts of the forest. If there is a hell, there will be more priests in it than any other description of people."
—*Journalist Anne Newport Royal, in a letter dated April 21, 1821*

The serving line at a dinner at the Stoney Creek Primitive Baptist Universalist Church, Carter County, Tennessee, near Elizabethton
(© Howard Dorgan)

Holiness hands with serpent and bible, Happy, Kentucky, 1987
(© Shelby Lee Adams)

Old-Time Camp Meetings

There was an era when people in the mountains would travel miles to hear a preacher during "old time camp meetin' days." The first large camp meeting occurred on August 6, 1801, and continued for six days, day and night. It was estimated by historians to have had a crowd of 10,000 to 25,000 in Cane Ridge, Kentucky. People traveled by foot, horse, or wagon to reach the area. Around the same time, communities began holding "all-day singin' and dinner on the grounds," usually on a Sunday but occasionally during the week. On a Sunday, there would be the regular preaching, then a huge feast with home cooking, where everyone brought out their specialties, which were placed buffet-style on long tables under the trees. These tables were crafted from long planks, sometimes reaching a hundred feet in length, stretching across saw horses. After dinner, the "singin'" would commence. This tradition still takes place in parts of Appalachia today.

with the early Wesleyan movement as a "second blessing" form of sanctification, emerging for a life of especially high spiritual dedication. Initial salvation was the "first blessing," and this "sanctification" consequently became the "second blessing." This version of Holiness thought is weak in the Appalachian Holiness-Pentecostal movement, however. When it does exist, it surfaces primarily as another conceptualization of Holy Spirit possession. Therefore, initial salvation is the first blessing, but to be chosen by the Holy Spirit for anointment is the second blessing, also referenced as "baptism in the Spirit" or "baptism by fire."

Doctrinal and behavioral issues have split the Holiness-Pentecostal movement into countless divergent units. One of the most interesting doctrinal divisions lies between the Jesus Only, or Oneness, believers and the Trinitarians. The former baptize "in the name of Jesus," while the latter use the more traditional "Father, Son, and Holy Spirit." The Oneness believers further divide between those who formally denounce the Trinity and those who seem to hold that baptism should be in the name of Jesus only.

Perhaps the most "extreme" Holiness-Pentecostal group is that which observes "practicing signs," based on the biblical scripture Mark 16:17–18, proclaiming "these signs shall follow them that believe": casting out devils, speaking in tongues, handling serpents, drinking deadly things, and healing the sick. Among these Holiness groups, only those who handle serpents and also consume poisonous liquids, such as strychnine, manage to practice all of the signs. Pentecostals who follow two or three of the signs, but not all, argue that this is just an example of the optional "spiritual gifts" referred to by Paul (I Cor. 12). There is additional dispute over the execution of glossolalia, since Paul mentions both the gift of tongues and the gift of interpreting tongues. Consequently, some Holiness churches practice both aspects of this sign.

Overall, the Holiness-Pentecostal package of doctrines and practices is a malleable one, resulting in great fluctuation of precise congregational formats. Considering the Holiness-Pentecostal picture of dynamic variability alongside the immense diversity of the region's Old Baptists, it is little wonder that observers find it difficult to understand the Appalachian religious landscape. Nevertheless, that landscape should be appreciated for its wonderful variability and uniqueness.

PREACHING TO THE CHICKENS

GARY CARDEN

I told my first stories to 150 white leghorns in a dark chicken house when I was six years old. My audience wasn't attentive and tended to get hysterical during the dramatic parts. It was hardly an auspicious beginning, but I guess it helped me to develop a sense of structure. A few nights before my "debut," I heard a Pentecostal preacher describe the most terrifying aspects of hell: molten brimstone, roasted flesh, and endless pains on the Devil's rotisserie. As I sat, mouth agape, and watched this inspired performance, I found myself memorizing details. When he described the screams, weeping, and lamentations of the tormented, I heard a Mormon Tabernacle choir of grief and saw the lurid red lights. As he stalked the platform, miming the antics of the damned—writhing, whispering, and shouting—I sneaked a look at the people behind me. They were riveted, hanging on to every word, swaying like trees in this aural wind. "Wow!" I thought, as the hairs stood up on my neck, "I want to do that!" And so I came to that dark chicken house with a graphic message about chicken hell.

(Gary Carden/photographed by Marian Steinert)

Eventually, I got a human audience. In the third grade, my classmates encouraged me to repeat the stories that our teacher had read aloud. If I said, "You've already heard it," they responded, "Not your version." I enjoyed telling "augmented" renderings of Saturday Westerns, Tarzan movies, and afternoon serials. I enjoyed the attention I received, and I enjoyed the suspense of discovering what I would say next. Sometimes, well-meaning teachers brought me home and made diplomatic comments to my anxious grandmother about problems regarding an "overly active imagination." They noted that I spent too much time in the world of "make-believe," which could cause problems when it came to adjusting to "the real world." My grandmother usually said, "Well, he can't help it. His grandfather on his mother's side told lies, too." The teachers were right, of course. An uncontrollable desire to improve on the truth has caused me endless problems.

THE JOLO CHURCH OF
THE LORD JESUS

SHANNON BELL

*Member of Jolo Church
of the Lord Jesus*
(Chuck Conner)

Deep in the coalfields of southern West Virginia lies the small town of Jolo, where the mountains are rich with precious natural resources, and the people are rich with Appalachian hospitality and friendliness. It's not unlike many of the West Virginia towns south of Interstate 64–towns whose steep mountains and treacherous terrain keep the generic tendencies of city life from encroaching upon the land and affecting the wonderful character of the Appalachian culture. You won't find any strip malls, office buildings, traffic lights, or McDonald's fast-food places there–mostly just mom-and-pop diners and the occasional small grocery store. Jolo seems like the type of town that wouldn't usually receive much attention from the outside world, except from the coal company honchos, who drool over the seemingly endless supply of coal that lies beneath these great mountains.

Surprisingly, however, this quiet and isolated little town has had its fair share of visitors, from scholars and newspaper journalists to the Discovery Channel and *National Geographic Explorer.* Most of these visitors have breezed in and out in a flash, leaving once they've extracted the sensational story they were after. Some have been gracious and respectful, others not so kind. So what is the attraction? What could possibly be so exciting in this small, isolated West Virginia town that curious people have come from as far away as Belgium to visit? The draw is actually a church–the Church of the Lord Jesus. This church is the most eminent Pentecostal signs-following, or "serpent-handling," church in Appalachia.

The Signs Followers have historically been one of the most misunderstood and misrepresented sects of Christianity. Many people in mainstream America think that the Signs Followers are members of a "snake-worshiping cult" or that they are "testing God" in their services. Even a great number of native Appalachians believe these stereotypes, and many have a strong aversion to the production of books, articles, or television specials about this faith because they feel that it contributes to Appalachia's "hillbilly" stereotype. Sadly, most of the media pieces have portrayed these Christians in a not-so-flattering light, simply because they have focused on the most sensational aspects of the worship services. The media has dwelled almost entirely on the snake handling, which is only a very minor part of this faith. There is an entire story that has been neglected by the media, one that looks more deeply at this religion and its followers. This is the story that photographer Chuck Conner and I have sought for the past two years through our visits to the Jolo church.

Although the exact number is not known, there are Signs-Following churches scattered throughout the entire Appalachian region. This faith is a sect of Pentecostal-Holiness, which is known for speaking in tongues and for its intense spirit-filled worship services. What sets the Signs Followers apart from other Pentecostal-Holiness churches is that they believe in reading *all* parts of the King James Bible literally, including Mark 16:17–18, which states:

> And these signs shall follow them that believe; in my name shall they cast out devils; they shall speak with new tongues; they shall take up serpents; and if they drink any deadly thing, it shall not hurt them; they shall lay hands on the sick, and they shall recover.

"I praise my God—I'd rather lose my mama, my daddy, even my children. Welfare come in and wanted to know where I kept my serpents at. I told them, 'The best thing for you to do is turn around and go back out that door.' When I take up serpents, I'm willin' to lay down this life for what I believe. If this wasn't right, I wouldn't even fool with it, sure wouldn't take up serpents. My daddy-in-law died this way, and I sure wouldn't want to die of a serpent bite if I thought it wasn't right. I been bit five times. They had a copperhead up there that nobody wanted to fool with. I mean he was mean. I said, 'Lord, I want to handle that copperhead,' and He told me to go ahead. I said, 'Lord, I want victory!' He said, 'You have victory.' I went up thar and it bit me! And I said, 'Lord,' I shouted out loud, I said, 'Lord, you said I had victory, and it bit me.' I know God when He speaks. He said, 'You won't swell.' I been bitten five times after that, and I ain't swelled yet. I got victory."

—*Jolo congregationalist Larry Hagerman*

Thus, as they read the passage, it is a *command* that they cast out devils, speak with new tongues, lay hands on the sick, and handle poisonous snakes, simply because they are believers. Furthermore, if they drink a deadly poison—such as strychnine, frequently imbibed during the services—they will not be hurt. To put it quite simply, the serpent handlers are merely following the word of God literally as it is written in the Scripture. However, they believe that they follow the Scripture not through their own power, but through the power of the Holy Ghost. These church members believe that they are anointed by the Holy Ghost, giving them power to enact supernatural signs.

Church members in Jolo
(Chuck Conner)

BROTHER RAY'S SERPENT BITES

One of the first pieces of information that Chuck and I learned through talking with congregation members at the Church of the Lord Jesus was that congregant Dewey Chafin had been bitten 133 (now 142) times throughout his forty-plus years of serpent handling. Almost all of the men and some of the women in the church exhibit some sort of deformity on their hands and fingers from a rattlesnake or copperhead bite. An atrophied finger, the loss of movement in part of a hand, or tiny holes from a serpent's fangs are proudly exhibited by these church members when asked about their "battle scars." These serpent bites represent an undying faith in the word of God.

Because of their faith in these words of Mark in the Bible, speaking in tongues, casting out devils, laying hands on the sick, drinking strychnine, and handling rattlesnakes and copperheads occur in almost every church service as a testament to their faith in the power of the Lord.

According to Brother Bob, pastor of the church, the serpents "are the visible sign of the devil," and when one has power over these serpents through the anointing of the Holy Ghost, he or she is, in effect, exerting control over Satan. At one of the first services that Chuck and I attended, we witnessed Brother Ray being bitten five times by a handful of copperheads. Though he was not seriously injured, his hands and arms swelled pretty badly. None of the church members request medical attention when a poisonous snake bites him or her; in fact, Brother Bob's stepdaughter was killed by a serpent bite in the 1960s. But what does it mean when someone is bitten or when someone dies of a bite? Has the power of God failed that person in some way?

Brother Ray was eighty-two years old and had been with the church since its beginning in the late 1940s. (He has since passed away, dying in November 2000 of a heart attack not related to serpent handling.) He was a very powerful force in the church, and I absolutely loved to hear and watch him sing and dance in the services. Always one of the first to handle the serpents during services, Ray brought to church his own boxes of the creatures, which he had caught himself. His right hand was bitten more than twenty years ago by a diamondback and became extremely atrophied. His index and middle fingers were completely unusable, and both of his hands had a swollen appearance. Before that service, Ray had been bitten eighty-nine times during the nearly fifty years he had been with the church. On that Sunday morning, while holding a handful of copperheads, Ray was bitten five more times on both hands.

Jolo man with serpents
(Chuck Conner)

When bitten, Ray did not yell out or even drop the serpents. The only indication of the bites' having occurred was a slight jolt in Ray's body. He gently put the copperheads back into their box, and immediately the members of the church gathered around and laid hands on him. At that point, I expected this to be a tragedy, that the music would stop and the service be halted so all attention

(Chuck Conner)

could be focused on Ray. I expected him to sit down and care for his body.

But none of these things happened. Someone gave Ray a cloth to soak up the blood on his hands, and the music continued, full force. While the congregation gathered around Ray, praying over him, touching him, and caring for him, he remained standing. In fact, another church member, Ruby, who appeared to be in an ecstatic state, dumped out another serpent box, picked up a huge rattlesnake and two other smaller copperheads, and handled them right there beside Ray. As she was about to put them back in the box, Ray took the serpents from her and handled them again. Then he danced, demonstrating that despite the poison coursing through his body, he was protected from its effects by the power of the Lord.

After Ray had finished handling, Brother Dewey came from behind the pulpit and took the three serpents. He began to preach, asserting that the Bible "didn't say these snakes wouldn't bite you or wouldn't hurt you . . . there's death in these things." He continued, "[The Lord] said, 'these signs *shall* follow.' These are the signs nobody wants to follow." Later, Brother Bob emphasized this point: "If we're led by the Spirit and [the serpent] bites us, then it was God's will." Furthermore, "If it bites you and you're under the anointing, and you die, you've just done God's will. That was your way to go. Because there's going to be something that takes everybody out of this world. To me, it's fulfillment of the Word. . . . The Bible says, 'Happy are you if you die in the Lord.' What better way would you find to die than doing what God said to do?"

Thus, the church members accept a certain degree of mystery associated with the will of God. No one knows for certain why God might allow a serpent to bite an individual, but one must simply have faith that there is a reason.

At the end of the service, Ray's hands had swollen a great deal, but he wasn't feeling sick, nor did he exhibit any effects other than being a little "itchy." He stood up to testify and said:

> I'd like to praise God for being here . . . thank Him for the Spirit. I'd like to thank him for the bites I got today, all five of them.
>
> I praise Him for it because they're not hurtin'—they're itchin', but they're not hurtin'. They're swellin'. But you know, I thank and praise Him for it because that lets me know that He's able to take care of me if I just trust Him. If I do what He says to do, I'll be all right. . . . I praise Him for puttin' His Spirit on me to lead me and guide me. I praise Him for each and every thing He does for me. . . . I started to go to that box of rattlers over there, but He moved and led me to the copperheads. I got the copperheads and I got bit. But that was for somethin'. That was done for somethin'—to show me that He's still able to take care of me even if I'm an old man. I praise Him for it. And I'll pray for you all the best that I know how.

A Jolo member possessed with the spirit falls to the floor.
(Chuck Conner)

Ray felt that there was a reason for what, to an outsider, would appear to be a breakdown in the power of the Spirit. His getting bitten was not a breakdown at all but was God's way of showing Ray that He would still take care of him, even though Ray was an "old man."

According to the members of the Church of the Lord Jesus, God has a reason for everything that He does, and they as His children must simply trust that will, even if they do not understand it. They are receptacles for His supernatural powers, and through Him they can perform certain miracles, but they are not in control—God is. And most important, it is through their ability to surrender their control and to have complete faith in Him that they are able to tap in to the powers of the Lord.

THE PICTURE MAN

SHELBY LEE ADAMS

The home of author Adams'
grandparents in eastern
Kentucky
(© Shelby Lee Adams)

I was born the son of native east Kentuckians. Because my father's job required that he live all over the country, I saw lots of America. East Kentucky became the place where I felt most at home. We spent our holidays and vacations there on my grandparents' farm located in a holler.

One of the most momentous events during my childhood was witnessing my beloved grandmother slowly go blind. I learned to walk the farmland paths with my eyes shut, to experience what it was like to be blind. The blindness was a great injustice to my grandmother, whom I deeply loved, and it was an unexplainable and unacceptable tragedy to me as a child. She gave me my first watercolor kit, and when I visited her, she would ask me to paint what I had seen each day. I learned to observe closely the world around me. I wanted to develop my own visual sensibilities so acutely that I could see for her. I know now that, as my grandmother was becoming blind, I was learning to see.

I remember in the 1960s, while my family was briefly residing in Florida, we saw a television special about President Johnson's War on Poverty. I was shocked to see photographs of the area of Kentucky where my grandparents lived. We tried to spot people and places we knew depicted on the TV screen. I had never thought of my grandparents or their neighbors as "living in poverty." They treated the land and the mountains as a precious treasure that was theirs. The worst thing you could ever say to a holler dweller is that he or she lives in poverty.

In *The Autobiography of Mark Twain,* Twain says of his childhood home, Hannibal, Missouri, "The class lines were quite clearly drawn, and the familiar social life of each class was restricted to that class. It was a democracy." Eastern Kentucky is such a democracy, but its class lines are less rigid. All my life I have crossed back and forth between those lines, yet I hated this social reality. My family was one of the middle-class families of Appalachia: I could afford to go to college.

As a college art student in Ohio, I discovered photography and became acquainted with the Farm Security Administration and the Depression-era photography done in the South. My professors always talked about this work in the past tense, as if the problems examined in these photographs were solved long ago and had little social or political importance during the Vietnam War period of my college days. The work of Walker Evans, Marion Post Wolcott, Russell Lee, and others moved me in an intensely personal way, jogging numerous childhood memories. Those recollections of Kentucky and the FSA photographs stirred me to begin my own photographic search. I studied the work of Diane Arbus, Ralph Eugene Meatyard, and Clarence John Laughlin, and later I found inspiration in the work of Mary Ellen Mark, Bruce Davidson, Emmet Gowin, and Frederick Sommers.

Doc Adams, 1973
(© Shelby Lee Adams)

In Cincinnati, I began to photograph immigrants from Appalachia who'd moved to Ohio in search of work. In a few cafes and bars, they would congregate with others from Kentucky and West Virginia with whom they felt at home. One elderly lady was introduced to me as a member of the feuding Hatfield clan. I found these people to be wonderful subjects for my budding portraiture work.

During my summer vacations, I took Depression-era photography books home with me and shared them with my family in eastern Kentucky. My uncle, a country doctor, upon seeing the photographs,

Leddie with children, 1990
(© Shelby Lee Adams)

said, "These people still live around here; they haven't changed in fifty years. You need to come with me when I make house calls in the heads of these hollers." My uncle, known as "Doc Adams," was and still is a folk hero to the mountain people of eastern Kentucky, and he made the perfect introduction to them for me in the early 1970s. On his calls, Doc Adams packed his doctor's bag with medical supplies and equipment and a .38 caliber Smith & Wesson. When people couldn't afford to pay, my uncle would barter his services, accepting a bag of potatoes, a mess of green beans, or a quart of moonshine as payment. I learned how to trade and barter, to joke, to eat wild game like raccoon, squirrel, possum, and rabbit, shoot guns, and drink. Most important, I came to respect the mountain people and to enjoy their company.

Since that first visit thirty years ago, I have photographed throughout twenty-two eastern Kentucky counties, with my portraits comprising three books published over the past decade. I've become known to the mountain people as "the picture man." Photographing in Kentucky has been an experience of continual discovery of new people and of new approaches to photography. I am still amazed by what I find. Every valley is a new community. Although places may appear very similar on the outside, each one is different within. I may find a Holiness church service filled with frenetic psychic energy or a family that is quiet and remote.

The mountain people I photograph are not simple country people. They have a complex cultural legacy that resists the modern media culture that surrounds and invades them. Their religious and cultural values are passed along from person to person and handed down from generation to generation. For them, belief in a personal god is essential, and the spiritual world of devils and angels is a part of daily life. The only way to achieve greatness, in their eyes, is through spiritual redemption here on earth, for which the reward is eternal salvation with God the Father and Jesus the Son in heaven. They see life on earth as a test and a burden to endure; what matters is where one goes after this life. For the mountain people, material things may be beneficial, but they are often burdensome; education is good for those who are so inclined, but books and possessions do not necessarily lead to the gates of heaven.

The Napiers' living room, 1989
(© Shelby Lee Adams)

Each summer and fall I return to Kentucky with two or three hundred eight-by-ten glossy photographs made the year before, which I give to my subjects. They, in turn, introduce me to neighbors and friends whom I photograph, and the following year, I return with their photographs. I prefer to work with a single subject or a family over time. On the first visit, I show pictures of other family members, and I may not even set up the camera. Other times, however, I discover the family eager to have their pictures made, and I occasionally get a photograph I really like on the first visit. If the first attempt is not successful, I study the image over a period of time and get better results the second or third visit, even when the sessions are a full year apart. A successful image results from an intimate interaction between photographer and subject.

Things have changed greatly in Appalachia over the past three decades. Today, there are superhighways, fast-food restaurants, strip mines, discount stores, mobile homes, satellite dishes, and the usual

Old couple at Stenger's Cafe,
Cincinnati, Ohio, 1979
(© Shelby Lee Adams)

plastic that decorates the rest of the country. My pictures are by no means typical of the area and should not be interpreted as a general representation of all Appalachian people or their culture today. Rather, my work is a study of a people cut off from the mainstream, bypassed by much of the ephemeral development of modern America. The subjects of my photographs exist in isolated areas and experience what most Americans would consider impossible living conditions. I know the back roads and paths to which most visitors are denied access.

Every summer and fall, traveling through the mountains photographing, I am somehow able to renew and relive my childhood. I regain my Southern, mountain accent and approach the people with openness, fascination, and respect; and they treat me with respect, too. My psychic antennae become sharpened and acute. I love these people. Perhaps that is it, plain and simple. I respond to the sensuous beauty of a hardened face with many scars, the deeply etched lines and flickers of sweat containing bright spots of sunlight. The eyes of my subjects reveal a kindness and curiosity, and their acceptance of me is gratifying. For me, this is a rejuvenation of the spirit of times past, and I am better for the experience each time I have it. My eastern Kentucky photographs are, in a way, self-portraits that represent a long autobiographical exploration of creativity, imagination, repulsion, and salvation. My greatest fear as a photographer is to look into the eyes of a subject and not see my own reflection.

Self-portrait with grandma, 1974
(© Shelby Lee Adams)

—A different version of this essay was originally published in *Appalachian Portraits,* by Shelby Lee Adams, University Press of Mississippi, 1993.

Mrs. Jacobs viewing book dummy (she and her daughter are in the layout), 1999
(© Shelby Lee Adams)

THE QUARE GENE

Tony Earley

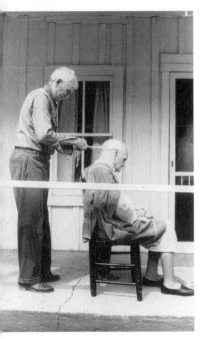

Sixty-four years of marriage, 2001
(© Shelby Lee Adams)

I do not like, have never liked, nor expect to like, watermelon. For the record, I consider this a private dietary preference, not a political choice, neither sign of failing character, nor renunciation of Southern citizenship. I simply do not like watermelon. Nor, for that matter, grits, blackberries, cantaloupe, buttermilk, okra, baked sweet potatoes, rhubarb, or collard greens. I don't even like to look at collard greens. But, because I am a Southerner, a North Carolinian of Appalachian, Scots-Irish descent, offspring of farming families on both sides, my family finds my failure to like the foods they like somehow distressing. Whenever I eat at my grandmother Ledbetter's table, my relatives earnestly strive to convince me that I am making a mistake by not sampling this or that, that I do not know what I am saying when I say no, that I should just *try* the greens, have just a little *slice* of watermelon, a small *bite* of cantaloupe, that I would eventually get used to the seeds in blackberries, the mealiness in grits, the swampy odor of greens boiled too long in a big pot. And when I refuse, as I have been refusing with passion and steadfastness for as long as I have known how to talk, they stare at me for a few seconds as if they do not know me, their mouths set sadly, then look down at their plates as if preparing to offer up a second grace. Then my grandmother says, "Tony Earley. You're just quare."

According to my edition of the *Shorter Oxford English Dictionary*, *quare* is an Anglo-Irish adjective from the early nineteenth century, meaning "queer, strange, eccentric." Most dictionaries, if they list it at all, will tell you that it is dialectical, archaic, or obsolete, an anachronism, only a marginal, aging participant in the clamoring riot of the English language. But when spoken around my grandmother's table, by my parents and aunts and uncles and cousins, *quare* isn't archaic at all, but as current as the breath that produces it, its meaning as pointed as a sharpened stick. For us, *quare* packs a specificity of meaning that *queer, strange, eccentric, odd, unusual, unconventional, or suspicious* do not. In our lexicon, the only adjective of synonymous texture would be *squirrelly,* but we are a close bunch and would find the act of calling each other squirrelly impolite. No, in my grandmother's house, when quare is the word we need, quare is the word we use.

Nor is *quare* the only word still hiding out in my grandmother's dining room that dictionaries assure us lost currency years ago. Suppose I brought a quare person to Sunday dinner at Granny's house, and he ate something that disagreed with him. We would say he looked a little peaked (pronounced peak-ed). Of course, we might decide he is peaked not because he ate something that disagreed with him, but because he ate a bait of something he liked. We would say, why, he was just too trifling to leave the table, and ate almost the whole mess by himself. And now we have this quare, peaked, trifling person on our hands. How do we get him to leave? Do we job him in the stomach? Do we hit him with a stob? No, we are kinder than that. We would say, "Brother, you liked to have stayed too long." We would put his dessert in a poke and send him on his way.

When I was a child I took these words for granted. They were simply part of the language I heard in the air around me, and I breathed them in. I knew that if I ran with a sharp object I might fall and job my eye out; the idea of *jabbing* my eye out would have sounded as foreign to me as French. My grandmother's table was the center of the universe. Only when I began to venture away from that center did I come to realize that the language of my family was not the lan-

Mr. Dixon, 1985
(© Shelby Lee Adams)

Appalachian roadside stop
(Mary Almond)

guage of the greater world. I was embarrassed and ashamed when my classmates at Rutherfordton Elementary School corrected my speech, but by the time I entered college, I wasn't surprised to learn in an Appalachian studies class that my family spoke in a *dialect*. I had begun to suspect as much and was, by that time, bilingual. I spoke in the Appalachian vernacular when I was with my family and standard English when I wasn't. This tailoring of speech to audience, which still feels to me a shade ignoble, is not uncommon to young people from this part of the world. In less generous regions of the American culture, the sound of Appalachian dialect has come to signify ignorance, backwardness, intransigence, and, in the most extreme examples, toothlessness, rank stupidity, and an alarming propensity for planting flowers in painted tractor tires.

This is not some misguided, Caucasian appeal for ethnicity, nor is it a battle cry from the radical left against the patriarchal oppression of grammar, but the fact is that, for me, standard English has always been something of a second language. I have intuitively written it correctly from the time I started school, but speaking it still feels unnatural, demands just enough conscious thought on my part to make me question my fluency. When I am introduced to a stranger, when I meet a more showily educated colleague in the English department at Vanderbilt, when I go to parties at which I feel unsure of my place in the evening's social pecking order, I catch myself proofing sentences before I say them—adding g's to the ends of participles, scanning clauses to make sure they ain't got no double negatives, clipping long vowels to affectless, Midwestern dimensions, making sure I use *lay* and *lie* in a manner that would not embarrass my father-in-law, who is a schoolteacher from California. I try, both consciously and unconsciously, with varying degrees of success, to remove words of Appalachian idiom from my public vocabulary before the person I'm talking to decides I'm stupid. Occasionally my wife, whose Southern accent is significantly more patrician than mine, will smile and ask, "What did you just say?" I realize then that I have committed a linguistic faux pas, that I have unwittingly slipped into the language of my people, that I have inadvertently become "colorful." I'll rewind my previous sentence in my head so I can save it as an example of how not to speak to strangers. I say, "What did you think I said?" Only inside the sanctity of Granny's house do I speak my mother tongue with anything resembling peace of mind.

I began thinking about the language I learned as a child, compared to the language I speak today, after reading Horace Kephart's book *Our Southern Highlanders*. Kephart was a librarian and writer who, following a nervous breakdown, left his wife and children and moved to the mountains around Bryson City, North Carolina, in 1904. Although he traveled there initially to remove himself from human contact, he soon recovered enough to take an active interest

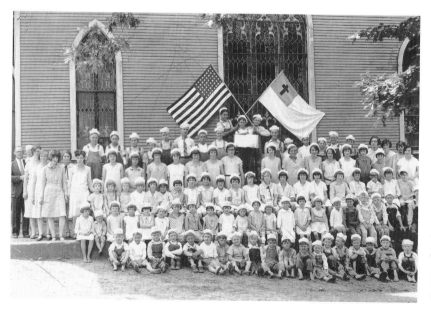

Rutherford County Baptist youth group, circa 1942 (Photographer unknown, Holly George-Warren Collection)

in the world in which he found himself. An avid gatherer of information and a compulsive list maker, Kephart spent the rest of his life compiling exhaustive journals and records detailing the geography, history, culture, and language of the southern Appalachians, a pursuit that resulted in innumerable magazine articles and two editions of *Our Southern Highlanders.*

Although Kephart had chosen the Appalachians over the deserts of the Southwest simply because it was the wilderness area closest to home, he arrived in western North Carolina at a particularly fortuitous time for a man of his particular talents. In the roadless hollows of the Blue Ridges and the Smokies, Kephart found a people living largely as their ancestors had lived in the latter half of the eighteenth century, when the great Scots-Irish migration out of Pennsylvania first peopled the region with settlers of European descent. The hostile geography of the mountains had simply walled off the early settlers from the outside world and precluded, for almost a century and a half, extensive contact between their descendants and the greater civilization. "No one can understand the attitude of our highlanders toward the rest of the earth, until he realizes their amazing isolation from all that lies beyond the blue, hazy skyline of their mountains. Conceive a shipload of emigrants cast away on some unknown island, far from the regular track of vessels, and left there for five or six generations, unaided and untroubled by the growth of civilization. Among the descendants of such a company we would expect to find customs and ideas unaltered from the time of their forefathers. . . . The mountain folk still live in the eighteenth century. The progress of mankind from that age is no heritage of theirs," Kephart writes.

Silver City, Rutherford County, North Carolina
(Glenn James/Holly George-Warren Collection)

Kephart was particularly interested in the English dialect he encountered in North Carolina, which he believed was closer to the Elizabethan English of Shakespeare or the Middle English of Chaucer than anything that had been spoken in England for centuries. Because the Scots-Irish had spoken to, and been influenced by, so few outsiders, the language they brought from Scotland and Ireland, by way of Pennsylvania, had been preserved remarkably intact. Coincidentally, had Kephart come to the mountains a generation later, his research would have been by default less definitive. Within a few years of his death in 1931, road-building initiatives, radio, and the Sears-Roebuck catalog began to open even the darkest hollows of the Appalachians to twentieth-century America. In just a very few years, the resulting cultural homogenization turned the Southern highlands into a world vastly different than the one he discovered in 1904.

I have since learned that Kephart's research methods were primitive by contemporary standards, and he was one of the first purveyors of what have since become suspect Appalachian generalities, but *Our Southern Highlanders* held for me the power of a revelation. Before reading the book, I knew only that I had always been quare, and occasionally peaked. I just never knew why. Kephart's work told me who I was, or at least where I came from, in a way I had never fully understood. All of the words I thought specific to my family had entries in the dictionary compiled from Kephart's research of southern Appalachian idioms. And all of them—with the exception of quare, which is a mere two hundred years old—are words of Middle English origin, which is to say anywhere from five to eight hundred years old. Although most of the people I meet today wouldn't have any idea what it's like to eat a bait, Chaucer would have.

Of course, a word of Middle English origin is a mere babe com-

Jane, 1990
(© Shelby Lee Adams)

pared to the words of Latin, Hebrew, or Greek etymology that constitute much of our language. The Latin and Greek roots of the words *agriculture* and *barbarian* were old long before the primitive tribes of the British Isles painted their faces blue and grunted in a dialect resembling English. And, of course, no language is a static property; the life cycle of words mirrors the life cycles of individuals who speak them. For specific words to fall out of favor and be replaced by new ones is the natural order of things; every language, given enough time, will replace each of its own words, just as every population replaces the old with the young, just as every seven years the human body replaces each of its cells. The self-appointed guardians of English who protest that the word *celibate* means "unmarried" and not "abstaining from sexual intercourse" are wasting their time. "Sounds are too volatile and subtle for legal restraints," Samuel Johnson wrote in the 1775 preface to his *Dictionary of the English Language.* "To enchain syllables, and to lash the wind, are equally the undertakings of pride." Understanding this, I am not advocating a return to eighteenth-century Scots-Irish dialect for the residents of western North Carolina. I am less taken by the age of the words of the Appalachian vernacular that found their way into my grandmother's dining room than I am by the specific history they hold.

The word *quare,* for me, contains sea voyages and migrations. It speaks of families stopping after long journeys and saying, for one of a thousand reasons, "This is far enough." It speaks to me of generations of farmers watching red dirt turn before plow blades, of young men stepping into furrows when old men step out. It speaks to me of girls fresh from their mothers' houses, crawling into marriage beds and becoming mothers themselves. It bears witness to a chromosomal line of history, most of it now unmappable, that led to my human awakening beneath these particular mountains. If language is the mechanism through which we inherit history and culture, then individual words function as a type of gene, each bearing with it a small piece of the specific information that makes us who we are and tells us where we have been. My brother Greg and I came down with the same obscure bone disease in the same knee at the same age. For us the word *quare* is no less a genetic signifier of the past than the odd, bone-eating chromosome carried down through history by one wonders how many limping Scots-Irish.

The last time I remember talking to my maternal great-grandfather Womack, he was well into his nineties and my whole family had gathered at the house he built as a young man along Walnut Creek in the Sunny View community of Polk County. When I tell this story, I choose to remember it as a spring day, though it may not have been, simply because I like to think that the daffodils in his yard were blooming. My grandmother helped him plant them when she was a little girl. At some point, everyone got up and went inside, leaving Paw Womack and me alone on the porch. I was in high school, a freshman or sophomore, and was made self-conscious by his legendary

Sherman's porch, 2001
(© Shelby Lee Adams)

age. He had been born in another century. His father had been wounded at Gettysburg. He was *historical*. He had farmed with a mule well into his eighties. He never bought another car after the one he bought in 1926 wore out. A preacher's son, he had never uttered a swear word or tasted alcohol. He had voted for Woodrow Wilson. I felt somehow chosen by the family to sit with him; I felt like I had to say something. I got out of my chair and approached him as one would a sacred totem. I sat down on the porch rail facing him, but I had no idea where to start. I remember his immense, knotted farmer's hands spread out on the arms of his rocker. We stared at each other

Cecil, 1993
(© Shelby Lee Adams)

for what seemed like a long time. Eventually I blushed. I smiled at him and nodded. He smiled back and said, "Who *are* you?"

I said, "I'm Reba's boy. Clara Mae's grandson."

"Oh," he said. "Reba's boy." If we ever spoke again, I don't remember it.

It seems significant to me that when I told Paw Womack who I was, I didn't give him my name. My position as individual was secondary to my place in the lineage, his lineage, that led to me sitting on his porch. I identified myself as a small part of a greater whole. *Who are you?* I'm Reba's boy, Clara Mae's grandson, Tom Womack's great-grandson. *Where are you from?* Over yonder. *Why don't you like watermelon?* I don't know. I guess I'm just quare.

Ironically, just as I learned from Horace Kephart to fully appreciate the history contained in the word *quare*, I also have to accept the fact that it is passing out of my family with my generation. Neither I nor my cousins use it outside of Granny's house unless we temper it first with irony—a sure sign of a word's practical death within a changing language. I tell myself that the passing of Appalachian vernacular from my family's vocabulary is not a tragedy or a sign of our being assimilated into a dominant culture, but simply the expected arrival of an inevitable end. "Life may be lengthened by care," Dr. Johnson says, "though death cannot ultimately be defeated: tongues, like governments, have a natural tendency to degeneration." I tell myself that it is a natural progression for my children to speak a language significantly different from that of my parents, but the fact that it happened so suddenly, within the course of a single generation, my generation, makes me wonder if I have done something wrong, if I have failed all the people who passed those words down. Sometimes the truest answer to the question "Who are you?" is "I don't know."

A few years ago an ice storm splintered a large stand of pine trees on my grandmother Ledbetter's farm. When the broken timber was logged and removed, our whole family was shocked by how close the mountains were behind the ridge where the trees had stood. We all walked out the road past the barn to have a closer look, almost as if we had never seen them before. "These very mountains of Carolina," Kephart writes in *Our Southern Highlanders,* "are among the ancients of the earth. They were old, very old, before the Alps and the Andes, the Rockies and the Himalayas were molded into their primal shapes." Young's Mountain, Rumbling Bald, Chimney Rock, Shumont, World's Edge, White Oak—my family has apparently always lived in their shadow. They preserved in their hollows and laurel hell the words that tell us better than any others who we are. Words and blood are the double helix that connect us to our past.

As the member of a transitional generation, however, I am losing those words and the connection they make. And by losing language, I am losing the small comfort of shared history. I compensate, in the stories I write, by sending people up mountains to look, as Horace Kephart did, for the answers to their questions, to look down from a high place and see what they can see. My characters, at least, can still say the words that bind them to the past without sounding queer, strange, eccentric, odd, unusual, unconventional, or suspicious. "Stories," says the writer Tim O'Brien, "can save us." I have put my faith in the idea that words, even new ones, possess that kind of redemptive power. Writers do not write about a place *because* they belong there, but because they want to. It's a quare feeling.

–Reprinted with permission from *Somehow Form a Family: Stories That Are Mostly True* (Algonquin, 2002)

Holland family gathering, Rutherford County, North Carolina (Photographer unknown, Holly George-Warren Collection)

FULL CIRCLE

EDWIN SWEENEY

A final resting place in Appalachia
(Andy Sabol)

A few years back, I went to a funeral in a remote part of West Virginia. The warm October day and pungent scent of leaves seemed like an atavistic trigger for reflection on the departed woman's life. This was a life that began here, moved to New York and beyond, then came full circle back to the hills.

The country church could have come from a sixty-year-old Walker Evans photograph, and some of the mourners could have been Evans' subjects. Others were cosmopolitan types who, before this occasion, had only flown over the area on their way from New York to Atlanta or Miami.

An octogenarian man reminisced with one of his contemporaries about the dead woman's ability to "do sums" mentally. Although this facility is what led her to college and subsequently a job in New York City's financial district, it was her natural ability to sing and perform with ease that eventually steered her to success in the theater.

At an early age, she had been asked to lead the children's hymn in church. It was probably from there that her delicate soprano evolved into its strong onstage speaking presence. Along the way, she sought to put her southern Appalachian accent in the closet. She generally succeeded, except when speaking with acquaintances from home.

In a word, she could "pass" successfully from one culture to another. When she took to the stage, people who didn't know her background may have assumed she'd lived on the Upper East Side her entire life.

When she met the man she married, it was more than a year before she brought him back to her birthplace. Whether consciously or not, she had been preparing him for the way of life in that area he had only seen from a plane.

Perhaps she underestimated him during that year of preparation. A life so different from his could have caused him to disparage it. But this wasn't so. From his first immersion into this newly discovered subculture, he was intrigued. This was not the same Appalachian area he had seen depicted in comic strips and situation comedies. He discovered that people who were initially reserved offered condolences at his wife's funeral, they extended friendship and urged him to return. He didn't need such urging.

The brief biblical service was eloquent in its stark simplicity. A man with a full white beard played the guitar and sang "Amazing

(Andy Sabol)

The Hills of Appalachia

Playin' grandpa's fiddle on the front
   porch swing
I feel my fingers dancin' on the
   strings
I can almost hear grandma laugh
   and sing
In the hills of Appalachia

On that country road in the
   summer rain
I could drink the air like a sweet
   champagne
Honeysuckle vines swam around
   my brain
In the hills of Appalachia

We'd make maple syrup from the
   backyard trees
And steal the honey from the
   honeybees
Skip flat stones from across the
   stream
In the hills of Appalachia

As I close my eyes and draw that
   bow
I can feel the mud wet between my
   toes
From down by the river where we
   used to go
In the hills of Appalachia

This old fingerboard is worn and
   thin
And the wood remembers my
   grandpa's chin
Every note I play takes me back
   again
To the hills of Appalachia

Now the songs I play have a touch
   of home
And the memories linger even
   though I'm grown
I play grandpa's fiddle and I'm not
   alone
In the hills of Appalachia
                    —*Arlene Faith Kortright*

Fiddler Jilson Setters
(Jean Thomas, The Traipsin'
Woman Collection/University
of Louisville Photographic
Archives, courtesy of Charles
Wolfe)

Grace." As a pallbearer that day, I followed the funeral director's instructions when he said, "Boys, it's time." As we bore the coffin from the church to its final destination, I noticed another group behind us: the "flower girls," teens to past-middle-aged women, who carried baskets of flowers to cover the mound of soon-to-be-distributed earth.

A gentle breeze coaxed leaves to the ground as if to make a protective blanket for the graveyard inhabitants. Distant ridges were visible, and the hills offered a similar sense of protection.

The four men who opened the grave—and would soon close it—waited by a pickup truck. As the minister began the final prayer, they ceased talking, removed their caps, and lowered their eyes as a mark of respect.

How reassuring to know that some characteristics that set us apart also bring us together at such sorrowful times, helping us to survive as an enduring culture.

THIS TRAIN PASSES THROUGH BUT DOESN'T STOP

Jason Ringenberg

Rolling through an Appalachian holler, a train can seem to just materialize out of the mist, then disappear as quickly and mysteriously. So it has always been with the outside world's influence on this isolated, remote region of America. In spite of Appalachia's proximity to major urban/industrial areas, it somehow has maintained its distinct, exclusive personality. The outside world may pass through, but its impact is usually rather insignificant.

I am not from Appalachia, but I have always related to its fierce independence and resistance to change. When pioneers began crossing the Appalachian Mountains in the eighteenth and nineteenth centuries, many of the hardy folk of Tennessee, Kentucky, Virginia, and North Carolina saw no need to join the land-feeding frenzy across the Mississippi. Their fathers and mothers were buried in those hills; how could one leave that? When the Civil War began, many of them resisted both Confederate and Union attempts to impose agendas on their valleys and hills. When New Dealers arrived in the 1930s and 1940s, some ended up on the bottom of rivers and caves. Even today, that independence still lives in the hearts of those who disdain the tackiness, commerciality, and upward mobility of the "New South."

It is that independence that has spawned the region's most sacred

A Shay engine building up steam outside Cass, West Virginia, where at one time it was used to haul lumber to the sawmill from logging camps
(© Mary Almond)

The Kentucky Hill Billies, 1933
(Photographer unknown,
Charles Wolfe Collection)

"Bill Monroe was very special and still is very special to me. I'd get my mandolin and go over to his house, and we'd play for two hours and wouldn't say five words in two hours. And I'd say, 'Well, I need to go pick the kids up at school,' and he'd say, 'Okay, come on back and see me. I believe we did good today.' And here we hadn't said nothin'. We just played and said everything our hearts needed to say. I just respected him so much for that. He pioneered a music America can call its own."

—Cordell, Kentucky–born
musician Ricky Skaggs

and lasting export: its music. Bluegrass, mountain music, country, Americana—call it what you will—it is the pure product born of those hills and hollers. Its sound conjures memories of train whistles dying in the mist, great-grandparents buried in the backyard, babies crying for lack of nourishment, back-porch dances during mountain sunsets, family, and home. It was that music that originally inspired me to move to Nashville from an Illinois hog farm on July 4, 1981. When I arrived in Music City, I rented a shotgun shack on Neighborly Drive, a little hamlet that had yet to be gentrified and suburbanized. Most of the folks in this backward valley lived in the same wooden, tin-roofed houses that their grandfathers had built in the twenties and thirties. "Picking parties" were still held regularly in some of the shacks. I frequently attended those evening hoots and was welcomed as one of their own. There was no self-important pretense, just folks soulfully playing banjos and guitars, as chickens scratched the hard clay for ticks. Although down Interstate 40 just a piece, Nashville's slick Music Row might as well have been 10,000 miles away. But the little holler had kept its identity and spirit in spite of the suburban monster that devoured all originality at its borders, just as Greater Appalachia had kept its primordial separateness in the backwaters of twentieth-century America's march toward political and cultural world dominance.

It is this paradox that is so striking to me about Appalachian music: It is without a doubt one of America's most unique and lasting products, yet it completely goes against the grain of the Greater American Manifest Destiny—i.e., the continuous expansion of territory, wealth, and material goods, as well as the never-ending geographic migration to "a place with better opportunities." There is hardly anywhere else in America where families still farm land that their ancestors worked. There is nowhere else where you see so many folks trace their roots to their current home, and nowhere else where you find so many people so determined to stay. Such loyalty to a place may account in large part for the development and vitality of mountain music. It gave the singers, listeners, and pickers a way both to codify their roots and to mentally leave their circumstances behind for a bit. Having done that, the musicians and their audiences were then completely satisfied to stay put.

It is also important to note that those folks who did leave the hills in the 1950s through the 1970s—for economic opportunities in the great Midwestern industrial centers—found they could never spiritually or mentally break from the past. Detroit did not become home. Dry Gulch, Kentucky, always would be home in their minds. No amount of money or material gain could change that. Some of the finest country songs of that generation ("Detroit City," "Streets of Baltimore") dealt with an endless longing for their ancestral homeland. Homesickness was a chronic condition that never left their spirits. Good American citizens, they first and foremost were tied to their mountain heritage with bonds that no materialism or "progressive" circumstance could break.

It was into this culture that Jason and the Scorchers first started fusing mountain music with modern punk rock. In that little shack (where one-hundred-degree heat was the summer norm), we started jamming on songs I had learned at neighborhood hoots. The other boys in the band were enamored of first-wave punk rock, and I was the roots guy. It was an absolute chemical explosion. The neighbors on Neighborly Drive could, of course, hear what we were doing through those thin walls and readily gave their support and encouragement. I guess they thought we were carrying on their tradition by

The Tennessee Ramblers
(Photographer unknown,
Charles Wolfe Collection)

"Bluegrass is just timeless stories about home and family. It reminds me of the good old days when life was simpler—like my favorite songs. Not that times were easy, but definitely simpler. I love the love stories and the bluegrass tunes—daydreams accompanied by five-string banjo."
—*Champaign, Illinois–born Alison Krauss*

Sir Cordell Kemp, Defeated Creek, Tennessee
(Marty Stuart/Holly George-Warren Collection)

Flatt and Scruggs and the Foggy Mountain Boys entertaining from the top of the concession stand at a drive-in theater in West Virginia. From left: *Curly Seckler, "Cousin Jake" Tullock, Lester Flatt, Paul Warren, Earl Scruggs, "Uncle Josh" Graves.* (Photographer unknown, Charles Wolfe Collection)

"Lester Flatt and Earl Scruggs performed once during intermission at the drive-in movie. They were performing on top of the concession stand. The next day out in the yard, I went around pretending I was up on that concession stand singing."

—*Pikesville, Kentucky–born musician Patty Loveless*

putting a little punk-tinged moonshine into the mix. It was a heady time. We took our music on the road throughout the South, and I was always honored when children of mountain folk dug our stuff and understood our passion and respect for their roots—even though we played at hyperspeed, with volumes regularly exceeding 110 decibels. It was our independence and respect for musical traditions that kept them coming back to our shows over and over again, in some cases even bringing their parents!

It's no surprise that roots music continues to grow, develop, and win new converts. Music has always been a central part of Appalachian culture, dating back to the first wave of Scots-Irish immigrants who carried the fiddle jigs and dance tunes of the static, closed Old World to the vibrant, open, and dangerous New World.

Here, those tunes found new life in the isolated hills and valleys of Appalachia. Unlike the settled, navigable eastern seaboard, the Appalachians were a remote, cold, and damp environment where people had to learn to entertain themselves. A neighbor might have lived only a few miles away, but it was up- or downhill those few miles. Just getting to town was a day trip. These mountain settlers had to rely on family for everything, including music. So in most of the old families, every member played an instrument or sang. Songs were handed down through the generations, changing to fit new times while still honoring the old. Even the smallest children would join in singing. It bonded folks to their ancestors and made it difficult to even consider leaving their ancestral valleys. As each generation passed, it became harder to imagine leaving. The rest of America continued to migrate westward, but the people of Appalachia stayed on, buried their parents in the old family plots, raised children, and in turn were buried beside their parents. At these passings, the old songs were always sung, blending it all together denser than Georgia red clay.

So what happens now to this ancient culture and its music? Will its foundation of heritage and history survive in a world that increasingly puts premium value on speed, evolution, innovation, and change? All evidence suggests that it will not only survive but prosper. People around the world, of every stripe and history, are finding solace and deep peace in Appalachian music. As life continues to accelerate for every one of us, it's good to know that someplace, in a Kentucky holler or a European concert hall, Appalachian music is taking folks back to the mountains and home. The train whistle's echo may die in the holler's mist, but its spirit lives on.

Hawthorn's Cabin Mountain, Randolph County, West Virginia
(Karl Badgley)

Thread

You fall asleep beneath a willow
in autumn woods near pine-pitched
water. When you awake, you
    discover
an orb weaver has chalked some
    lines
from a nearby branch to your
    shoulder,
a few silken joists for a web.
As the sun sinks below the tree
line,
frogs and whip-poor-wills, crickets
and doves entice you to stay. You
    linger
awhile as you watch your lodger
pay her silver down. The stars
have made you forget your name,
the trees are whispering *rain*,
and it's time for you to go.
As you leave the dark woods, you
    scythe
your way through strands of thread
that connect everything to
    everything.

—*John Sokol*

AFTERWORD

My introduction to the haunting land and people of Appalachia began with migrants in the inner city of Cincinnati. It soon extended to the far hollows of east Kentucky in the 1970s while filming *Appalachian Heritage,* a documentary dealing with the great migration out of Appalachia and the profound impact of strip mining. That experience led me to return to the mountains a few years later to film the story of a young girl growing up in an Appalachian coal town: In the 1980s, I went into the rugged mountains of West

Virginia to write and direct a drama set in a coal town in the 1930s. Each of these films added to my understanding of and emotional attachment to the remarkable story of the people and the land.

When Mari-Lynn Evans shared with me her life experience and passion for the land, it rekindled my long-time affinity for the mountains and my desire to make a comprehensive film on the history and culture of the Appalachian people.

My most vivid memories of creating the film *The Appalachians* are of first meeting the people we became honored to know. On a rainy night in Cobin, West Virginia, we met ninety-one-year-old master fiddler Melvin Wine, who played ancient mountain tunes with hands gnarled by arthritis. "Good for the soul of man," Melvin whispered about his music. "And it keeps you out of meanness."

Dewey Fox was 103 years old when we interviewed him. The son of a slave, Dewey survived the KKK, the Great Depression, and Jim Crow with a spirit unspoiled by hate. Jack Hatfield told us the bloody stories of his grandfather's legendary feud and of his experiences in the moonshine trade. In Jolo, West Virginia, a serpent handler who'd been bitten 139 times by rattlers and copperheads referred to these episodes as "water under the bridge."

Indeed, the heart of our film, as well as the book *The Appalachians*, lies in the stories of the people who reside in Appalachia. They have made an indelible imprint on American history and culture.

—*Tom Robertson*
Director, The Appalachians
Nashville, Tennessee
December 2003

CONTRIBUTORS

Shelby Lee Adams is a photographer whose work has been exhibited in numerous galleries and museums in the United States and Europe. His photographs have been included in more than fifty solo and numerous group exhibitions, both nationally and internationally, as well as in many private and museum collections. He has been awarded two National Endowment for the Arts grants. Three books of his photographs have been published: *Appalachian Portraits* (1993), *Appalachian Legacy* (1998), and *Appalachian Lives* (2003).

Mary Almond is a self-taught landscape photographer and digital artist who calls the mountains of West Virginia home. Her eye for capturing the beauty and mystique of a place has made her a well-known artist throughout the world. Her website is themerrycat.com.

Karl Badgley is a wildlife artist whose work reflects an intricacy of detail resulting from his continuing appreciation and growing knowledge of wildlife. Badgley has traveled extensively from British Columbia to Maine, and his nature subjects, though varied, always reveal his intense research. His stand on the preservation of wildlife has prompted him to donate his work to a variety of programs, including the Canaan Valley Refuge, to which he has given one hundred signed and numbered "American Woodcock" prints to aid in the establishment of a national wildlife refuge in Canaan Valley, West Virginia. He has illustrated publications for the National Audubon Society as well as others. Many of Badgley's original works are found in private collections throughout the United States. His former vocation as television art director led to nine Emmys and numerous other awards. He is the staff photographer for mountainmade.com.

Shannon Bell and photographer **Chuck Conner** have attended more than sixty church services at the serpent-handling Church of the Lord Jesus, in Jolo, West Virginia, in order to document their faith. Bell received degrees in religion and biology from Washington and Lee University in 2000 and a master of social work degree from West Virginia University in 2004. She currently works in Cabin Creek, West Virginia, in community development and public health.

Julia Bonds is the director of Coal River Mountain Watch. In 2003 she was awarded the Goldman Environmental Prize for her work in the fight against mountaintop-removal mining in the mountains of West Virginia.

Judy Prozzillo Byers is Abelina Suarez English Professor and Director of the West Virginia Folklife Center at Fairmont State College.

Paul Burch is a musician, songwriter, and producer who grew up in Virginia, Mississippi, and Indiana. Since moving to Nashville in 1994, Burch has released five CDs, including *Fool for Love* and *Last of My Kind,* a companion to Tony Earley's novel *Jim the Boy.*

Robert C. Byrd made his first run for political office in 1946 and was elected to the West Virginia House of Delegates. After two terms, he was elected to the West Virginia Senate; then to the United States House of Representatives for three terms; and finally, in 1958, to the United States Senate, where he has represented West Virginia continuously ever since. He has served longer in the United States Senate than anyone else in West Virginia's history. Senator Byrd became a member of the Senate leadership in 1967, when he was selected by his colleagues to be secretary of the Democratic Conference. In 1971, he was chosen Senate Democratic whip. In 1977, he was elected Democratic leader, a position he held for six consecutive terms. He served as Senate Majority leader six years and as Senate Minority leader six years. On two different occasions, Senator Byrd has served as chairman of the Senate Appropriations Committee. Also twice, Senator Byrd unanimously was elected president pro tempore of the Senate, a post that placed him third in line of succession to the presidency. Byrd has the distinction of having held more leadership positions in the U.S. Senate than any other senator of any party in Senate history. In May 2001, Senator Byrd received what he considers his greatest honor, when Governor Bob Wise and both Houses of the West Virginia legislature named him "West Virginian of the Twentieth Century."

Gary Carden is a folklorist, storyteller, artist, and the author of *Mason Jars in the Flood and Other Stories.*

Stephanie Chernikowski left her home in Texas in 1975 and moved to Gotham, West Virginia, where she became a photojournalist specializing in music. Her work has appeared in publications such as *The Village Voice, The New York Times,* and *Rolling Stone,* and has been reproduced and exhibited around the world. In 1996 she published a book documenting the original punk and new wave scene in New York, *Dream Baby Dream: Images of the Blank Generation;* she is currently working on a second book documenting her Texas heritage.

Chuck Conner has been a photographer for more than thirty years. From his beginnings in high school, in the U.S. Air Force, and at the Library of Congress to stints as a professional lab processor and printer, he has traveled down various avenues in the medium. His current project with writer Shannon Bell documents the faith and lives of congregation members of the Church of the Lord Jesus, in Jolo, West Virginia. This and other work by Chuck Conner can be viewed at chuckconner.com.

Howard Dorgan is a Professor Emeritus of Communication at Appalachian State University, in Boone, North Carolina, where he has spent the last thirty-three years of his professional career. Dorgan has written four books on Appalachian religious traditions and has published more than forty essays on Appalachian religious history and culture. He served as the editor of the religion section of the forthcoming *Encyclopedia of Appalachia*.

Tony Earley is the author of the novels *Jim the Boy* and *Here We Are in Paradise* and a book of essays, *Somehow Form a Family*. His short stories earned him a place on *Granta*'s list of the twenty Best Young American Fiction Writers in 1996 and a National Magazine Award for fiction. He is a professor of English at Vanderbilt University.

Mari-Lynn Evans is the executive producer of many television and video programs including the four-part PBS documentary series *The Appalachians* and *Living Well: A Guide to Healthy Aging*, a twenty-six-week series for PBS and the Fox Health Network. In addition, she has produced and directed the *Living Well* five-part video, as well as *Geezbo's Alley, Changes,* and the documentary *Standing in the Safety Zone*. She is the executive producer of *Integrative Medicine: Body, Mind, and Spirit,* a thirteen-week series for American Health Network and the Fox Health Network, hosted by Naomi Judd. Evans is the recipient of several national awards, including the 1999 U.S. Small Business Administration Tibbetts Award and a Bronze National Mature Media Award.

Rita Forrester is the director of the Carter Fold, a performance space in Hiltons, Virginia, dedicated to the work of the Carter Family and the music inspired by their legacy.

Holly George-Warren is coeditor of *Martin Scorsese Presents: The Blues, American Roots Music,* and *The Rolling Stone Encyclopedia of Rock & Roll,* among other books. The author of *Cowboy: How Hollywood Invented the Wild West* and the coauthor of *How the West Was Worn,* she is currently at work on a biography of Gene Autry, which will be published by Oxford University Press.

David Giffels, a columnist with the *Akron Beacon Journal,* is coauthor of *Are We Not Men? We Are Devo!* and *Wheels of Fortune: The Story of Rubber in Akron.* He is also a contributor to the forthcoming *Encyclopedia of the Midwest.* He has written extensively for newspapers and magazines and also wrote scripts for the MTV cartoon *Beavis and Butt-Head.*

Martha Hume was born and raised in east Kentucky coal country and has written extensively on country and pop music for publications such as *Rolling Stone,* the New York *Daily News, GQ, In Style,* and *People.* She currently lives in Nashville, Tennessee, where she is at work on a memoir, *Missing Scarlett.*

Jonathan Jessup is a nature and landscape photographer who specializes in the environs of West Virginia. Documenting their rugged, majestic mountains to their swampy, peaceful bogs, Jessup has been exploring the hidden treasures of the Appalachians for many years. His love affair with West Virginia wilderness began when he was just six years old, when his family bought property near Slanesville in Hampshire County. His deep spiritual connection to the mountains has inspired him to share his experience with others. His work can be viewed at jonathanjessup.com.

Arlene Faith Kortright is a songwriter and musician whose Celtic fiddle music is featured in the documentary *The Appalachians.*

Ronald L. Lewis is the Robbins Chair in History at West Virginia University. His teaching and research specializations are West Virginia history, Appalachian history, and the social history of industrialization.

Jim Marshall's photographs have been exhibited in galleries and museums around the world, including the Smithsonian Institution. He has published a retrospective of his photography, *Not Fade Away,* and his photographs can be seen in other books including *Rolling Stone: Images of Rock & Roll; Garcia; Early Dylan;* and *Martin Scorsese Presents: The Blues.*

Gordon B. McKinney was born and raised in the White Mountain region of New Hampshire. He has taught history at Valdosta State University, Western Carolina University, the University of Maryland, and Berea College. He was also a program officer in the research division of the National Endowment for the Humanities and executive director of National History Day. He is the author of *Southern Mountain Republicans, 1865–1900, Zeb Vance: North Carolina's Civil War Governor,* and *Gilded Age Political Leader;* editor of *The Papers of Zebulon Vance,* microfilm edition; and coauthor of *The Heart of Confederate Appalachia: Western North Carolina in the Civil War.* He is presently a professor of history and director of the Appalachian Center at Berea College.

Alan B. Mollohan, a native of Fairmont, West Virginia, was first elected to the U.S. House of Representatives in 1982 and has been reelected to each successive Congress. A senior member of the House Appropriations Committee, he has focused his efforts on defending northern West Virginia's traditional industries and diversifying the district's economy to also include information technology, aerospace, and government service sectors. In addition, he works to support local communities in areas such as downtown and neighborhood revitalization, watershed management, and cultural and historic preservation.

Ted Olson teaches Appalachian studies and English courses at East Tennessee State University, where he also serves as director of that school's Appalachian, Scottish, and Irish studies program. Olson is the author of *Blue Ridge Folklife;* the editor of James Still's *From the Mountain, From the Valley: New and Collected Poems;* the coeditor (with Charles Wolfe) of *The Bristol Sessions: Writings About the Big Bang of Country Music;* and the editor of *Crossroads: A Southern Culture Annual* and the music section of the forthcoming *Encyclopedia of Appalachia.*

Bill Richardson is a lifelong resident of central Appalachia and an assistant professor for the West Virginia University Extension Service. He has created numerous plays, films, and other works about the history and culture of the region.

Jason Ringenberg is a founding member of Jason and the Scorchers, with whom he's recorded numerous albums since 1981. His most recent solo release is *A Day at the Farm with Farmer Jason,* a children's album.

Tom G. Robertson is a writer, producer, and director of film and television projects that have been honored with more than one hundred national and international awards, including the George Foster Peabody Award, multiple Emmys, and the National Achievement in Children's Television Award, along with top honors from the New York Film Festival and many other major film and television festivals. Robertson's programs have been seen on ABC, NBC, HBO, Showtime, the Disney Channel, PBS, A&E, the History Channel, TNN, Nickelodeon, and in worldwide syndication. His work includes a premiere film for Disney and Wonderworks on PBS, as well as after-school specials for ABC and NBC, more than seventy young people's dramas, numerous music and variety specials, TV series, prime-time historical documentaries and miniseries, and a daily reality-based magazine show.

Robert Santelli is coeditor of *Martin Scorsese Presents: The Blues* and *American Roots Music;* author of *The Big Book of Blues,* among other books; and the executive director of the Experience Music Project in Seattle, Washington.

Van Slider is a well-known West Virginia photographer who lives in his hometown of Paden City, West Virginia. His main focus is on photographing nature and the rural countryside. His work has appeared in numerous calendars, magazines, and commercial pieces. His website is ovis.net/~vslider.

Lee Smith is the author of many bestselling novels, including *Black Mountain Breakdown, Fair and Tender Ladies, The Devil's Dream, Family Linen,* and *The Last Girls,* as well as the musical *Good Ol' Girls,* a collaboration with Jill McCorkle, Marshall Chapman, and Matraca Berg.

Andy Sabol, originally from Pittsburgh, Pennsylvania, trained as a photographer at Middle Tennessee State University in Murfreesboro, Tennessee. He settled in Akron, Ohio, and worked as a medical photographer in a children's hospital for fifteen years and spent another ten years as a nomadic photographer/truck driver. He no longer drives a truck but still loves to travel in his Airstream and photograph landscapes and nature.

John Sokol is a writer and painter living in Akron, Ohio. His poems have appeared in *America, Antigonish Review, The Berkeley Poetry Review, Georgetown Review, New Millennium Writings, The New York Quarterly,* and *Quarterly West,* among others. His short stories have appeared in *Akros, Descant, Mindscapes, The Pittsburgh Quarterly, Redbook,* and other journals, and he has published a collection of his poetry entitled *In the Summer of Cancer.*

Marian Steinert is an art teacher in the Akron public school system and an award-winning photographer who has worked with artist/writer Gary Carden for several years and photographed many of his works.

Vivian Stockman has resided in Spencer, West Virginia, since 1990. Her maternal grandparents were from West Virginia and she credits her grandfather with instilling in her a deep respect for the natural world. Stockman graduated with a B.S., cum laude with distinction, in environmental communications from Ohio State University. In 1999, Stockman received the West Virginia Environmental Council's highest honor, the Mother Jones Award. She works for the Huntington, West Virginia–based Ohio Valley Environmental Coalition, a group striving to halt mountaintop-removal coal mining. Her articles and photographs have appeared in numerous publications.

Edwin Sweeney, a native and resident of Weston, West Virginia, is a writer who has spent much of his life collecting the customs of the southern Appalachian area and chronicling its way of life. He has taught writing at the college level and holds a master's degree in journalism from West Virginia University. He currently works for the West Virginia High Technology Consortium Foundation in Fairmont, West Virginia.

John Trew gave up the editorship of the world's oldest daily newspaper, the *Belfast News Letter,* to undertake the considerably less stressful role of travel writer. He has visited all the states where his Ulster-Scots heroes were pioneers. Although European by birth and upbringing, he feels more at home in the Shenandoah Valley than in Sheffield, Sorrento, or Seville, and prefers bluegrass, barbecue, and Dave Barry to Beethoven, brandy, and Balzac.

Charles Wolfe is a professor of English at Middle Tennessee State University and is the author of *Kentucky Country; Grand Ole Opry: The Early Years;* and *Tennessee Strings,* among many other books.

ACKNOWLEDGMENTS

J
ust as the Appalachian mountain chain is comprised of numerous summits, hollers, and sweeping valleys, so this book was created by a diverse roster of talent and expertise. First and foremost, the indefatigable team of designer Harry Choron and literary agent/book producer Sandy Choron transformed the film project *The Appalachians* into the book you now hold in your hands. Also essential were the scholars who gave both the film and the book their undivided attention and shared their vast knowledge with us: Led by Howard Dorgan, *The Appalachians'* advisory committee consisted of Judy Byers, Ron Eller, Ron Lewis, Gordon McKinney, Ramie Barker, Laura Kuhns, Steve Fesenmaier, Ted Olson, Ed Sweeney, Charles Wolfe, Naomi Judd, and Dena Divito. We also wish to thank Anne McLaine at the Library of Congress; Cheryl Head and Susan Ross at The Corporation for Public Broadcasting; David Thompson, Dalton Delan, Karen Fritz, and Sharon Rockefeller at WETA; and Adrienne Bramhall at The Sierra

Club. We also want to acknowledge Fred Armstrong, Dick Fauss, Ed Hicks, Kay Goodwin, Phylis Geller, Senator Robert C. Byrd and Congressman Alan B. Mollohan and their staffs for all their help with this project. Kudos, also, to director Tom Robertson for his help in transferring his cinematic vision to the printed page, and to producer Mari-Lynn Evans for her creative direction and enthusiasm. We're also grateful to all the wonderful writers, photographers, and illustrators whose work has made this book such a pleasure to put together. In addition, *The Appalachians* benefited from the editorial expertise of Nina Pearlman, Robin Aigner, Elizabeth Gall, Robert Warren, Nita Freedman, Janet Wygal, Richard Elman, and the rest of the Random House team. We also greatly appreciate Random House editors Dan Menaker and Bruce Tracy for their support and expertise. Others who helped in this regard include Sarah Lazin, Bob Santelli, Adele Hauk, Lisa Howorth, Kathy K, Nancy Heidel, Ann Griffin, Wayne Griffin, Bob Oermann, Mary Bufwack, Chet Flippo, Frances Spratt, and Jean Ware. *The Appalachians* is, indeed, the fruit of many labors—we hope the result gives you many hours of pleasure.

–Holly George-Warren

INDEX

"Hill Billys" (animated cartoon short), 110
"Hills of Appalachia, The" (Kortright), 217
Hillsville, Virginia, 92
Hiltons, Virginia, 101–2. *See also* Maces Springs,
    Virginia
Hinton, West Virginia, 127, *127*
Hispanics, 25–26, 68
Hobbs, Roy, 95
"Hobnobbing with Hillbillies" (W. A. Bradley), 110
Hoffman, Elisha, 90
Holcomb, Roscoe, 115, 118
Holiness-Pentecostals, 184, 188, 189–91
  Signs Followers, *190*, 195–202
Holland, Beulah Mooney, xxxii
Holland, Herbert Roland, xxxii
Holland, Martha Jean, *xxxi*, xxxii
Holland family, xxxii, *215*
Holy Spirit (Holy Ghost), 189–90, 196–97, 199
Honeybee, Kentucky, graves, *132*, 138
Hooterville, Kentucky, *188*
Hoot Owl, Kentucky, 164
Hopkins, Al, 110
Hotel Stearns, Stearns, Kentucky, 135, 136, 137, 138, 139
House of Representatives, U.S., 128, 129
Houston, Sam, 31
"How Can a Poor Man Stand Such Times and Live"
    (song), 91
Howe, Julia Ward, 34
Huguenots, 25
Hume, Hattie Carter, 135, 136–37, 138
Hume, Martha, 131–41, 231
Hume, Whitman, 134–37, 138, 140
Hungarian immigrants, 25, 42, 80, 144–45
"Hunkitchy Man, The" (legend), 55–56
"Hunters of Kentucky, The" (song), 58–60
Huntington, West Virginia, 75
Huntsville, Alabama, 45

"I Am Bound for the Promised Land" (song), 92
Illinois, 29–30, 188, 220
"I'm Redeemed" (song), 94
Indiana, 30, 188
Indian Territory (Oklahoma), 21
Industrial Revolution, 41, 51, 71
Inez, Kentucky, 177–78

Internal Revenue Service, U.S., 85, 130
International Church of the Foursquare Gospel, 189
International Pentecostal Church of Christ, 189
International Pentecostal Holiness Church, 189
Interstate 40, 220
Interstate 64, 194
"In the Pines" (song), 95
Iranian immigrants, 25
Irish immigrants, 42
Irish war of 1690, 32
Iroquois tribe, xxi,
Irwin, John Rice, 21
Island Creek, Kentucky, 164
"It" (Sokol), 18
Italian immigrants, 25, 42, 52, 79, 144
"I Want to Go Where Jesus Is" (song), 90–91

Jack (folk legend character), 46, 47
Jackman, John S., 36–37
Jackson, Andrew, 31, 58
Jackson, Thomas ("Stonewall"), xxii, 34
Jack Tales, The (record), 47
Jacobs, Mrs., *205*
Jagger, Mick, 100
Jamaican immigrants, 25
James, Henry, 28–29
James, Mr., 123
James, Skip, 116
James Valley, xxi
Jane, *212*
Japanese immigrants, 25
Jason and the Scorchers, 221
"Jealous Sweetheart, The" (song), 91
Jefferson, Blind Lemon, 116
Jefferson, Thomas, 124
Jennings, Waylon, 101
Jessup, Jonathan, xxxii, 231
Jesus Only (Oneness) Pentecostals, 190
Jim and Jessie (bluegrass duo), 87, 92
"John Brown's Body" (song), 34–35
"John Hardy" (song), 57–58
"John Henry" (song), 25, 44, 57, 60–61
John L. Lewis Day, 125
Johnny Cash Christmas special (television program), 102
Johnny Cash Show (tour), 101, 104

About the Editors

MARI-LYNN EVANS, born in West Virginia, is the executive producer of many TV and video programs, including *Living Well: A Guide to Healthy Aging* for PBS and Fox Health.

ROBERT SANTELLI is the author of seven books, including *The Big Book of Blues,* and coeditor of *American Roots Music.* He is executive director of the Experience Music Project.

HOLLY GEORGE-WARREN is coeditor of *Martin Scorsese Presents: The Blues* and *American Roots Music;* the author of *Cowboy: How Hollywood Invented the Wild West;* and the coauthor of *How the West Was Worn.*

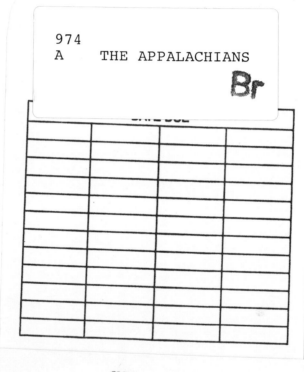